The Perennial Philosophy
Series

World Wisdom
The Library of Perennial Philosophy

The Library of Perennial Philosophy is dedicated to the exposition of the timeless Truth underlying the diverse religions. This Truth, often referred to as the Sophia Perennis—or Perennial Wisdom—finds its expression in the revealed Scriptures as well as the writings of the great sages and the artistic creations of the traditional worlds.

On the Origin of Beauty: Ecophilosophy in the Light of Traditional Wisdom appears as one of our selections in the Perennial Philosophy series.

The Perennial Philosophy Series

In the beginning of the twentieth century, a school of thought arose which has focused on the enunciation and explanation of the Perennial Philosophy. Deeply rooted in the sense of the sacred, the writings of its leading exponents establish an indispensable foundation for understanding the timeless Truth and spiritual practices which live in the heart of all religions. Some of these titles are companion volumes to the Treasures of the World's Religions series, which allows a comparison of the writings of the great sages of the past with the perennialist authors of our time.

On the Origin of Beauty

Ecophilosophy in the Light of Traditional Wisdom

John Griffin

Foreword by
Satish Kumar

World Wisdom

On the Origin of Beauty:
Ecophilosophy in the Light of Traditional Wisdom
©2011 World Wisdom, Inc

Library of Congress Cataloging-in-Publication Data

Griffin, John.
   On the origin of beauty : ecophilosophy in the light of traditional wisdom /
John Griffin ; foreword by Satish Kumar.
      p. cm. -- (The perennial philosophy series)
   Includes bibliographical references (p.   ) and index.
   ISBN 978-1-935493-98-3 (pbk. : alk. paper)
   1. Aesthetics. 2. Ecology--Philosophy. 3. Human ecology--Religious aspects. I.
Title.
   BH39.G685 2011
   111'.85--dc23
                                                                        2011023548

Printed on acid-free paper in the United States of America

For information address World Wisdom, Inc.
P.O. Box 2682, Bloomington, Indiana 47402-2682
www.worldwisdom.com

O World! O life! O time!

Shelley

There are two birds, two sweet friends,
who dwell on the self-same tree.
The one eats the fruits thereof,
and the other looks on in silence.

Mundaka Upanishad

CONTENTS

FOREWORD

"Beauty is truth, truth beauty," said the poet John Keats, "—that is all ye know on earth, and all ye need to know."

When we discover the unity of truth and beauty then goodness, happiness, and wellbeing flow through our lives of their own accord. Where there is no beauty there is no truth and where there is no truth there is no beauty. When beauty and truth are in residence in the house of human life then harmony and wholeness, joy and delight, integrity and balance occur automatically.

If beauty is truth then beauty has to be more than a visual appearance. Beauty is the intrinsic quality of right relationship within and between objects and subjects, individuals and communities, nations and continents, religions and races and, above all, people and the planet earth. When these relationships break down then there is no truth, no beauty, no peace, and no freedom.

When true balance and proportions are maintained between rights and duties, order and freedom, intellect and intuition, science and art, and all the other apparent opposites then we experience the conditions of beauty.

Where there is right relationship between the observer and the observed then there is no distinction between the beautiful and the useful or the natural and the artistic. In the state of right relationship nature inspires artists and the artists are filled with gratitude to nature.

Social injustice, environmental degradation, religious and racial conflicts, terrorism and wars are ugly because there is an intense breakdown of right relationship between the self and society, between producer and consumer, between ruler and the ruled, and between humankind and the natural world.

Globalization of economy, industrialization of manufacturing, and militarization of the nation states make ugly situations uglier. They undermine the right relationship among diverse human groups, between people and the planet earth and within the biodiversity of the wild. The result is an unhappy, unequal, insecure, and discontented humanity; moreover we are left with a polluted, depleted, contaminated, and exhausted natural world. This is not the beautiful utopia we were promised during the twentieth century.

Beauty is the original and fundamental principle of the universe based on a harmonious relationship between the entire ecosystem, but through the pursuit of unlimited and continuous economic growth, endless consumerism, and mindless materialism, humankind has embarked upon a suicidal assault on our beautiful biosphere. If we wish to escape from the catastrophic consequences of ecological degradation we have to shift our attention from the pursuit of economic growth to the pursuit of beauty. We have to re-establish the integrity of the biotic community which is the earth itself.

This we can do by honoring and celebrating the sublime beauty of the wild, through the re- enchantment of the color, light, magic, and mystery of the universe. We can restore beauty in the human world by safeguarding the majestic beauty of the natural world. The origin of the human despair is in the destruction of the wild beauty in nature. Conversely the healing of the human soul is entirely dependent on rejoicing in natural beauty.

The environmental movement has no real purpose if it is not a movement for the protection and conservation of natural beauty. There is nothing more urgent than recognition of this reality.

In this context, John Griffin's book, *On the Origin of Beauty*, is a profoundly challenging manifesto. He has performed an immense service to humankind by writing this book. *On the Origin of Beauty* is bound to become a catalyst in transforming human consciousness. This book reminds us that environmental sustainability, economic resilience, social justice, and spiritual fulfillment are by-products of beauty. Therefore, by addressing the subject of beauty, John Griffin has addressed all these concerns by implication; it is a seminal book, a book of reason and wisdom, at once convincing and inspiring.

Satish Kumar
Editor,
Resurgence Magazine

INTRODUCTION

There can be no more worthwhile task for a writer than to confront and make sense of the pivotal event upon which their age turns. What is the defining event of our own times if not the ecological crisis and our sudden awakening to our long-standing role as antagonist in the greatest of all tragedies? We have, it is evident, pitted ourselves against the earth itself in a battle we could not possibly win. A ghastly sense of inevitability has come to pervade this drama, and we play on, now with full awareness of what we do, awaiting only the final act and the disclosure of our fate. One thing that is becoming ever clearer as we watch the ecological crisis unfold is that we have forfeited whatever freedom we once had to influence that fate. When the north polar icecap retreats and does not return, the glaciers of Greenland melt away into the sea, the ice shelves of Antarctica are sheared away, and the frozen tundra of Siberia and Alaska thaws, we may sense "Gaia" quietly, as if with determination, closing ranks against a threat to her life-sustaining capacity. The destructive tendencies of those she has nurtured through all their time on earth will be stopped one way or another. For her to defeat such an adversary is not difficult; all that is required is the disabling—by flooding or other means—of the organizational centres of what is now a global technological and economic system. If this is achieved relatively quickly there is no hope that humanity can "re-group" in time to continue to wreak the same level of damage. It is in the death throes of modern civilization, though, where the greatest threat lies. Before it has been so reduced in power that it is unable to continue the assault, the body of Gaia may be severely weakened by the effects of a desperate struggle for declining resources.

An accepted expert on the Earth system, James Lovelock, in early 2006, made one of the gloomiest forecasts to date, prophesying that it is all but too late to prevent the environmental changes that will lead to the demise of modern civilization and the death of a huge proportion of the human population, and that we should prepare for a retreat to the few habitable places that will be left.[1]

---

[1] James Lovelock, *The Independent*, January 16, 2006.

It is an extraordinary state of affairs that the span of a human life might include not only the first awareness and declaration of an environmental crisis, the emergence of coherent discussion and research, the establishment of relevant data, the proposal of solutions (which engage science, philosophy, politics, and religion), and an active response to such a crisis (at all levels from the individual to the global), but also the witnessing of a finality of such proportions as to make all such enterprises entirely redundant.

We might look to the effect of Rachel Carson's *Silent Spring*, published in 1963, for one of the earliest signs that the humanist concerns of the post-Renaissance era were beginning to yield. "The 'control of nature,'" Carson wrote, "is a phrase conceived in arrogance, born of the Neanderthal age of biology and philosophy, when it was supposed that nature exists for the convenience of man."[2] It would, of course, be possible to draw up a long list of *earlier* defenders of wild nature and the rights of other species (which would surely include John Ruskin, Jean Jacques Rousseau, William Wordsworth, William Blake, Henry David Thoreau, John Muir, Albert Schweitzer, and Aldo Leopold). Yet, as Roderick Nash in *The Rights of Nature* has asserted, "The emergence of [the] idea that the human-nature relationship should be treated as a moral issue conditioned or restrained by ethics is one of the most extraordinary developments in recent intellectual history."[3] The sense that environmental ethics is revolutionary is taken for granted in environmental thought, even prompting the extravagant claim from Nash that this ethics is "arguably the most dramatic expansion of morality in the course of human thought."[4] Such statements suggest a willingness to imagine pre-modern consciousness as something akin to that of our own day, yet bearing the additional handicap of an undeveloped moral sense. The irony is that the so-called "expansion" is taking place within a milieu that is beyond doubt far more destructive towards nature, and generally far more oblivious to its "rights" than ever before. The damage inflicted in the past was trivial in comparison, both in terms of scale and

---

[2] Rachel Carson, *Silent Spring* (London: Hamish Hamilton, 1963), p. 243.

[3] Roderick Nash, *The Rights of Nature: A History of Environmental Ethics* (Sydney: Primavera Press, 1990), p. 4.

[4] Nash, *The Rights of Nature*, p. 7.

severity, and a relative harmony with nature prevailed for thousands of years, not just among primal peoples but in most agrarian cultures.

It is perhaps only when we step back from an immersion in our own times and survey the past with a sympathetic eye that we become aware of this fact and are led to wonder about what lay at the heart of this difference. Certainly it is easy to forget, in all the mental hubbub of philosophical and legal definitions and the formulation of elaborate arguments to show how and why the environment should be saved, that we are dealing now, as in the past, with a response to nature not based on reason, but on *feeling* or *perception*. Peter Hay, in *Main Currents in Western Environmental Thought*, expresses it thus:

> *The wellsprings of a green commitment—at both the activist and more passive levels of identification—are not, in the first instance, theoretical; nor even intellectual. They are, rather, pre-rational.* . . . It is a deep-felt consternation at the scale of the destruction wrought, in the second half of the twentieth century, and in the name of a transcendent human progression, upon the increasingly embattled lifeforms with which we share the planet.[5]

This insight is crucial and may be taken as a point of departure for a book that deals with beauty. For, the term "pre-rational," here, both suggests the sense of *non*-rational experience and hints at a corresponding mode of consciousness that comes *prior* to discursive thought. In parting company with a forward-marching rationality and instead setting out to investigate the path of the pre-rational, we are inevitably led towards an encounter with an earlier understanding. Along this same path lies beauty and its origin, for the perception of the beauty of nature is just as evidently not first and foremost a conceptual reality but an experience which, when it manifests deeply, arises before thought. Hay's appraisal provides an opening into the whole question of beauty precisely because it is a conclusion which lacks but invites an initial premise. If it be asked *why* the loss of nature is lamented so deeply, it can only be because we appreciate in nature a quality or qualities of a subtle order that we treasure, love, or find meaningful or significant. And since beauty in nature is an almost univer-

---

[5] Peter Hay, *Main Currents in Western Environmental Thought* (Sydney: University of New South Wales Press, 2002), pp. 2 and 3, author's emphasis.

sally experienced quality, it is perhaps beauty that most invites study. The quest to discover the fundamental nature of beauty is also a search for the deepest roots of perception.

A return to fundamentals suggests the entire movement of this work, which finds its justification in the profound need to recover a lost wisdom. For the philosopher Seyyed Hossein Nasr,

> the environmental crisis is so critical that it is necessary to quickly go beyond what has been done during the past few decades to solve it. What is required is the re-examination of our very understanding of what it means to be human and of what nature is, along with the re-establishment of the harmony between man and nature.[6]

It is in the spirit of answering to this requirement that the search for the origin of beauty is undertaken. However, travelling in the land of beauty is fraught with difficulties, not least because reason, obliged to take part in the journey, would prefer to be the guide as well, convincing us, perhaps, that the terrain is unstable; that trails embarked upon will prove to be dead ends, obliging one to return and set out once again; that others will give way altogether and prevent any discovery. Alternatively, it may claim that each person's trip must be an expedition undertaken alone, and therefore that what one attempts to describe may be countered by a hundred other equally valid descriptions of the landscape. Or worse, that the travel has been illusory after all: there is no such land—the traveller has not stepped beyond their own imagination.

The modern age is the first to have denied the relevance and even the reality of beauty. If beauty now seems vague and nebulous, subjective and open to debate, it is because we are used to the pronouncements of modern science on such matters, and science has failed to measure beauty. No account of beauty, therefore, would be possible without understanding the influence of the scientific enterprise. As inheritors of the great movement in human thought that slowly took place over more than five hundred years, and which comprises the nominalism of the later Middle Ages, the humanistic thought of the Renaissance, the scientific revolution, and

---

[6] Seyyed Hossein Nasr, "Man and Nature: Quest for Renewed Understanding," *Sophia*, Vol. 10, No. 2 (2004): p. 6.

Enlightenment rationalism, we now "inhabit" two worlds. The first is circumscribed by the boundaries of empirical method. Science, through the use of instrumentation and by reasoning, has provided a mental picture of a universe comprising star-filled void, orbiting planets, and a complex organization of atoms, elements, molecules, amino acids and proteins. In this world composed of matter and psyche, beauty has a tenuous existence consigned to the subjective realm of individual consciousness. Virtually all aesthetic theory is subordinate to the assumption that beauty belongs only to this subjective realm. When beauty has been contained in the brain, as it were, it is more likely that philosophy will be satisfied with conceptualizing it, determining the criteria by which beauty is to be assessed rather than seeking the origin of beauty elsewhere. In his introduction to *Timeless Beauty*, the writer and artist John Lane admits,

> the history of aesthetics is littered with unsuccessful attempts to rationalize and systematize this hugely evanescent experience. In the course of researching this work, I read a number of books on aesthetics, but none took me closer to any understanding of the beautiful; often the opposite. So much abstract, cerebral speculation may even take one away from the vivid beauty of a spray of cherry blossom.[7]

Lane perceptively identifies here the problematic nature of aesthetic theory. Whether we endorse the objective position (that beauty inheres in the object) of philosophers like Plato and Aristotle,[8] or the subjective position (that it exists only in the experiencer's mind) of those such as Hume, Kant, and Edmund Burke,[9] is beside the point. To imagine one has captured beauty within the net of elaborate description is to confuse the description of beauty with beauty itself. It is to invite both surprise and disappointment, for the net, in fact, contains nothing of substance. Lane rightly sees that beauty resides elsewhere and that its manifestation in consciousness

---

[7] John Lane, *Timeless Beauty in the Arts and Everyday Life* (Dartington: Green Books, 2003), p. 24.

[8] See, for instance, Plato's *Symposium* and Aristotle's *Rhetoric*.

[9] See, for instance, David Hume's "Of the Standard of Taste" in *Four Dissertations* (1757); Immanuel Kant's *Critique of Judgment* (1790); and Edmund Burke's *On the Sublime and Beautiful* (1757).

relies precisely on not casting the net in the first place, on not conceptualizing. This might suggest, after all, that nothing worthwhile can be written about beauty. Three points may persuade us otherwise. Firstly, if we approach beauty by way of investigating the path of the pre-rational we may hope to avoid the impasse to which an exclusive faith in rational discourse brings us. Secondly, if we skirt the quagmire of debate surrounding the nature of art and the criteria of artistic judgment, and instead are content to tread a path familiar to all—that of natural beauty—we are straightaway on firmer ground.[10] Thirdly, if while journeying towards beauty we are also interested in whatever allows it to be seen more clearly, we are at once involved in *praxis*—in a practical application of aesthetics. Seeking to investigate the subject consciousness and its perceptive capacity is a way of avoiding the pitfall that is the chief failing of aesthetics: its externality to its object.[11] Beauty, the twentieth century philosopher Theodor Adorno claimed, is not to be understood from the outside, but from an immersion in it.[12] A goal of this book is to demonstrate the validity of a subjective or

---

[10] The beauty of nature is readily agreed upon. It was Theodor Adorno who said, "The song of birds is found beautiful by everyone; no feeling person . . . fails to be moved by the sound of a robin after a rain shower" (Theodor Adorno, *Aesthetic Theory* [London: Continuum, 1997], p. 87). Kant refers us to, "The superiority of natural beauty over that of art," and writes, "A man who has taste enough to judge the products of fine art with the greatest correctness and refinement may still be glad to leave a room in which he finds those beauties that minister to vanity and perhaps to social joys, and to turn instead to the beautiful in nature, in order to find there, as it were, a voluptuousness for the mind in a train of thought that he can never fully unravel. . . . We shall ourselves regard this choice of his with esteem and assume that he has a beautiful soul, such as no connoisseur and lover of art can claim to have because of the interest he takes in his objects" (Werner S. Pluhar, trans., *Critique of Judgment* [Indianapolis: Hackett Publishing, 1987], pp. 300-301).

[11] Robert Hullot-Kentor observes: "Anyone turning to aesthetics would expect that, to call itself aesthetics, it would be allied with what is exceptional in the experience of its object. But what is discovered instead is a discipline that throughout its history has worked at the conceptual undergirding of standards of beauty, the sublime, taste, art's dignity, and so on, while failing to achieve the standard of the experience of what it purports to treat" (Robert Hullot-Kentor, introduction to *Aesthetic Theory*, by Theodor Adorno [London: Continuum, 1997], p. x).

[12] "We don't understand music, it understands us," he pithily wrote. (Theodor Adorno, *Beethoven*, ed. Rolf Tiedemann [Frankfurt: Suhrkamp, 1993], p. 15.) His programme—and advice—was "to use the strength of the subject to break through the fraud of constitutive subjectivity" (Theodor Adorno, *Negative Dialectics*, trans. E.B. Ashton [New York: Routledge, 1990], p. xx).

epistemological approach to beauty, and show how a seemingly limited or narrow way opens onto a much broader avenue allowing a vision of beauty which vastly transcends what we first see.

The path opens to us when we stand before nature and acknowledge that while we may *imagine* the conceptual, extrapolated, world of science referred to above, we do not actually experience it. Instead, we experience another world of very different proportions, makeup, relationships, operations, and qualities. Its compass extends to the horizon, and to the sky over our head. The sun, a comparatively small object, rises, moves, and sets over a nearly flat landscape. Normally, we know only what occurs in our immediate environment, what can be seen and heard and touched. When we encounter the world's varied forms of life, and its mountains, rivers, and seas, these entities display no signs that they are somehow invested with the classifications of geology or biology, or that they are composites of carbon, hydrogen, and oxygen, or molecules and genes, or that they operate mechanically or unconsciously. Before we subject nature to measurement it displays for us only immediately perceptible *qualities*.

The perception of beauty in nature may be termed an *immediate* or intuitive response to a world that is not of our making, to the dazzling array of brightness, colour, form, sound, scents and textures we experience. One of the significant aspects of this world is that it is alive and engaged in an ongoing process of unfolding which our creations do not manifest. We seem to stand in the presence of something that, because it infinitely transcends our own being, our understanding, may provoke a reaction that is quite *extra*-ordinary. In the immediacy of our encounter with the quiet green of rainforest, or the limitless expanse of desert under a vast blue sky, the sound of waves moving over sand, or the star-filled vault at night—if one is not assessing, analyzing, conceptualizing, or anticipating, but just listening, looking, touching, breathing—there may come a sense of awe, the sublime, profound beauty, the significance of which seems to far surpass ordinary consciousness. It is this profound sense of beauty—the *aesthetic experience* itself—that is a central concern of this book: the pre-rational experience of beauty, rather than theories concerning the beautiful which reason is wont to offer.

The validity of an immediate perception of the world is what phenomenology attests. Yet, while the philosophy of Husserl and Heidegger drew attention away from the conceptual world constructed by scientific rationalism and towards a more intuitive and traditional way of seeing the world, it is unable to represent all that the traditional perspective embraces. And this is because, having arisen consequent to the worldview that modern science imposed, it exists now in the shadow of science, and is therefore cut off from the light of what went before. Indeed, nearly all modern thought is coloured by the paradigm of modern science, including philosophy, sociology, psychology and anthropology. As distinctive expressions of a limiting doctrine, they have been encapsulated by the term "modernism" by a body of writers who distinguish what is really a recent anomalous vision from an age-old and virtually universal one.[13] In journeying from the lonely outpost of modernism back across desolate waters to a forgotten shore where beauty's real nature resides, I offer as guides the expounders of *traditionalist* thought, uncommonly discerning when it comes to navigating the past.

"Traditionalism" stands in opposition to modernism. In one sense it might be said to have had its birth in the perennialist "school" of René Guénon, the French metaphysician whose devastating critique of the modern West[14] helped to focus or inspire the writings of various intellectuals in the second half of the twentieth century. Yet, this would be to pay undue attention to the messenger, and risk overlooking the key fact that the message itself—the *sophia perennis*—concerns an always-existing and unchanging wisdom. The essential condition of this wisdom is a *participative perception* to which human consciousness is always potentially heir—a vision that is both revelatory and inspirational. Its manifestation is the genesis of many traditional teachings, the esoteric essence of a religion, and the understanding behind much great art and poetry. Successors to Guénon, who have continued to explicate the *sophia* from different vantage points, are now numerous, and many are included in this book.[15] Frithjof Schuon—whose seminal *The Transcendent Unity*

---

[13] Lord Northbourne's own account of modernism as "anti-traditional, progressive, humanist, rationalist, materialist, experimental, individualist, egalitarian, free-thinking and intensely sentimental," shows how broad the term is, and also how the emphasis on the role modern science plays may vary. See Lord Northbourne, *Religion in the Modern World* (Ghent, New York: Sophia Perennis, 1994), p. 12.

[14] See René Guénon, *The Reign of Quantity and the Signs of the Times* (New York: Sophia et Perennis, 1995).

[15] Besides those already mentioned—Guénon and Nasr—the significant ones include Frithjof Schuon, Martin Lings, Ananda Coomaraswamy, Lord Northbourne, Titus Burckhardt, Whitall Perry, William Stoddart, Huston Smith, Charles Le Gai Eaton, James Cutsinger,

of Religions[16] (published in 1953) must be considered providentially suited to our eclectic times—speaks from a profound knowledge of a number of different spiritual traditions, while remaining always mindful of the foundational vision upon which their metaphysics are built. Others, such as Philip Sherrard, are more concerned to enunciate the *sophia* as it is channelled by a particular religious tradition. Complementing these authors are those like Kathleen Raine—not part of this lineage—who seek the *sophia* outside these channels in the "living source" within. The writings of more diverse thinkers, such as Aldo Leopold, David Bohm, or David Ehrenfeld—more or less independent of the traditionalist influence, but familiar for their deep mistrust of modernism—lend support to the vision of these guides, and help to close the distance between modernism and the traditional outlook.

It is indeed the oft-assumed dichotomy of scientific "truth" and religious "belief" that makes urgent the need to save true intellectuality from continuing to fall prey to the stranglehold of modern science. If it be thought reasonable to identify "Darwinian" thought as lending the chief support to the scientific outlook—even determining it—then the significance of the book's title will be recognized. To provide a counterpoint to the ubiquitous and insistent melody of *material evolution* is to bring back depth and richness to an otherwise flat composition. Science decrees that the world be measurable, and establishes its reality upon just this criterion. Beauty can never make its home in such a world, for there it has no chance to reveal all that it is. An intuition of this truth, of a mysterious non-material or transcendent quality, makes the usual empirical rules we apply to things seem absurdly inadequate. Such an intuition lies at the heart of religion as much as at the heart of the environment movement. It is precious, but also precarious since it has to endure a rationality that would make beauty a part of the world science describes. This is why to envisage this subtlest of entities as belonging to another realm entirely is to take the first step away from the modernist world. Beauty's role as catalyst begins here. Re-establishing a link with the world of tradition requires overcoming the restrictive barrier imposed by modern science, and by its very nature beauty lends wings to such a venture. The determination to keep beauty in

William Chittick, Rama Coomaraswamy, Harry Oldmeadow, and Reza Shah-Kazemi.

[16] Frithjof Schuon, *The Transcendent Unity of Religions* (Wheaton, Illinois: Quest Books, 1984).

sight, to dwell upon it and so allow it to dwell within our being, is what facilitates the process of return.

Now, although environmental thought has roots in a secular, humanistic and scientific past, it maintains a willingness, in view of the desperate times in which we live, to engage with all ideas—whether contemporary or historical—in defence of nature. Environmental philosophy, the area of philosophical study that deals with environmental ethics (or the question of moral community) and with a redefining of the human-nature relationship (which involves questions of epistemology and ontology), has opened the way to an intelligent reappraisal of the conceptual resources of the great religious traditions. However, this form of environmental discourse often proceeds from a human-centred perspective, where our seemingly unique standing as moral agents or rational beings enables us to make judgments and pronouncements regarding nature. *Ecophilosophy*, on the other hand, attempts to shift this frame of reference by placing nature in the position of central importance. The term "ecocentrism" describes a radical outlook where an acceptance of the intrinsic value of the natural world requires that we transcend our merely human assessments of it and thus extinguish any claim to sovereignty over it. Since ecocentrism is now an established principle within ecophilosophy, one of ecophilosophy's major undertakings has become the identification of just those conceptual resources that serve to support this new vision and the rejection of those which do not.

Certainly, the paramount importance of the natural world can hardly be denied. It is the *sine qua non* of the whole philosophic venture, simply because it is the foundation which upholds human life itself. This is why it is held as axiomatic in what follows that a humanistic and anthropocentric approach to philosophy is no longer defensible, and why the ecocentrism of ecophilosophy is a focus of interest. Yet, if ecophilosophy earns the right to respectful attention, it does so more by virtue of relinquishing *genuinely* outworn philosophies than by its perspicacity. When vision lacks acuity, not only may we overlook what is normally apparent but we may be persuaded to see what is not there at all. To apply this metaphor to ecophilosophy is to find adequate reason to question the world it shows us, to look again at what it has passed over, and to seek the renewal of a vision all but obscured.

Part One

WILDERNESS

CHAPTER ONE
Lake Pedder

What work of philosophy does not in some way have its origin in reflections on personal experience, whether they be voiced or remain a story left untold? When the subject is beauty, it may well begin in a child's encounter with the natural world.

In the summer of 1972, my father, having been told he must see Lake Pedder before it was gone, took three of his children walking into what was then considered the heart of the Tasmanian wilderness, an area encompassing nearly a third of the island State. The lake and its surrounds—one of the glories of the earth—along with much of the south-western part of the island had been preserved against settlement due to a mountainous and inaccessible terrain. It was now to be flooded to provide an impoundment for hydro-electricity generation, and by the following year its life would be at an end. How easy to recall that still afternoon, nearly forty summers past, walking upward through flowering melaleuca and banksia and first glimpsing, from the crest of a hill, that wide lake, at peace under a shimmering sky filled with birdsong. There are places, they say, where the veil between this world and the next becomes translucent, and to gaze upon them brings an ache to the heart. All hope that the fate of this lake could be altered was over, as even now the flood waters were backing up behind a distant and unseen dam and imperceptibly creeping over the sands of Pedder's beach far below.

We stayed only one night, and I recall no laughter or high spirits as we pitched camp near a creek below the dunes, then walked barefoot to the lake's edge as the light faded from the sky. Such symbolism as might be found in standing before a darkening landscape would not elude adult sensibilities. Yet I was only dimly aware of what it meant to destroy such a vast entity, or even what it meant to be a witness thereto. The soothing waters conspired to remove all objectivity, imparting their own untroubled nature.

In the morning mist, we set off for home. After climbing for an hour, we were in the sun and could turn to watch the white shroud covering the lake being slowly burnt away. More symbolism, offered not to the eyes of the child who would never again see this place, but to the imagination of one who, half a lifetime and half a world away, must now bear witness not only to what was, but to everything that such beauty represents. There are those who will be haunted by Pedder's beauty for the rest of their lives. No doubt some feel the tragedy of her loss more keenly, though they have set down not a word in her praise. Who indeed can speak for the unfathomable grace with which nature occasionally displays her work?

Lake Pedder embodied just those elements that enchant the heart and eye. Its beauty was in the colour and light that radiated from it. An anomaly amidst the rugged mountains, rainforest, and plains of the South-West, it shone as a sapphire under the blue heaven of summer, or glowed deep amethyst under storm-filled skies. Its crystalline beach of white and pink quartz sand formed a gleaming wide crescent that curved around to embrace it and threw dazzling light upward and out onto the surrounding hills. At its edge, amber coloured streams flowed beneath stands of tea tree, fragrant and alive with insect hum, through dunes covered in green mosses, and out across the sand to the transparent shallows. While the sun shone, it was a natural playground. The quietness of dusk brought wildlife to the water's edge. And at night, as constellations wheeled and more heavenly creatures traced their path overhead, it captured the stars and played with the light of a thousand suns, sending each one dancing over its waves.

For those who knew Pedder it seemed to represent the essence of natural beauty, where the various elements which go to make up an ideal wilderness—flowing waters, open plains and forests, wildlife and wild-flowers—were refined, distilled, and concentrated in one place. Moreover, the historical Lake Pedder remains a pre-eminent example of the confluence of the various streams that arise from the theme of the beauty of the natural world. Here, the recognition of natural beauty, the refusal to see this beauty, and the destruction of beauty, all coalesce at a particular time and mark the beginning and the impetus of the environment movement in Tasmania. Although the jewel that was Pedder was crushed in the grip of a technological hubris and an arrogance deliberately blind to its beauty, the spirit of the lake flows like a great undercurrent within this movement. Hidden most of the time, it can be discerned in a sigh, a wistful look, or the gleam in an eye when the name "Pedder" is mentioned; in that strange combination of passion and despair that can only come about when one has known the beautiful and then seen it destroyed.

Yet, as the artist Max Angus once observed, "Communication between those who have seen Lake Pedder and those who have not, has always been difficult and must remain so."[1] For, to speak of the beauty of Pedder is to speak of far more than aesthetic appreciation in the usual sense. To choose Pedder as the starting point of a book about beauty is to consciously introduce that in nature which has the power to transform our understanding of what beauty and what nature *is*. It has remained a truism in environmental thought to say that before we can justifiably pronounce upon what our relationship to nature should be, it is important to establish what the nature of nature is, and what our own nature is.[2] It is in this respect that the beauty of the natural world may be seen as a catalyst by which more profound philosophical questions regarding ontology and epistemology may be brought to the surface and examined.

The wilderness that Pedder exemplified has been identified as central to an understanding of environmentalism and ecophilosophy.[3] The nature writers of the eighteenth and nineteenth centuries, whose work later became influential in the development of environmental thought, often extolled the value of wild nature, seeing in it a contrast to the human world and a remedy for the shortcomings of civilization. But in the twentieth century, the passion for wilderness established itself on a non-anthropocentric (or non-human-centred) platform.[4] However, it is no coincidence that this manner of looking at things—of "absolutizing" nature—has evolved within a civilization where the complete de-sanctification of nature had taken place and where traditional principles pertaining to the relationship between humanity and nature were already forgotten. It is no longer possible to defend the conception of wilderness as nature that is unaffected by humans, without also denying the place of primal people in nature, and without denying their vision which is at once more holistic and more sacred.

---

[1] Max Angus, *The World of Olegas Truchanas* (Hobart, Tasmania: Olegas Truchanas Publication Committee, 1975), p. 37.

[2] In a 1983 paper, Po-Keung Ip proposed: "Any environmental ethic . . . should provide adequate answers to three questions: (1) What is the nature of nature? (2) What is man's relationship to nature? (3) How should man relate himself to nature?" (Po-Keung Ip, "Taoism and the Foundations of Environmental Ethics," *Environmental Ethics* 5 [1983]: p. 335).

[3] See, for example, Hay, *Main Currents in Western Environmental Thought*, chapter 1.

[4] Significantly, the writings of prominent ecophilosophers such as J. Baird Callicott, Bill Devall, George Sessions, John Seed, and Warwick Fox—which defend the intrinsic value and rights of the non-human world—were developed in regions of the world (America and Australia) still possessed of substantial areas of wild nature.

Considering that people have lived upon and modified all the continents, "wilderness" must now be reconceived as *largely* untouched areas, where the processes of nature continue relatively unhindered by human actions. To embrace the idea of wilderness today is to acknowledge that nature, left to its own design, will continue to unfold in its own way, and that there is a special value in this unfolding. Wilderness might be thought akin to "Gaia," in that it exemplifies the Earth system in its autonomous mode of being. It is what used to be designated "virgin nature," inviolable by virtue of its being sacred creation. As "unmodified nature," it is an index by which to measure the relative "freeness" of nature that *has* been so modified. Its beauty, accordingly, is an index by which to measure what beauty in nature *is*.

Significantly, Lake Pedder lay at the heart of a nearly pristine wilderness of considerable size. No road ever reached it and, until 1898, not even a walking track. Indeed, few saw it until after the Second World War. When, in 1835, the first of the Tasmanian government surveyors, George Frankland, wrote of Pedder he described it as a beautiful lake "lying in the heart of the most romantic scenery."[5] In 1837, James Calder wanted "to portray the beauty of this delightful and secluded scene . . . we were much struck with the landscape and conceive that the most careless observer cannot behold Lake Pedder with the hundred peaks of the Frankland Range without admiration and almost amazement."[6] George Innes first sighted Pedder in 1896 and remarked: "Lake Pedder is a beautiful sheet of water about three miles across, bounded on the north by a rugged range, on the east by a beautiful white beach, on the south by the rugged walls of the Frankland Range, and west the Serpentine valley." He brought back the first photographs, which he hoped would give "some idea of the beauty of this gem of southern Tasmania."[7] However, for fifty years after the first walking track was made it was known firsthand only to a few hardy bushwalkers who took between one and two weeks to make the trip in. Its remoteness meant it attained to near-mythological status. Then, in 1946, the photographer Lloyd Jones discovered he could land a small aircraft on

[5] George Frankland quoted in Bob Brown, *Lake Pedder* (Hobart, Tasmania: Wilderness Society, 1985), p. 14.

[6] James Calder quoted in Brown, *Lake Pedder*, p. 14.

[7] George Innes quoted in Brown, *Lake Pedder*, p. 15.

Pedder's beach— exposed in the summer months—and it came to be visited and appreciated by thousands.

Yet, how can one describe all that it was, or what it meant to those fortunate enough to set eyes on it before it was gone? In *Lake Pedder,* environmentalist Bob Brown admits: "Pictures cannot portray Lake Pedder's living complexity and changing moods. Nor can words convey the compelling presence with which it bonded the people who went there."[8] And for Angus, "No map, no description, however detailed could remotely convey the sense of awe and wonder felt by those who saw this place."[9]

This is perhaps the first thing to point out in our quest: the perception of beauty is, and can only be, an *immediate* perception. Beauty in nature cannot be wholly grasped by *re*-presenting it in image, whether painting or photograph, or through language (a representation in abstract form), simply because the *referent* is not actually present. Some of the sense of beauty evoked by the original may be gleaned through these media, but we are mistaken if, when we see beauty in a photograph for example, we believe we are experiencing the beauty of what it represents. We may say, "That is beautiful," yet we are not really talking about the thing itself because we are not responding to it. Ultimately, we must acknowledge that it is to the beauty of the photograph we are responding. Precisely because the reality has so much more substance to it, is so much more complex, intricate, detailed, usually alive, far larger, and so on, it is essential, when gauging nature's beauty, that the opportunity to experience it through direct perception is allowed. And this highlights the tragic element in the Pedder story, for virtually none of the people responsible for the fate of the lake went to see it.

Being present before nature gives us access to all that nature may reveal. And this lived experience is, necessarily, holistic. The fallacy of imagining that beauty can be withdrawn from nature and put into the receptacles of images and words, is echoed in the notion that beauty is composed of separate elements. Reasoning may well identify components of sensory experience connected with the perception of beauty in nature—things like light, colour, form, and texture. Yet, we cannot say that beauty *is* these things, anymore than we can say that a beating heart or breathing is life. Similarly, using reasoned analysis to isolate aspects of the phenomenologi-

---

[8] Brown, *Lake Pedder*, p. 13.

[9] Angus, *The World of Olegas Truchanas*, p. 37.

cal experience of beauty may give us much that is of interest, but it does not give us the *experience*. If we find beauty disappearing under such analyses, we may justly suspect the reasoning process itself to be in conflict with the aesthetic experience. In which case, the only way to transcend paradox, and develop a greater understanding of the subtlety that is beauty, is to view what follows—an appraisal of the more subtle elements that were associated with or seemed to heighten the sense of beauty for those who experienced Pedder—as a type of palimpsest where, beneath the surface of things, may be discerned the hazy and indistinct outline of another language. We must look, as it were, *through* the elements of experience to what the experience indicates about perception itself. The ability to read the "language" of perception is made possible because beauty is the subject of the main text. In the *contemplation* of beauty, and not in its objectification, lies the means of refocusing our vision.

COMPLEXITY AND CONTINUITY

> Lake Pedder bore the intricate marks of millennia on its face; and this cannot be, in the flick of a wrist, even remotely paralleled. To look upon Pedder as it was gave a reassurance of the continuity of natural equilibrium from the most magnificent to the most exquisitely small.[10]

The significance of this statement by Angus lies in its contrasting of nature with our own works, whether they be created by the flicking of a mechanical switch which floods and irrevocably alters a natural landscape, or the deft wielding of paintbrush to create a landscape on canvas. Human artefacts rarely compare with nature, and this is because they lack the layer upon layer of richness found in nature. If we examine our own artistic works in detail, we find they are all surface expression. They are a portrayal of their subject that masquerades as the real thing, but upon close examination is seen to be illusory. And this need not be surprising, since the raw materials for our architecture, sculpture, painting, photography even, are rather simple "non living" compounds, basic elements and minerals drawn from the earth itself. All art uses nature; we easily forget, as we "create," that we do so by dismantling nature, and often beautiful nature at that.

---

[10] Max Angus quoted in Brown, *Lake Pedder*, p. 16.

In nature, we are able to look and look and find seemingly no end to its richness. In the examination of a handful of sand, or shells piled on the shore; the reflection in a pool of the movement of clouds in the sky or of snowflakes as they fall; the flow of water between two different coloured stones in a mountain stream; the lichens on one of those stones; or the veins in one leaf of one small plant there—all this we must accept as a minute fraction of what lies around us, because everything we see seems to be positioned about halfway between an infinite range of both greater and smaller.

In considering wilderness, or nature that has not been greatly modified and is still free to follow its own course, this richness is usually—perhaps always—greater than in nature that *has* been modified. Human-altered environments are often simplified ones, the number of species in a given locale and the populations of many of those species being diminished. This is certainly true where complex ecosystems, like tropical or temperate forests, are modified, and is probably so even when areas of desert—which appear empty to our eyes—are converted.

The richness of nature is closely associated with its long-term existence. The intricate marks of millennia, to which Angus refers, "gave a reassurance of the continuity of natural equilibrium . . . [and] the effect on the spirit was indescribably healing."[11] The link between nature's undisturbed expression and the sense of beauty has its parallel in the human sphere. We know of the relevance of elapsed time to our own creations, such as the lustrous patina of an antique tabletop. By contrast, the removal of centuries of grime from Michelangelo's Sistine frescoes somehow seems like the removal of those intervening years—a putative good, since something seems to have been lost. And we hardly like to imagine the Greek temple that now lies before us, ruined but clothed in beauty, as it was—pristine, and painted gaudily in primary colours. Significantly, it is the hand of nature herself that, over time, lends beauty to our art. Our works are subject to entropy from the day they were created, and, if beauty is perceived to grow, it is through nature having reasserted its influence.

When, in 1965, then, it was suggested that a "modification" be made to Lake Pedder, and that it might consequently become more beautiful, this was almost universally rejected as a foolish statement. The modification would utilize just one element—water—to obscure, or destroy a mul-

---

[11] Brown, *Lake Pedder*, p. 16.

tiplicity of existing elements. As the environmental photographer, Olegas Truchanas, expressed it,

> Lake Pedder, to me, is the very heart of the South-West. When it is "modified" as it is called, into a . . . big inland sea, it will *not* be a more beautiful lake. It will be an artificial manmade pond in the middle of the natural wilderness area. It will affect, in my thinking, the entire atmosphere, the entire make-up of the South-West.[12]

As part of the water impoundment behind a new hydroelectric dam on the Gordon River, it was determined that the lake be flooded to a depth of fifty feet. The seeming failure, by those involved in this decision, to appreciate the beauty of Pedder, may be partially explained by the effect of post World War II technological vigour. Hydropower was seen as the means by which the small island State might progress materially and contribute towards the wealth of the nation. Technology, industry, and economic development were considered throughout the 1950s and '60s as, by and large, an unalloyed good. In the face of such practical concerns, there exists a determination to keep sentiment at arms length. The mind that must deal with technical and mechanical problems and solutions tends to apply this same mindset to the environment. Technology becomes the tool whereby the "machinery" of nature can be modified and harnessed to suit our ends. It becomes necessary to, as it were, turn a blind eye to the beauty that is, nevertheless, always evident in a moment's reflection when one turns from the task at hand. Significantly, those who were instrumental in seeing that the proposal would eventuate declined to visit the site:

> Incredibly, at Parliament House, in Hobart, decisions of the gravest consequence were reached by references to maps and documents alone while the reality lay less than sixty air miles from the seat of government.[13]

The aerial view of Pedder was breathtaking. It has been said that American helicopter pilots who flew the investigative missions for the great dams on the Gordon and Serpentine rivers were astounded at what

---

[12] Olegas Truchanas quoted in Brown, *Lake Pedder*, p. 16.

[13] Angus, *The World of Olegas Truchanas*, p. 37.

was being planned, having no doubt that at home their own governments would have gone to any lengths to preserve such sites. When one Parliamentarian, Louis Shoobridge, *was* persuaded to go to Pedder, the view from the air was decisive:

> It was from a height of about 2000 feet . . . that I caught sight of it and I think it was then that I realised the enormity of what the State was going to do. . . . It was no use landing on the lake floor . . . going home and saying it's still expendable. It wasn't to me any more expendable.[14]

But Pedder's glorious seclusion had worked against her. Historically, too few had come under her influence, and now too many were unwilling to be swayed by "sentiment." It can be surmised that those who stayed away somehow knew they needed to literally distance themselves from what was at stake. And it is this that indicates beauty is more than subjective judgement. The fact that Pedder had a profound impact on those who experienced it suggests a two-way interaction between nature and ourselves. It suggests that beauty belongs to nature, but that it can be ignored, and its influence can be masked by a particular mental proclivity. Angus is clear in this respect: "only one thing emerged with any clarity—something supremely beautiful was about to be destroyed."[15]

TRUCHANAS

A sense of the beauty in nature very easily evokes feelings of protectiveness and obligation. We are drawn to beauty, and when we are, we want to preserve it. Olegas Truchanas (1923-1972) was one such lover of nature. It is sometimes given to émigrés (Truchanas was from Lithuania) to see in their adopted country what others do not see, and so re-awaken dulled sensibilities. As a walker, canoeist and photographer, Truchanas had delighted in Pedder's wild beauty and became deeply saddened by its imminent loss. An employee of the Hydro Electric Commission in Tasmania, he felt he could not become too outspoken. However, in a great effort of altruism he almost single-handedly galvanized public sympathy for the cause of saving

[14] Louis Shoobridge quoted in Brown, *Lake Pedder*, p. 19.

[15] Angus, *The World of Olegas Truchanas*, p. 37.

Pedder by the public presentation of his own photographs of the lake, believing this could be done "without offending anybody," while conveying his "very special feeling for Lake Pedder."[16]

Here at last were images to evoke Pedder's "subtle and mysterious beauty,"[17] her moods and her glory. Truchanas' pictures have an unsurpassed quality about them, and he is recognized today as a master of environmental photography. In the manner of any great artwork, the images he produced reflect not as a mirror, rather they contain something of the artist's perception or insight into his subject; they reflect an intimacy with, and an appreciation of, its essence. His photographs are suggestive of an underlying quality lying beneath outer form, which he had seen and was endeavouring to show.

It seems reasonable to claim, from what he said as well as the images he produced, that Truchanas fully accepted that the beauty we find in nature is an inherent quality. He did not deign to question its reality, much less feel the need to subject it to analysis as a scientist (or philosopher) might, but unhesitatingly accepted it as part of the nature of nature. His photographs are, indeed, testimony to this recognition. In other words, he was not saying, "This is my *interpretation* of what is there"; he was attempting to capture what he believed existed:

> This vanishing world is beautiful beyond our dreams and contains in itself rewards and gratification never found in artificial landscape, or man-made objects, so often regarded as exciting evidence of a new world in the making.[18]

For the sake of this precious content, we should, he said, "try to retain as much as possible of what still remains of the unique, rare and beautiful."[19]

We have no more-detailed expositions from Truchanas which would have shed more light on his thinking. Tragically, he would never publish; he died while gathering more photographic material. His legacy, instead, resides in the visual record he made of the beauty of Tasmania's wilderness,

[16] Truchanas quoted in Brown, *Lake Pedder*, p. 16.

[17] Angus, *The World of Olegas Truchanas*, p. 38.

[18] Angus, *The World of Olegas Truchanas*, p. 51.

[19] Angus, *The World of Olegas Truchanas*, p. 51.

and especially Lake Pedder, and we may be content that this is indeed the expression of his thought.

As the lake was filling, the campaign to save Pedder continued with great vigour, and from it came some of the most impassioned declarations of the existence in nature of a quality that cannot be measured in the usual empirical way, but which is nonetheless considered as real as any quantifiable characteristic. It was left to Angus to fashion from Truchanas' simple language an elegy in prose to reveal the spirit within the man that responded to nature's spirit, and drove him to return time and again to this wilderness. He would fashion, too, from the disparate thoughts and writings of the campaigning "Pedder people," a testimony that bespoke a hidden essence within Pedder with the power to move the human spirit. What he attested, and what he so eloquently enunciated before a Senate Select Committee of Enquiry into the fate of the lake, was both the inescapable reality of this essence, and a way of knowing that went beyond the usual sensory or rational limits.

SENSE OF PLACE

High above the lake, where the walking track began the descent to the beach, Pedder could be encompassed in a single sweep of vision. In this, it was exceptional. So often it is the case that some threatened area of the world, such as river or forest, is too extensive to be seen as a whole, making it hard to visualize. Yet, all of Pedder could be pointed to and described. It could be kept in the mind's eye, and herein lies an explanation for the strong sense of place visitors experienced. Pedder was an *obvious* locus, a place in the way that a room in a house, a building in a street, or a park or square in a town is a place. As a self-contained entity, it was somewhere to go, reside in, be at peace from that which surrounded it, whether that be conceived as the immediate wilderness, or the artificial world one had left behind. The lake itself was not huge—about four square miles of water. It was encircled by mountains and hills. One might venture into them, yet the lake, its beach and its dunes, remained the focal point, a place to return to. The water of the lake was shallow and warm in summer, safe even for children. Pedder's geomorphology was the embodiment of a nurturing and protective environment. In Mary Hewitt's words, "In a very rugged area, it was home—it was shelter, and protection."[20]

---

[20] Mary Hewitt quoted in Brown, *Lake Pedder*, p. 17.

It is almost impossible not to evoke here the sense of the feminine, and I have already used the term "her" when referring to Pedder. Environmental thinkers learn to be wary of such easy designations; one is not supposed to anthropomorphize nature these days, or at least not remain unaware of what is being done. And yet, until recently, it was an obvious way of expressing what has always been a fundamental intuition about nature—that it is animate or conscious.

CONSCIOUSNESS

Even an early environmentalist, Aldo Leopold (whose writings are to be discussed shortly), was, when describing nature, in the habit of lending human-like consciousness and will to animals, birds, trees, and even rivers. The trees on his land are masculine entities, almost conscious of their role in providing food or shelter for the birds that come to sit in their branches. A river will deliberately "procrastinate," and consciously seek a particular way to the sea. If there is anything in this to object to, it is, perhaps, that it does not do adequate justice to the traditional outlook. For strictly speaking it is not *pantheism* (which considers the existence of individual conscious agents in nature), but *panentheism* (which treats the whole of nature as alive and conscious simply because it shares with humanity a common ultimate ground of being), which is the universal heritage. As Harry Oldmeadow has observed,

> In reality, pantheism, if ever it existed as anything other than an anthropological fiction, could never have been more than a degenerate form of what is properly called "panentheism," which is to say a belief in the overwhelming presence of the spiritual within the natural world.[21]

The failure of this vision and the confusion now surrounding it are, as should become clear, both rooted in the anomaly that is modern science. Indeed, it is a measure of the influence of the modern scientific outlook and the empirical method that informs it, that green thought is now wary of pantheistic tendencies. Reflecting current scientific knowledge, there

---

[21] Harry Oldmeadow, "The Firmament Sheweth His Handiwork," in *Seeing God Everywhere: Essays on Nature and the Sacred*, ed. Barry McDonald (Bloomington: World Wisdom, 2003), pp. 34-35.

may be a growing acknowledgement of developed awareness within some animals. By the same token, there is little tolerance for the idea of awareness within trees, "inanimate" matter, or the earth as a whole. And the subtlety of interpretation that anthropomorphism calls for is likely to be lost altogether in the scramble to remain objective, in which case anthropomorphism will be labelled anthropocentric to the extent that it conceives of nature in terms of our own particular viewpoint, which, because it is *only* ours, does not describe a quality that is actually "out there."

Setting aside these observations for now, it is nevertheless true that even a "casual" reading of anthropomorphism has the potential to create for us a richer beauty, because it is in keeping with our own nature to love what is animate and conscious more readily than what is not; and while we may love what is beautiful, we more easily see beauty in what we love. A generation after Leopold we find few overt references to Pedder as "she," but anthropomorphism continues in at least two ways, as for instance when Melva Truchanas can say, "the moods of the Lake were continually changing."[22] This form of anthropomorphism is to ascribe to nature human traits in a metaphoric, rather than literal-minded, way. When it is said that the lake is "glowering" or "sombre," we are not saying the lake *has* a mood; more that *we* feel a particular mood when experiencing, say, bad weather. This form of anthropomorphism might be likened to Lovelock's view of Gaia: a *conscious* entity does not exist, but the workings of the natural world enable one to draw comparisons.

Another sense of anthropomorphism, though, suggests the actual presence of a *somewhat* conscious entity that shares human traits, as when Peter Donnelly can find at Pedder, "the *kindest* balmy feeling—it was there all day"[23]; or when Kevin Kiernan says, "I have loved many . . . wild places. . . . But only at Lake Pedder did I feel somehow loved in return."[24] Here, Pedder is experienced as something more than an inanimate object. This second sense of anthropomorphism corresponds to the way some environmentalists like to appreciate the concept of Gaia—a conscious entity directing, in some way, the processes of life on the planet.

[22] Melva Truchanas quoted in Brown, *Lake Pedder*, p. 17.

[23] Peter Donnelly quoted in Brown, *Lake Pedder*, p. 17, author's emphasis.

[24] Kevin Kiernan quoted in Brown, *Lake Pedder*, p. 18.

In both these grades of anthropomorphism, it is easy to see the "pantheistic fallacy" reflected. When human consciousness is conceived as preeminent, it becomes like a standard by which to measure consciousness elsewhere. In one sense, this liberates nature to be more than inanimate thing. In another, it actually delimits nature by requiring that it wear a human-like mask. Only by trying to relinquish this form of human centeredness do we permit whatever else is there to reveal itself. Sometimes the consequence of removing the mask is that at first we see nothing clearly at all.

SYMBOLISM

Often the reaction to Pedder does not entail specific reference to an entity but rather hints at an indefinable quality that lies "behind" or "beneath" what is seen, the recognition or perception of which cannot be shown or given to another. The fact that it is referred to in vague terms should not tempt us in the least to assume that the referent is vague also—there is no logical connection here; all that can be deduced is that the nature of what is being experienced is not easily communicable. (The indefinable character of the more straightforward aspects relating to beauty, like colour or sound—the scientific explication of which only hints at the experienced reality—helps to remind us of this.) The following selections from Brown's *Lake Pedder* betray the sense of reaching for underlying essence:

> I was not prepared for the enormous dynamic of the place, the combination of grandeur and intimacy.[25]

> There was a special magic about Pedder: that much is clear. How else may one explain the passion, the almost mystical fervour, with which these people have fought for its retention. . . ?[26]

> I can only say that that lake is something quite unique, quite different from any other place I have ever seen. . . . There is some quality about Lake Pedder which makes it different.[27]

[25] Beverly Dunn quoted in Brown, *Lake Pedder*, p. 17.

[26] Edward St John, QC quoted in Brown, *Lake Pedder*, p. 17.

[27] Clive Samson quoted in Brown, *Lake Pedder*, p. 17.

"Responsible people," writes Angus, cogently formulating such expressions,

> do not get upset as a rule about an issue from which they can never hope to gain a single cent. They have been deeply moved in a way they can only comprehend *in terms of spiritual response, and know themselves to be in the presence of something beyond themselves.* It is this that has provided them with the faith to continue to fight for *the life of this lake.*[28]

While allusions of this type seem to fall short of their target, a *symbolist* approach may reach it, and begin to make clear what seems nebulous. Now, normally, to speak of symbolism is to speak of that which *by general consent,* represents or recalls something else. When *this* particular understanding is applied to the natural world, certain aspects of the environment are seen to bear analogy with the life of the human being. Hence, we find Pedder referred to as the "heart" of the South-West Wilderness. Lying hidden, untouched, perfect, and unique, it was conceived to stand in relation to this wilderness as a real heart to the body of a person, providing life to the whole and, while there, a sense that the whole was unimpaired, its integrity preserved. Thus, Kiernan, in one of the finest pieces ever written on Pedder, would "wonder at the worth of fighting for the remnants of a wilderness which had had its heart torn out. The whole will not be healthy again until that heart is restored."[29]

Yet, to be convinced that this way of representing nature can be no more than poetic analogy is to succumb to the same error that can be made in relation to anthropomorphism. As long as we believe we have *arbitrarily* imposed upon nature something of ourselves, rather than begun to uncover a basic truth about nature, we are bound by a limited version of symbolism. If, on the other hand, we are willing to draw a distinction between *nature that is invested with our humanness* and *nature set free,* we are on the way to a wholly different understanding of symbolism. For, nature set free is not nature free of symbolism, but nature free of the usual assumptions about what symbolism is. Traditionally, the whole of nature has been viewed as the expression of something which transcends the nor-

---

[28] Max Angus quoted in Brown, *Lake Pedder*, p. 16, emphasis added.

[29] Kevin Kiernan, "I Saw My Temple Ransacked," in Brown, *Lake Pedder*, p. 23.

mally perceived outer form. In the way that a painting of a rose may be held to symbolize or represent the real thing, so, analogously, nature may be regarded as a symbol for something more real. That is to say, its normally perceived expression is taken to be a simplified or less-rich rendition of what its overall reality is; its straightforward appearance "concealing" or "containing" another level of reality altogether. Symbolism of this type may be best illustrated here by invoking Kiernan's experience while observing a friend at Lake Pedder:

> As she gazed across the lake she seemed to become one with it, and both of them seemed to become part of something greater. I can't explain that sensation. [Her] vision of Pedder was as an expression of the divine.[30]

Here, the underlying or deeper reality is not an *aspect* of the more outward or superficial one; this would be to reverse the true ordering and confuse the symbol with what is being symbolized. Instead, the world we normally experience is but an aspect of what we do *not* see. Nor do the two bear the same relationship to each other as they do in the familiar version, where the symbol really exists in an abstract elsewhere. Here, there is no question of a manufactured analogy. The more real and the apparently real are coexistent, being not different things but different modalities. Understandably, however, nature can only "become" symbolic in this way when the *familiar* experience of nature *can be compared* with a deeper reality. Clearly, this comparison is not always made because the deeper level is not always known. To speak, then, of this type of symbolism is, inevitably, to be talking of perception as well; what is perceived relies on perceptive *capacity*.

ENVIRONMENTAL ETHICS

In the end, Pedder was lost, drowned under many fathoms of floodwater. Its demise was felt keenly, like the loss of a beloved friend. Having stared into the face of those waters from high above, one could easily find cause to personify it as a living presence of beauty on earth. When it had been effaced, the words of one QC left some reason to dream: "There is very fortunately, in this case," declared Edward St John, "an opportunity to repent. . . . If not we ourselves, the day will come when our children will

---

[30] Kiernan, "I Saw My Temple Ransacked," p. 19.

undo what we so foolishly have done."[31]

The treatment Pedder suffered was not unique. Who, reading this, cannot recall a place of beauty which once existed and now is gone? How we shrink, confused and outraged, from what has replaced it, as though we personally have betrayed the nature we once loved. And how at a loss we are to convey such feelings to those who seem indifferent to this beauty. Yet, would we falter before the wholly unfamiliar opportunity to set things right again? Lake Pedder was nearly resurrected at the turn of the century. Incredibly, a geo-morphological study showed the beach (now the lake floor) to be intact; covered by only the thinnest layer of silt, the sand still displayed its characteristic ripples. Engineers deemed the draining feasible. When the waters had receded, the lost vegetation would return, creeping down the hills to fill the desolate basin, perhaps in only years. But it did not happen. Somehow, the lake as it had become swayed popular imagination. Does repentance, then, last but a generation, or is it our trust which fails us? Once, I revered and drew solace from the old judge's words. Now I am no longer sure it would be a good thing to reclaim what we once had, perhaps because I no longer have faith that we would know how to manage the consequences. Might we have to live with yet more regrets? When the sun last shone on Pedder's face, there was no "ecotourism." Left alone, no more can be done to desecrate it; resurrect it and we would have the chance to destroy it all over again. For all the ways we could do this we need only look to any of the once-beautiful areas of the world that have succumbed to the unending requirements of those who demand to see them. Such outcomes are a sign that the beauty we initially respond to is *not* matched by an inner perception, that we have not beauty enough within to reciprocate in kind. Ignorance before beauty makes ruinous the hand raised to touch it, and since, as time passes we seem ever less able to put forth a hand without destroying, our ignorance becomes more evident. Pedder, snatched away in innocence, has guaranteed a memory soul-wrenchingly beautiful. We should be grateful for this at least.

* * *

A mountain stands behind Tasmania's southern capital; a vast sandstone and dolerite sentinel whose buttresses are the hills upon which the city

---

[31] Edward St John quoted in Brown, *Lake Pedder*, p. 13.

clings. For a time, my family lived in one of the valleys at the very edge of the settled areas, and it was possible to walk from a suburb still entangled in the bush, up along the mountain's winding tracks where, in spring, wattles blazed yellow in the sunlight and silver peppermints made the air heady with scent. Climbing for an hour or two, and skirting the last soaring columns of rock three thousand feet above the Derwent River, a great plateau opened up. Here, cushion plants, pineapple grass and kerosene bush mingled with lichen-covered boulders and exquisite rock pools where endemic mountain shrimp swam. Walking out over this gently sloping plain, one first heard the trickle of water as tiny streams began to merge. The river that formed led past huge boulder fields, over rock ledges, and then to a waterfall. Facing southwest, there were no more houses or roads, only the convoluted and thickly forested contours of a mysterious world. Lost in the blue haze somewhere out there was the new "Pedder," and all around her range upon range of high mountains. In the winter, the snow-capped peaks shone white under a winter sun; and in the summer, long after the melting snows had turned streams and rivers into foaming torrents, some were still white with the gleam of quartzite. At the foot of these mountains, under the trees' canopy, where leatherwood blossom and swallow-tailed butterflies drifted in the filtered sunlight, limestone caves had once offered shelter to the first nomadic inhabitants of this country before they journeyed on to the open buttongrass plains of the south-west coast. Their first passage through this landscape was made perhaps ten thousand years ago after ice-age glaciers had retreated. Their last came less than two hundred years ago when their link with the land was forcibly broken by the European invasion. Over the years, along with one or two companions, I would come to know some of the places in that wild land known to them. For many who grew up in Tasmania or came to live there, the wilderness became an alternative dwelling place, holding an attraction seemingly primordial. Here, it was possible to walk for many days and come across nothing reminiscent of civilization. The countenance of those who returned from such expeditions was changed. And when they strode through the city's streets with the bushwalker's stride, it was as though they were only passing through and did not really belong there. Even those who had spent but a day or two in the wilderness knew they had experienced the real Tasmania and had now returned to a world of diminished significance. To become nomadic for a time was to lose interest in, or commitment to, the life of the town. Yet, if it became an unstated maxim that it was only to the bushwalker that the wilderness really spoke, and if "green" thinking was often sparked by immersion in the world known to the first "Tasmanians," nevertheless one must retreat from it in order to explore instead a landscape of thought fashioned in the attempt to understand this mysterious beauty and our relationship to it.

Once, when returning from the Vale of Rasselas, where the Gordon River swings westward and escapes through a narrow gorge before its wild energy is spent upon the indifferent body of the new dam, we were frozen by an unexpected vision. Above a distant hill, in a clear sky, a mushroom cloud was slowly forming. Behind us, at one end of the long valley, lay Lake Rhona, a miniature Pedder caught in the crags and caught in time, unchanged and scarcely visited since the days when native huts stood upon the open plains below. Less distant, the place we had left at midday, an old homestead in ruins, its beams, planks and shingles hewn from a single tree; once a hermit's refuge from the modern world, it had exuded the peace of another age. Now, stamped upon the pale sky ahead, this hallmark of the twentieth century was enough to stop the breath, as momentarily the inconceivable impressed itself. No noise reached us, and the sweet air around remained still. Then, the faraway clatter of a helicopter's rotors brought comprehension: way to the south a clear-felled forestry coop had erupted in fire.

A bushwalker's peace of mind lies in a freedom from the sights and sounds of modernity, and especially from its destructiveness. It is a contrived illusion though, and the long valley had carried us that day from a type of fool's paradise, an immersion in a remnant oasis of beauty, to face the real world. Since Pedder, the high dams that drowned the wild country had become the uppermost concern for environmentalists, and, by the early 1980s, the Franklin, "the last wild river," had been saved from inundation. But while one beauty holds our attention, another is lost. A desecration of unimaginable proportions had been unfolding across hidden and holy places; a war against the ancient forestlands of Tasmania was being waged with increasing ferocity and skill. The helicopter we heard was not there to *tackle* the fire. It was the very instrument of war, brought to bear after another great stand of eucalypts had been felled and dragged away to be chipped. Spewing incendiaries of napalm, it had wreathed a shattered mass of rainforest in flame, a firestorm whose sudden ignition forced this colossal pillar of smoke and ash skyward.

This fire of sacrifice, in which the intricate splendour of rainforest is burnt in exchange for the dull monotony of plantation timber and fleeting material gain, was to grow ever more common. The bright days of autumn would become smoke stained and darkened, as immense areas of primeval forest were incinerated with no hope of return. In this way, the frontiers of the Eden of our youth, visited in silent wonder, retreated each year. Once glorious walks now started ignominiously in the blackened wasteland of a clear-felled coop. It seemed our exile, though resisted, was eventually to be assured at the hands of those who had learnt nothing from Pedder.

By such ways are environmentalists made, and the company of those who speak in defence of the earth sought out. Throughout the 1970s and '80s, environmental thinkers were busy arranging the elements of a world that would transcend the extremes of an arrogant humanism. Wilderness was in a sense the bedrock of this project, for while it existed it made meaningful the term "nature." In turn, the wilderness experience—the human response to what are in fact the original conditions of our existence—provided a chance to fathom the depths of our own nature.

CHAPTER TWO
Leopold

In Aldo Leopold's 1949 book, *A Sand County Almanac*,[1] wilderness is the touchstone which reveals, through our contact with it, the true nature of our experience of beauty. Leopold, like Truchanas, accepted beauty as a characteristic of nature. His "land ethic," now famous within green thought, specifically and deliberately includes this quality:

> A thing is right when it tends to preserve the integrity, stability, and beauty of the biotic community. It is wrong when it tends otherwise.[2]

In a work that seeks to appraise the validity of a contemporary philosophy by exposing it to the light of a traditional one, Leopold's writings, because they contain elements of both, may act as a bridge between the two. As a respected pioneer of environmental thought, his ideas continue to have standing for ecophilosophy. Yet, as someone who treats the quality of beauty on a par with more easily defined qualities, his outlook is also controversial. However, the following study, as well as providing insight into Leopold's conception of natural beauty, begins the process of re-establishing beauty on a sure footing by showing the way in which the beautiful and its perception can be linked. The "problem" of beauty, normally conceived in terms of opposing approaches (the objective, which asserts that beauty inheres in the object; and the subjective, which finds beauty a matter of personal taste) is seen to be resolvable in a manner quite different from Immanuel Kant's attempt to mediate between the two by claiming the universal validity of aesthetic judgment.[3] In this way, Leopold's work lends credence to, and may engender sympathy for, the traditional perspective as it is revealed.

---

[1] Aldo Leopold, *A Sand County Almanac: and Sketches Here and There* (New York: Oxford University Press, 1989).

[2] Leopold, *A Sand County Almanac*, pp. 224-5.

[3] See Immanuel Kant, "Analytic of the Beautiful," in *Critique of Judgment* (1790).

In the land ethic, we face the question which Leopold and anyone similarly concerned with the relationship they have with nature, must answer: what *is* integral, stable, and beautiful? Upon his beloved "sand farm" in Wisconsin (land once cleared, briefly productive, and thence abandoned) Leopold is aware of many beauties, many wonderful relationships between its plants, animals, and birds. Yet his attitude is one of making the best out of what is there, for he is working towards re-establishing some semblance of what was, all the while remaining unsure of how rightly to proceed with this "husbandry of wild plants and animals."[4] When we find him engaged in the task of remedying the damage done, he concedes:

> the aspen is in good repute because he glorifies October and he feeds my grouse in winter, but to some of my neighbors he is a mere weed, perhaps because he sprouted so vigorously in the stump lots their grandfathers were attempting to clear. . . . Again, the tamarack is to me a favorite second only to white pine, perhaps because he is nearly extinct in my township . . . or because he sprinkles gold on October grouse . . . or because he sours the soil and enables it to grow the loveliest of our orchids, the showy lady's-slipper. . . . I like the wahoo, partly because deer, rabbits, and mice are so avid to eat his square twigs and green bark and partly because his cerise berries glow so warmly against November snow.[5]

Leopold is trying to put back what has been lost through degradation. He admits to being unsure of what exactly to include in the one patch of land for which he can be personally responsible, partly because he has no way of knowing with surety what was once there, and so what "should" be there. He knows, though, that to a certain extent nature will take its own course, so he can strive to help it in its meandering and circuitous route back through succession towards a stable, integral, and beautiful state. One of the pre-requisites, surely, for such a project is as deep a knowledge of the land as is possible, based on detailed observation of what is there already and how these several parts interact: an *ecological understanding*. The perception of beauty is a guide here too, for it registers absence and inclu-

[4] Leopold, *A Sand County Almanac*, p. 158.

[5] Leopold, *A Sand County Almanac*, pp. 71-2.

sion. Significantly for Leopold, the index for both nature that is whole, and for natural beauty, is wilderness.

It is in the encounter and engagement with wilderness that Leopold's mind, feelings and sense of poetry soar. Within the wilds of the Colorado Delta, there once existed the glories of a world as yet unspoilt. In 1922, as youths, Leopold and his brother went canoeing there, and in weeks of travel did not see "a man or a cow, an axe-cut or a fence."[6]

> When the sun peeped over the Sierra Madre, it slanted across a hundred miles of lovely desolation, a vast flat bowl of wilderness rimmed by jagged peaks. On the map the Delta was bisected by the river, but in fact the river was nowhere and everywhere, for he could not decide which of a hundred green lagoons offered the most pleasant and least speedy path to the Gulf. So he traveled them all, and so did we. He divided and rejoined, he twisted and turned, he meandered in awesome jungles, he all but ran in circles, he dallied with lovely groves, he got lost and was glad of it, and so were we. For the last word in procrastination, go travel with a river reluctant to lose his freedom in the sea.[7]

The delta is teeming with wildlife and an abundance of food for all, and although

> We could not, or at least did not, eat what the quail and deer did. . . . We shared their evident delight in this milk-and-honey wilderness. Their festival mood became our mood; we all reveled in a common abundance and in each other's well-being. *I cannot recall feeling, in settled country, a like sensitivity to the mood of the land.*[8]

But "all this was far away and long ago."[9] Once again, we encounter an unspeakable sadness in the face of the inevitable onslaught of development which has rung down the curtain on all this. After acknowledging the

---

[6] Leopold, *A Sand County Almanac*, p. 141.

[7] Leopold, *A Sand County Almanac*, pp. 141-2.

[8] Leopold, *A Sand County Almanac*, p. 146, emphasis added.

[9] Leopold, *A Sand County Almanac*, p. 148.

delta's death, from Leopold we have first the wry comment, "I am told the green lagoons now raise cantaloupes. If so, they should not lack flavor."[10] And then, in resignation to the tragic element that seems always to end the drama of humanity on the stage of nature:

> Man always kills the thing he loves, and so we the pioneers have killed our wilderness. Some say we had to. Be that as it may, I am glad I shall never be young without wild country to be young in. Of what avail are forty freedoms without a blank spot on the map?[11]

Leopold, like so many environmentalists, is prepared to claim for wild nature a quality that is distinct and unique. And for him it is the presence of this quality that corresponds to—and *may result in*—the perception we call beauty. Although it may be tempting to deny the objective reality of the quality behind the perception, and say it is a thing that is lent to nature by us, Leopold clearly did not believe this. For him, the perception of beauty occurs as a response to the existence of beauty, *or something we may call beauty,* in the world. When he includes beauty as an element whose presence in the world contributes to its "rightness," it is evident he is not using words casually or inaccurately. Hence, it would be a mistake to imagine he would, if faced with the more recent language of environmental ethics—which is now too cautious to include such terms—readily abandon "beauty" in favour of a more "scientific," less "subjective" word.

To familiarize ourselves with Leopold's particular vision of nature, we might look to the opening words of "Sketches Here and There":

> A dawn wind stirs on the great marsh. With almost imperceptible slowness it rolls a bank of fog across the wide morass. Like the white ghost of a glacier the mists advance, riding over phalanxes of tamarack, sliding across bog-meadows heavy with dew. A single silence hangs from horizon to horizon. . . . At last a glint of sun reveals the approach of a great echelon of birds. On motionless wing they emerge from the lifting mists, sweep a final arc of sky, and

[10] Leopold, *A Sand County Almanac*, p. 148.

[11] Leopold, *A Sand County Almanac*, pp. 148-9.

settle in clangorous descending spirals to their feeding grounds. A new day has begun on the crane marsh.[12]

What immediately follows alerts us to his way of seeing and is an example of Leopold at his most profound:

> *Our ability to perceive quality in nature begins, as in art, with the pretty. It expands through successive stages of the beautiful to values as yet uncaptured by language.* The quality of cranes lies, I think, in this higher gamut, as yet beyond the reach of words.[13]

There is so much in this deceptively simple statement that it has to be looked at carefully. Here we find the terms "quality" and "beauty" inextricably associated. There is a quality which resides in nature and which is perceivable, and that quality may come to be known or successively uncovered. The inference here is that the quality spoken of may not be known to everyone, or at least to the same depth, yet it exists independently of whether any individual endorses or denies that existence. Our ability to perceive varies and follows an open-ended, graded series. The perception of this quality begins with the feeling of the "pretty" and then, as more is seen or perceived, beauty of more and more depth is realized. The sense of the sublime surely enters here. And then, as Leopold recognizes, language fails to express the heights of perception that are possible in the confrontation with the essence of nature. Nevertheless, it is still "beauty" which most nearly answers to our question: "What is it that is there?"

Leopold recognizes that beauty exists in all of nature, including human-altered landscapes, or he could not delight so much in his own farm. Yet he values most what nature would like to "see" there, which is why he would rather follow where she leads than create exclusively what *he* wants. To the ecologist's eye, there is a special beauty in what nature brings about when free from our own designs. When this process is thwarted by the removal of flora and fauna, the degradation of soils, or the introduction of foreign species, there is the feeling that beauty, as well as integrity and stability, has been lost. Leopold's acknowledgement of the special type of beauty found in nature that is free and does not bear the obvious imprint of

---

[12] Leopold, *A Sand County Almanac*, p. 95.

[13] Leopold, *A Sand County Almanac*, p. 96, emphasis added.

humanity, is confirmed by the fact that whenever he has something to say about natural beauty it is not to the meadow or the cropland, but always to the wild element that he refers:

> The physics of beauty is one department of natural science still in the Dark Ages. Not even the manipulators of bent space have tried to solve its equations. Everybody knows, for example, that the autumn landscape in the north woods is the land, plus a red maple, plus a ruffed grouse. In terms of conventional physics, the grouse represents only a millionth of either the mass or the energy of an acre. Yet subtract the grouse and the whole thing is dead. An enormous amount of some kind of motive power has been lost.[14]

If this statement is to be taken seriously then it implies several things. Firstly, that nature is inherently beautiful: that is, it does not depend on our say so. Secondly, that its beauty resides in the way that it actually *is*; it is not subject to our particular whims (for example, whether we like grouse or not). Thirdly, that its beauty to some extent resides in its freeness from human interference. And fourthly, that certain parts of nature are invested with more significant quality than others.

"It is easy," Leopold continues, "to say that the loss is all in our mind's eye, but is there any sober ecologist who will agree? He knows full well that there has been an ecological death, the significance of which is inexpressible in terms of contemporary science."[15] It is here that we get to the crux of the issue of beauty and its perception. The quality that resides within nature as a whole, or within an individual species, and that provokes, gives rise to, or causes the perception of beauty, is an inner essence, not a surface thing. It is very real, but lies behind, or within, form:

> A philosopher has called this imponderable essence the *noumenon* of material things. It stands in contradistinction to *phenomenon*, which is ponderable and predictable, even to the tossings and turnings of the remotest star.[16]

---

[14] Leopold, *A Sand County Almanac*, p. 137.

[15] Leopold, *A Sand County Almanac*, p. 138.

[16] Leopold, *A Sand County Almanac*, p. 138.

Leopold infers that the essence or *noumenon* is perceivable or knowable. And, unhesitatingly, he proclaims that "the grouse is the numenon of the north woods, the blue jay of the hickory groves, the whisky-jack of the muskegs, the piñonero of the juniper foothills."[17] For those who would like to have Leopold fit the position currently held by ecophilosophy, it is always tempting to dismiss this aspect of his thought as a curiosity unworthy of serious consideration; to excuse this talk of "noumenon" as casual writing, appealing more to the *poetic* sensibility than the philosophic or ecological. Such thinkers, having been persuaded by the modernist outlook, are wont to agree with Kant that the noumenon is unknowable since it would have to be the object of non-sensuous intuition, and only sensuous intuitions exist; to talk about it, therefore, is pointless. However, for Leopold, the "sober ecologist" is not one who believes the true nature of things to be somehow commensurate with their phenomenal appearance, but one mindful of an *essential* nature (to which any particular species may give relatively less or more adequate expression). Furthermore, he is not one who believes all knowledge to be based on *sensory* perception, but acknowledges a perception that corresponds to this essence. To recognize the bias of modernist thought in regard to perception is to be more open to following where Leopold leads.

It has been said that Leopold accepted that there was more intrinsic quality in wild nature than in managed nature. Now, it is true that much of Leopold's early life was spent interacting with the environment in a way that, today, we would question as being at odds with the respect and care which he urges. Yet if it be thought that some of the experience of quality pertains to the "hunting and fishing" side of things, Leopold is the first to assure us that this is not the case. It is evident from his writings that he made the transition of thought that many make as they grow in appreciation for nature: an increasing reluctance to destroy, since destruction often leads to impoverishment of wild nature. His oft-quoted piece "Thinking Like a Mountain"—in which he comes to see the terrible error of the US Forestry's wolf eradication programme—is testimony to a *metanoia*, or profound change of thought, in this regard.[18] For Leopold, the experience of quality does not depend on a vigorous interaction with the environment, or on the perceiving senses. It depends in the end on perception itself, be-

[17] Leopold, *A Sand County Almanac*, p. 138.

[18] See Leopold, *A Sand County Almanac*, p. 129.

cause "*like all real treasures of the mind, perception can be split into infinitely small fractions without losing its quality.*"[19]

What is Leopold doing here? He is making a subtle correlation between the perception and the perceived. When he says, "perception can be split," he means that to whatever part of nature we direct our attention, we can find quality or beauty there. And if we are possessed of the heightened perception to which he has alluded, we will find a *corresponding level* of beauty there too. But he also means that that which is *perceived* can be split into small fractions without losing any of the quality. Natural beauty has almost a holographic nature: the same quality that is found in the whole is found in each part of nature; in Leopold's language, beauty and quality can be found at "home."[20] Experience readily confirms this. It is possible to be as profoundly moved by the beauty of a single flower as by a vast landscape. This characteristic of "infinite" divisibility recalls the point made earlier about the seemingly infinite complexity or richness of nature.

To value perception—especially the deeper levels of perception—and to perceive beauty wherever one goes, is, for Leopold, to view the idea of "trophy" recreation as both unnecessary and possibly at odds with this perception: "As a search for perception, the recreational stampede is footless and unnecessary."[21] Indeed, the interesting thing to note here is that if the subtlest end of the spectrum of perception is engaged—that is, if the perception of beauty has become rarefied—it becomes its own reward, warranting less and less interest in a physical interaction with nature, because more and more may be "taken" through a passive or contemplative interaction. "The outstanding characteristic of perception," writes Leopold, "is that it entails no consumption and no dilution of any resource."[22] Moreover, an engagement with materiality actually hinders the perception. Leopold recognizes this when he refers to the overuse of various contrivances that purport to make our enjoyment of nature greater.[23] However, the experience of wild nature, free from the trappings

---

[19] Leopold, *A Sand County Almanac*, p. 174, emphasis added.

[20] Leopold, *A Sand County Almanac*, p. 174.

[21] Leopold, *A Sand County Almanac*, p. 174.

[22] Leopold, *A Sand County Almanac*, p. 173.

[23] Leopold, *A Sand County Almanac*, pp. 177-187.

of civilization, does not *automatically* entail the type of perception to which Leopold is referring. In earlier times, while free of just these encumbrances, the spirit which animated Daniel Boone's engagement with nature (Boone spoke of the "horror" of the wilderness) was no less distant from what Leopold is talking about:

> Recreation . . . is not the outdoors, but our reaction to it. Daniel Boone's reaction depended *not only on the quality of what he saw, but on the quality of the mental eye with which he saw it.*[24]

Once again in Leopold we have a great deal contained within a brief statement. Here is a reiteration of the idea that the quality—the essence—is there in reality; it is not subjective. But now, combined, is the understanding, stated explicitly, that its perception *does* depend very much on the particular quality or mode of consciousness brought to bear by the individual when seeing. In fact, it is vital. *Perceptivity* is one side of an equation, while the *perceived* is the other. And lest it be mistakenly concluded that Leopold's "mental eye" refers to a knowledge-based mode of thought—such as a familiarity with the principles of ecology—he dismisses this forthwith:

> Let no man jump to the conclusion that [a person] must take his Ph.D. in ecology before he can 'see' his country. On the contrary, the Ph.D. may become as callous as an undertaker to the mysteries at which he officiates. . . . Perception . . . cannot be purchased with either learned degrees or dollars; it grows at home as well as abroad, and he who has a little may use it to as good advantage as he who has much.[25]

Here, towards the end of *A Sand County Almanac*, Leopold concludes effectively that the perception of quality or beauty not only is not related to mental knowledge, but even that such knowledge or thinking may be a hindrance to its perception. The significance of the earlier quoted statement, "As a search for perception, the recreational stampede is footless and unnecessary," can hardly be overstated. Why at this point, then, does

---

[24] Leopold, *A Sand County Almanac*, pp. 173-4, emphasis added.

[25] Leopold, *A Sand County Almanac*, p. 174.

Leopold seem to abandon his train of thought and the conclusions reached, and turn once again to a more active approach to wilderness? He has already recognized the underlying paradox of wilderness: we end up destroying it, no matter how long it takes, simply by acknowledging it and then making provision for its enjoyment. Moreover, he has already concluded that "all conservation of wildness is self-defeating, for to cherish we must see and fondle, and when enough have seen and fondled, there is no wilderness left to cherish."[26] And yet he goes on, in the remaining sections of the book, to deal with a much more "hands-on" approach. Perhaps he felt the rather austere non-utilitarian outlook was too much to hope for, or he shied from the double standards of those who first enjoy a place, then proclaim it "off limits." Whatever the reason, his conclusion regarding wilderness is a significant realization, and one that continues to confront environmentalism at the deepest level. For many environmentalists there is a deep-seated need to experience wild places. Often the thing experienced becomes the thing fought for, which in turn becomes the reward for the fight. If there is a fundamental inconsistency in the treasuring of wild nature, because of where it leads, it is not something that many care to dwell on. The logical requirement of having nothing to do with that which one reveres seems a curious, even impossible, outcome.

If this conflict seems irresolvable on the level of discursive thought, there is a way out of the seeming impasse when we follow the promptings of Leopold as regards beauty. For Leopold, beauty is not of the same order as "stability" or "integrity" (which may perhaps be measured empirically) and this is why it seems as though it does not belong in a coherent environmental ethics, which deals with outward form. Beauty evades measurement because, ultimately, there is nothing about it that can be measured. Whenever people agree upon a concept like stability it is because it can be made to conform to measurable standards that are then viewed as independent of personal belief. When it comes to beauty, it is found that not everyone agrees on what is being talked about, and this lack of agreement becomes good cause for believing beauty to reside not "out there" but in the consciousness of individuals. Yet logically, as Leopold knew, this failure to account for beauty points not so much to its unreality, as to the variability of its perception. If it *is* a more subtle aspect of nature, which resides behind, or within, outward form, then agreement over its reality would

[26] Leopold, *A Sand County Almanac*, p. 101.

require that a correspondingly more subtle perceptive capacity become more common. The key to Leopold's vision of beauty is indeed perceptive consciousness, the form of consciousness brought to bear being paramount in our relationship to the natural world. In this insight lies great irony, for the very discipline of thought—ecophilosophy—which has sought to adopt Leopold but finds difficulty in incorporating his ideas on beauty, is itself influenced by a mode of consciousness that works to counteract the emergence of the sort of vision Leopold expresses.

Part Two

ECOPHILOSOPHY

CHAPTER THREE
The Distinctiveness of Ecophilosophy

Within the lifetime of today's children, the ecosphere—the fragile, gossamer-thin mantle of flourishing life and matter that covers the face of the earth—may have become dysfunctional and no longer able to support human life.[1] If this happens, it could be said that ecophilosophy will have been the last great Western philosophical response to an understanding of the human position *vis à vis* the world. For, in responding to the tragic collision between our own endeavours and the limitations of the earth to be manipulated—which started to become apparent during the twentieth century—ecophilosophy began to marshal all the thought and practical

---

[1] Tragically, not natural catastrophe but the extraordinarily careless actions of humanity will likely be to blame. We might isolate a dozen different ways we could be accountable, from the dousing of soils and water with chemicals poisonous to life, the stripping bare of vast areas of forested land and the unforeseen consequences of blasting it with nuclear bombs, to irradiating it with depleted uranium, tinkering with global weather patterns through electromagnetic means, or even effecting a shift in tectonic plates through our seismic experiments. But, at the time of writing, the catastrophe that looms larger than any other, and which threatens disruption of the ecosphere, is the effect of an increase in the level of a few gases—mainly carbon dioxide—in the atmosphere. The resultant "greenhouse effect" is producing a global warming. Extreme weather conditions, melting of the Arctic and Antarctic icecaps, hugely raised sea levels, a reduction of Earth's albedo, the extinction of oceanic phytoplankton, and the increasing likelihood of vegetation being set ablaze and producing a "runaway" effect, are all probable consequences. If James Lovelock is right, then "Gaia"—the ecosphere as a huge self-regulating system—has been operating to guard against just this scenario, the living matter of the Earth having worked to keep the planet cool enough to allow its ongoing existence. See James Lovelock, *Gaia: A New Look at Life on Earth* (Oxford: Oxford University Press, 1995), and *The Revenge of Gaia* (London: Penguin, 2006). Early in 2006, the US National Oceanic and Atmospheric Administration reported an abrupt increase in carbon dioxide levels over the previous four years. "Scientists believe this may be the first evidence that climate change is starting to produce itself, as rising temperatures so alter natural systems that the Earth itself releases more gas, driving the thermometer even higher" (Geoffrey Lean, "Global Warming to Speed up as Carbon Levels Show Sharp Rise," *The Independent*, January 15, 2006). In September 2007, the International Institute for Strategic Studies (IISS) conceded: "if the emission of greenhouse gases . . . is allowed to continue unchecked, the effects will be catastrophic—on the level of nuclear war" (IISS Report released by Reuters, September 12, 2007).

wisdom of past centuries and direct them towards one last enterprise: the preservation of the life of the world.

Ecophilosophy's *raison d'être* might be defined by just this goal. It may also be said that the goal—this particular commitment to nature—has shaped ecophilosophy. For countless generations the task ecophilosophy has set itself would have been unnecessary; the seemingly inexhaustible nature of the world we inhabited, its "self-sustaining" nature, and our relatively small population, meant our impact remained negligible and our ignorance of long-term consequences forgivable. "All the world's a stage," wrote Shakespeare, who might well have spoken for the generations of humanity absorbed in acting out the human drama against a "stage-set" that remained largely the same. At times, life was lived in a way we might term "sustainable." At other times, the backdrop was modified somewhat: fields replaced forests, and towns and cities the open spaces. If we caused degradation in one area, new frontiers were accessible to us.

We can no longer expect such a freedom. Nor, with our present knowledge, can we claim a freedom from responsibility. Human activity now encroaches upon complex weather systems that involve the movement of vast air masses and ocean currents. Like Bill McKibben, we are right to now doubt whether it is just "nature" that has brought the intensity of a summer's heat, the violent winds of autumn, floods in winter, or a drought in spring.[2] Consequently, we are right to view the stark and blackened landscape of a clear-felled forest, or clean air and fresh water poisoned by chemicals, as signs of a folly without bounds. For, it is to witness the stage itself—the life of the world—swept clean.

In such unprecedented times, we may sympathize with the sentiment of environmental philosopher J. Baird Callicott:

> The problems which taken together constitute the so called 'environmental crisis' appear to be of such ubiquity, magnitude, recalcitrance, and synergistic complexity, that they force on philosophy the task not only of applying familiar ethical theories, long in place, but of completely reconstructing moral theory (and a sup-

---

[2] Bill McKibben's *The End of Nature* (Harmondsworth: Penguin, 1990), a startling book only twenty years ago because of its forceful portrayal of an Earth that has become a partly human construct, already has the savour of old news.

porting metaphysics) in order adequately and effectively to deal with them.[3]

The inference here is that we have the problems we do in spite of—even because of—the metaphysical systems of the past, and therefore they are not adequate to the task at hand. Yet, although historical examples of "unecological" behaviour can be found in all cultures (whether of primal peoples or more developed civilizations[4]), destruction that is at once large-scale, is not done in ignorance of the consequences but often with full knowledge of them, and lacks any restraining wisdom, is a phenomenon only of recent centuries.[5] It would be a mistake, then, if we did not *ade-*

[3] J. Baird Callicott, "Conceptual Resources for Environmental Ethics in Asian Traditions of Thought: A Propaedeutic," *Philosophy East and West* 37, No.2 (1987): p. 115.

[4] Perhaps the most significant alteration of landscapes by relatively small numbers of people was achieved by the practice of "fire-stick farming." Continually setting light to the forests encouraged the growth of open grassland favourable to food species. In this way, both the Australian Aborigines and American Indians drastically altered their environment. Since the Agrarian Revolution, there have been many instances of land "degradation." The impact of Roman agriculture on the coastal lands of North Africa is a case in point. In more recent times—and still with simple technology—people have even created deserts in India and Africa. As Lovelock observes, "It is in these regions of vast disturbance, the dust bowls, that man and his livestock have most markedly lowered the potential for life" (Lovelock, *Gaia: A New Look at Life on Earth*, p. 105).

[5] For Edward Goldsmith it is modern humanity that is responsible for "rapidly destroying the natural world." In contrast, "the main features of the world-view of early vernacular societies were everywhere basically the same. They emphasized two fundamental principles that necessarily underlie any ecological world-view. The first is that the living world or Biosphere is the basic source of all benefits and hence of all wealth, but will only dispense these benefits to us if we preserve its critical order. From this fundamental first principle follows the second, which is that the overriding goal of the behaviour pattern of an ecological society must be to preserve the critical order of the natural world or of the cosmos" (Edward Goldsmith, *The Way: An Ecological Worldview* [London: Random Century, 1992], pp. xi and xvii). And Philip Sherrard observes that "In the great creative cultures of the world, human beings . . . do not look upon what we call the outer world, the world of nature, as a mere chance association of atoms or whatever, or as something impersonal, soulless, inanimate, which they are entitled to manipulate, master, exploit and generally to tamper and mess about with in order to gratify their greeds and their power-lusts. They look upon nature . . . as a divine creation, as full of a hidden wisdom. . . . They may in ignorance be excessive in their demands . . . in grazing their flocks or in felling too many trees. But they do not deliberately *trade in nature itself*, or at the expense of nature" (Philip Sherrard, *Human*

quately scrutinize the worldview of the modern West, or if we too quickly dismissed an older tradition.

The question of appropriate behaviour both in the world and towards the world—or ethics—is a timeless one, and has always been influenced by the particular image we have of ourselves and of the world. That image has traditionally been supplied by religion; and a religious ethics, restricting human behaviour through the use of sanction, or modifying it by urging "moral" behaviour, merely reflects and is made relevant by the existence of *underlying metaphysical principles*. Inevitably, if the metaphysics is weakened, so too is allegiance to the corresponding ethics, which may come to appear stultifying. Nevertheless, the attempt to develop a *secular* ethics based on reason and empiricism—a project of the last few hundred years—is both dubious and problematic. On the one hand, as Nasr points out, the norms by which secular ethics are considered ethical tend to remain those "which religion instilled in the minds of people in the West."[6] Alternatively, pushing the limits of a secular rational approach, as some theorists seeking to develop an environmental ethics have done, can yield a world in which even the stipulation against killing or eating each other (as other animals do), becomes nearly impossible to defend on rational grounds.[7] Such outcomes suggest grave problems once the principles of religion are set aside.

A faith in the utility of reason in such matters may be traced to a confusion over the supposed "non-religious" heritage of the Greek world. We know that in the *Politeia* ("Republic") Socrates looked for the foundations of appropriate behaviour in philosophy—the love or pursuit of wisdom (*sophia*). A human being, directed by a particular *internal conscious state*, would, he thought, be predisposed to approach the world justly. Yet the metaphysical principles that determine such a state are not different from

---

Image: World Image [Ipswich: Golgonooza Press, 1992], pp. 4-5).

[6] S. H. Nasr, *The Spiritual and Religious Dimensions of the Environmental Crisis* (London: Temenos Academy, 1999), p. 8. Nasr continues: "from a practical point of view the only ethics which can be acceptable to the vast majority, at the present moment in the history of the world, is still a religious ethics. The very strong prejudice against religious ethics in certain circles in the West, which have now become concerned with the environmental crisis, is itself one of the greatest impediments to the solution of the environmental crisis itself" (Nasr, *The Spiritual and Religious Dimensions of the Environmental Crisis*, p. 9).

[7] See Nasr, *The Spiritual and Religious Dimensions of the Environmental Crisis*, p. 8.

those which inform religion, and are just as certainly not *based* on reason. The overly rational interpretation of classical philosophy has tended to obscure or deny the importance which philosophers like Plato and Aristotle attached to a non-rational knowing. Indeed, as Algis Uždavinys observes,

> Modern Western philosophy . . . has been systematically reduced to a philosophical discourse of a single dogmatic kind, through the fatal one-sidedness of its professed secular humanistic mentality, and a crucial misunderstanding of traditional wisdom. The task of the ancient philosophers was in fact to contemplate the cosmic order and its beauty; to live in harmony with it and to transcend the limitations imposed by sense experience and discursive reasoning.[8]

Ecophilosophy, because it may be conceived as not only a system of environmental rights and human duties but also a shaper of a particular bent of mind or state of consciousness influencing the behaviour of an individual, more faithfully reflects the initial determination of Western philosophy.[9] The great merit of ecophilosophy is that its reach extends beyond conventional boundaries—historical, geographical and epistemological. It is as though humanity, despite the actions of imprudent youth, might be the inheritor of a wisdom born of an encounter with the knowledge of all the faiths, ideologies, and philosophies of the past few thousand years. It is to this extraordinary resource base that ecophilosophy has turned in an effort to determine both where we went wrong and what might still be done, even in the "eleventh hour." Ecophilosophy may be credited with a

---

[8] Algis Uždavinys, ed., *The Golden Chain: An Anthology of Pythagorean and Platonic Philosophy* (Bloomington: World Wisdom, 2004), p. xi. For Ananda Coomaraswamy, "Modern philosophies are closed systems, employing the method of dialectics, and taking for granted that opposites are mutually exclusive. In modern philosophy things are either so or not so; in eternal philosophy this depends upon our point of view. Metaphysics is not a system, but a consistent doctrine; it is not merely concerned with conditioned and quantitative experience but with universal possibility" (Ananda Coomaraswamy quoted in Kenneth (Harry) Oldmeadow, *Traditionalism: Religion in the Light of the Perennial Philosophy* [Colombo: Sri Lanka Institute of Traditional Studies, 2000], p. 88).

[9] The process by which environmental ethics developed from its roots in instrumental value theory and moral extensionism, to "ethical holism" and intrinsic value theory, and on towards the meta-ethical approach of deep ecology, has been documented well in Nash's *The Rights of Nature*.

relevance greater than mainstream philosophy by virtue of its subject matter, broad-ranging nature, and avowedly practical disposition.[10] In this, it is best placed to represent the aspirations of the age; to answer the urgent need for a change in thought that might halt the ongoing and appalling destruction of the natural world. A line from Callicott written over two decades ago still expresses well this striving:

> We may not hope to marry Truth to Reality, [but] we may hope to find an intellectual construct that comprehends and systematizes more of our experience and does so more coherently than any other.[11]

Yet, while the sincerity and idealism of this outlook may still motivate the ecophilosophy of today, it does not create the reality. For if, despite our access to the wisdom of the ages, we remain impressed by one particular and anomalous viewpoint—that of modern science—which stands not just in contrast with a traditional perspective but resists accommodating that tradition, can we really claim to be open to all that can be experienced? Freya Mathews has expressed this allegiance well: "if a new worldview is to attain legitimacy and take root in this [Western] culture, it must ultimately have the sanction of science"; and again: "the scope of science, and the values and attitudes to Nature that it presently embodies, may need to be transformed, but science in some form is nevertheless our 'reason to believe.'"[12] When armed with this view, and concerned to defend at least some of the world described by modern science, "abstractions" not thought to reflect human nature or the nature of nature tend to be dis-

---

[10] Faced with the destruction of the very foundation on which human life and its culture rest, many of the familiar philosophical questions and debates have come to seem irrelevant to say the least. As Karl Popper once observed, "the greatest scandal of philosophy is that, while all around us the world of nature perishes . . . philosophers continue to talk, sometimes cleverly and sometimes not, about the question of whether this world exists" (Karl R. Popper, *Objective Knowledge: An Evolutionary Approach* [Oxford: Clarendon Press, 1974], p. 32).

[11] J. Baird Callicott, "What's Wrong with the Case for Moral Pluralism" (paper presented at the sixty-third annual meeting of the American Philosophical Association, Berkeley, California, March 23, 1989).

[12] Freya Mathews, *The Ecological Self* (Maryland: Barnes and Noble, 1991), p.49.

carded. Hence, although most of the world's religions, ideologies, or world-views, past and present, have been assessed for their merits as suitable systems to inform our interaction with the environment, ecophilosophy has not shied from dismissing such philosophies if they seem inadequate.[13] And, as we shall see, such inadequacy usually rests on the verdict of modern science, or, more correctly, the verdict of *the mode of consciousness that science expresses*. Thus, the seemingly interminable debates between those who defend and those who oppose the relevance of religion or modern science, which Hay reviews in *Main Currents in Environmental Thought*,[14] invariably arise as a result of a confounding of the role of consciousness in the matter. Even to profess a dichotomy of "science supporters" and "science detractors" is misleading, precisely because the same environmentalists who are antagonistic towards the practical outcomes of modern science, feel obliged to agree with many of its pronouncements regarding ontology and epistemology, because *these are what define their ecological outlook in the first place*.

Whenever religion is dismissed outright it is usually because the world it describes is thought somehow fanciful, and the world modern science describes more true.[15] The naivety of this response is shown in the failure to see that the very practice of science might have resulted in a particular perception of the world: one, precisely, that *excludes another way*.

There are those who to some extent appreciate or are more attuned to the reality religion points to, but consider that science should (or must) inform our understanding of it. Thus, Charles Birch and John Cobb in *The Liberation of Life*[16] draw upon the process theory of Alfred North Whitehead (itself an attempt to come to grips with the profound re-conceptions wrought by twentieth century science) to establish a view of Christianity

---

[13] The best source of articles exploring traditional systems of thought in the context of environmentalism is the journal *Environmental Ethics*, which began in 1979.

[14] See the chapters "Religion, Spirituality and the Green Movement," and "Green Critiques of Science and Knowledge" in Hay, *Main Currents in Western Environmental Thought*.

[15] The "popularizers" of science are renowned for expressing this view. See, for example, Carl Sagan, *The Demon-Haunted World* (London: Headline, 1996), and *The Dragons of Eden* (London: Hodder & Stoughton, 1977); and Richard Dawkins, *Unweaving the Rainbow* (London: Penguin, 1998), and *River Out of Eden* (London: Phoenix, 1995).

[16] Charles Birch and John Cobb Jr., *The Liberation of Life: From the Cell to the Community* (Cambridge: Cambridge University Press, 1981).

that is not tied to any particular doctrine, but might change its beliefs in an evolutionary way. And, in *Toward a Transpersonal Ecology*, Warwick Fox is convinced enough by the cosmology of modern science to suggest a form of identification with nature based on this cosmology.[17] Here, although there is a recognition of there being more of value in the world than science studies, there seems little or no recognition that scientific consciousness itself may have acted to obscure the true depths of that reality; or obscured the existence of an alternative mode of consciousness adequate to that reality and already present "within" religion; or worse, thwarted the expression of this alternative mode of consciousness. Whenever the mode of consciousness is not fully taken into account we find the conclusions made are reasonable, but—precisely because of this oversight—fundamentally invalid. Thus, Hay finds Western religion in general either antagonistic to environmentalism (in the case of fundamentalism), or unsympathetic towards it (because Biblical injunctions or phrases like "subdue," "have dominion over," or "the fear of you and the dread of you shall be upon every beast of the earth . . . into your hand they are delivered"[18] suggest the subservience of nature). And, in regard to the Eastern religions, he believes

> It is difficult to avoid the conclusion that, when it comes to determining the public and private choice of ecologically relevant behaviour, the non-directive nature of eastern religious traditions renders them unsuited to serve as determinants of, or even moderators upon action.[19]

Such conclusions might be warranted by an overview of the operation today of the *exoteric*, or outward, dimension of religion. One can easily tire of the many attempts to portray a particular religion as "environmental" by either denying the influence injunctions like those above might have, or referring to doctrine and precepts that clearly are not followed by the majority of its adherents. One can also bewail the fact that there are not

---

[17] See Warwick Fox, *Toward a Transpersonal Ecology* (Boston: Shambhala, 1990), chapter 8.

[18] Genesis, 1: 28 and 9: 2. Obviously some distinction may be made here regarding Islam since, although it recognizes the authority of the Bible, the *Qur'an* and the *Sunnah* (or example) of the Prophet were always the chief guides in matters relating to the treatment of the Earth.

[19] Hay, *Main Currents in Western Environmental Thought*, p. 116.

enough religious proscriptions, or that they are not of the right kind. Yet to ask not how a religion *can* be interpreted, but how it may have *originally* been interpreted, is to create an opening into an *esoteric* world where the true dimensions of religion (and so the true dimensions of beauty) are to be found. It is to confront the reality of an alternative mode of consciousness more than adequate to the goal ecophilosophy seeks. It is also to discover a fateful interaction between religion and modern science, which suggests that they are, as Francis Bacon once claimed, implacably opposed.

An allegiance to scientific knowledge means a hesitancy over taking a first step into that world. At the beginning of the twenty-first century, ecophilosophy can be positioned at a juncture. To one side lies the familiar structure of modernist thought whose chief support—modern science—provides a comparatively arid appraisal of the world and of humanity's potential consciousness, and whose inventiveness continues to contribute to environmental devastation in both the human and natural world. To the other side lies what at first might be thought a more nebulous reality, positioned as it is in the glare of this science. This structure, ornate and many-levelled, represents the inheritance of the pre-scientific worldview. An attraction for it is evoked by a deeply felt allegiance to a world of subtleties alien to science, to an immaterial realm that art, poetry, philosophy, and religion once addressed. The language of this realm is foreign to science too, and bears testimony to an ontology which science is unable to confront: "Beauty," "Truth," and "Goodness" (Plato's three verities), the "Spirit," and the "Divine." If we can say that a motivating factor in the environment movement is a sensitivity to the beauty of the natural world, and an aversion to its destruction (a finding of the previous chapters), we have identified what is a common element in both environmentalism and this more traditional, non-scientific, understanding. In virtue of this correspondence, beauty and the perception of beauty represent a dynamic capable of effecting a substantial shift in the perspective of ecophilosophy. To follow where beauty leads is eventually to discover beauty's rightful dwelling place, a world of timeless relevance far removed from the one presently considered so real.

Environmental Ethics and Ecocentrism

Viewed with hindsight the ecophilosophy movement[20] seems to demon-

---

[20] There are, of course, various perspectives or "camps" within ecophilosophy, each of

strate an inevitable direction and momentum. Given the initial premise that the whole of the world's welfare was to be taken into consideration, and given the "discoveries" of science, the eventual positing of an *ecocentric* position could be seen as a logical outcome. Various historical streams had been flowing towards what would become the environment movement for decades. Indeed, one might even look back to the "worship" of nature itself—a phenomenon arising in the latter part of the eighteenth century—and to the attempt, in the following century, to preserve in national parks some areas of wild nature. The science of ecology, in the twentieth century, slowly awakened an appreciation of the complex and subtle interconnectedness and interdependence of all life on earth.[21] In the second half of that century, there was a focus on the despoliation and pollution of "our" environment—something largely due to the use and discarding of the products of industry. This anthropocentric and instrumental outlook, which sought to promote an environmental awareness by reference to the needs or wants of people,[22] was abruptly challenged in the 1970s with the

---

which makes important contributions to an understanding of the human-nature relationship. For instance, much of what ecofeminism has to say about an overly rationalistic masculine mentality is very much to the point. It is difficult to deny that whenever violence is done to the Earth it is done in the almost complete absence of the sympathetic feminine side of our natures. Indeed, the historian Richard Tarnas has summed up the whole enterprise of our civilization as the subversion of the feminine element in our consciousness: "the evolution of the Western mind has been driven by a heroic impulse to forge an autonomous rational human self by separating it from the primordial unity with nature" (Richard Tarnas, *The Passion of the Western Mind* [New York: Ballantine, 1991], p. 441). However, since the aim here is not to assess what is worthwhile about ecophilosophy, but rather to identify and deal with the significant features that are problematic, the following account restricts itself to the particular elements of modernism that steer ecophilosophy away from traditional thought.

[21] A significant parallel event was the first visual reminder of this holism: a photograph of Earth from space. The astronomer Fred Hoyle had remarked as early as 1948: "Once a photograph of the Earth, taken from the outside, is available . . . a new idea as powerful as any in history will be let loose" (Hoyle quoted in *This Island Earth*, ed. Oran W. Nicks [Washington, DC: NASA, 1970], p. 30).

[22] William Godfrey-Smith categorizes four ways in which the environment can be seen as useful and therefore worthy of being preserved: as "silo," "laboratory," "gymnasium," and "cathedral." See William Godfrey-Smith, "The Value of Wilderness," *Environmental Ethics* 1 (1979): pp. 309-19. Fox divides the last category into two—producing "aesthetic" and "cathedral"—and adds "life-support," "early warning system," "monument," and "psycho-

advent of a clearly argued moral extensionism, which expanded the field of ethical concern to include other sentient species.[23] This served the struggle to preserve certain endangered species such as the cetaceans, and promoted a concern for animal rights generally. However, this form of ethical consideration could not adequately cater for the protection or preservation of those species or aspects of the world not subject to pain or feelings, such as trees, mountains, or rivers. Thus it was recognised that all life, and finally "non living" elements of the earth—streams, mountains, the air, even the ecosphere in its entirety—needed to be included.[24]

The issue of ethical sentientism exposed the essential "problem" with any hierarchical system. Within such a structure there was, theoretically, always the chance that the "rights" of the more "important" members of the biotic community would override the rights of those considered less significant, even though the latter might be critically imperilled, and be critical, too, to the stability of the whole. Thus, in order to bring all life within the ambit of a fair ethical system and overcome such problems, it was believed necessary to treat all life, including humans, as somehow on an ethical par. This stipulation can take the form of an extension of moral consideration by us,[25] or, more subtly, an attempt by us to "see" intrinsic value in nature.

genetic" (that which pertains to psychological development), to arrive at nine arguments for preservation (Fox, *Toward A Transpersonal Ecology*, pp. 154-161).

[23] Two prominent philosophers in this field were Peter Singer (see *Animal Liberation: A New Ethics for our Treatment of Animals* [New York: Random House, 1975]), and Tom Regan (see *The Case for Animal Rights* [Berkeley: University of California Press, 1983]).

[24] Kenneth Goodpaster argued for the moral considerability of all life in "On Being Morally Considerable," *Journal of Philosophy* Vol.75 (1978): p. 310, while Christopher D. Stone proposed extending legal rights to non-human entities in "Should Trees Have Standing? Toward Legal Rights for Natural Objects," *Southern California Law Review* 45 (Spring 1972).

[25] Various ecofeminist authors argue that this extension of "rights" to *individuals* is indicative of a typically male "hierarchical" approach to ethics. In contrast, the female is considered innately more attuned to a sense of non-hierarchical "interrelatedness." On this subject see Susan Griffin, *Woman and Nature: The Roaring Inside Her* (New York: Harper Collins, 1978); Ynestra King, "The Ecology of Feminism and the Feminism of Ecology," in *Healing the Wounds: The Promise of Ecofeminism*, ed. J. Plant (Philadelphia, Pa.: New Society, 1989), pp. 1-28; Ariel Kay Salleh, "Deeper Than Deep Ecology: The Eco-Feminist Connection," *Environmental Ethics* 6 (Winter 1984): pp. 339-345; and Carolyn Merchant, *The Death of Nature: Women, Ecology and the Scientific Revolution* (San Francisco: Harper Collins, 1980).

Intrinsic value theory tries to escape the conventional ethical boundaries altogether. Instead of nature being contained within *our* value system, and therefore subject to our determinations, we are asked to see ourselves (along with our very species-specific interests) as positioned within the greater whole that is nature. However, this nature-centred philosophy or *ecocentrism*—which, according to Fox, "strives to be non-anthropocentric by viewing humans as just one constituency among others in the biotic community, just one particular strand in the web of life, just one kind of knot in the biospherical net"[26]—remains unacceptable to most people on the planet, even to many environmentalists. And this situation is unlikely to change, not just because it fails to answer to pressing social inequalities or tackle a devastating economic paradigm and so on, but because it largely ignores the overwhelming relevance of the traditional religious view as a determinant of an ethical outlook.[27] Fidelity to this view rests not—as an ecocentrist might suppose—on the desire to preserve human interests against those of the non-human world, but on the wish to preserve the human being *per se.*

When, in the 1980s, the social ecologist Murray Bookchin first waded into the debate over the anthropocentric-ecocentric divide, he was extremely critical of the legitimacy of the ecocentric position. In his attack on deep ecology, he voiced the common sense of outrage that is felt upon witnessing what seems an assault on human nature:

Nothing could seem more wholesome, more innocent of guile, than this 'we are all one' bumper sticker slogan. [But] . . . this all encompassing definition of 'community' erases all the rich and meaningful distinctions that exist between animal and plant communities, and above all between non-human and human commu-

---

[26] Warwick Fox, "Deep Ecology: A New Philosophy of our Time?" *The Ecologist* Vol. 14 (1984): p. 89.

[27] For Nasr, "The fact remains that the vast majority of the people in the world do not accept any ethics which does not have a religious foundation. . . . If a religious figure . . . goes to a village and tells the villagers that from the point of view of the *Shariah* (Islamic Law) or the Law of Manu (Hindu law) they are forbidden to cut this tree, many people would accept. But if some graduate from the University of Delhi or Karachi, who is a government official comes and says, for rational reasons, that it is better not to cut this tree, few would heed his advice" (Nasr, *The Spiritual and Religious Dimensions of the Environmental Crisis,* p. 9).

nities. . . . [Ecocentrism] essentially denies or degrades the uniqueness of human beings, human subjectivity, rationality, esthetic
sensibility, and the ethical potentiality of this extraordinary species.[28]

Bookchin's juxtaposing of the humanist's celebration of *human* attributes
with deep ecology's "cosmic night which lacks differentiation,"[29] may remind us of the nihilism in Shakespeare:

> What a piece of work is a man! how noble in reason! how infinite
> in faculty! in form and moving how express and admirable! in
> action how like an angel! in apprehension how like a god! the
> beauty of the world! the paragon of animals! And yet, to me, what
> is this quintessence of dust? man delights not me.[30]

In ecocentrism, for the sake of the environment, there is an abandonment
of the view that people are the chief players upon the world's stage, and
the rest mere backdrop. The players now are asked not to "hog" the stage,
or give such impassioned speeches about their own troubles, but to dis-
perse a bit, and look to what they have ignored. The script now includes
other, non-human, voices. The play has been recast to favour none as protagonist.[31]

   While Bookchin, as humanist and advocate of science, cannot be credited with defending the full range of human traits to which a traditional
religious view attests, his argument remains insightful, and it highlights
one consequence of attempting to adopt an ecocentric approach. At the
deepest level, ecocentrism contradicts the nature of what we experience,
both within ourselves and in the world around us. Embracing ecocentrism

---

[28] Murray Bookchin, "Social Ecology versus 'Deep Ecology,'" *Green Perspectives: Newsletter of the Green Program Project* 4/5 (Summer 1987): pp. 1-23.

[29] Bookchin, "Social Ecology versus 'Deep Ecology,'" p. 4. Bookchin's critique of the non-anthropocentric view is summed up in his *Re-Enchanting Humanity: A Defense of the Human Spirit against Antihumanism, Misanthropy, and Primitivism* (London: Cassell, 1995).

[30] William Shakespeare, *Hamlet*, Act II: Scene II.

[31] The adoption by some of this new view has meant that it is no longer so uncommon to encounter—while war rages and uncounted numbers of people are killed or maimed—an expression of concern for some particular species or other whose habitat will be devastated.

means not just a relinquishment of a traditional view of humanity and nature, but the adoption of a view imposed by *a particular reading of the insights of modern science.*

When Hamlet dismisses everything that man is or might be, he chooses instead to reflect on one aspect: his earthly nature. Seen as only a material entity, it is true that "man" indeed comes from the earth and returns to it. In the same way, *mutatis mutandis*, for the philosophy of ecocentrism to work, it must focus on outer form or materiality, the one thing all living and non-living entities possess. It must set to one side the clear evidence for a *vertical* dimension—a hierarchy displayed in the increasing complexity of life and consciousness in life-forms, and an inner, mostly human, hierarchy of consciousness (self-awareness, imagination, reason, and, most significantly in the context of the religious stance, the intuitive *Intellect*)—in favour of what amounts to a flat two dimensional view of the world.

The origin of a system of thought that believes it possible to dispense with the traditional view of hierarchy is not hard to find. Fox betrays it thus:

> where we have been able to check our anthropocentric assumptions against reality, we have discovered again and again that these views—views that have been of the first importance in determining our thinking about our place in the larger scheme of things—have been empirically incorrect and, hence, disastrous for the development of our theoretical understanding of the world. We do not live at the centre of the universe and we are not biologically unrelated to other creatures. . . . We are not even psychologically, socially, or culturally different *in kind* from all other animals and . . . we are not the "end point" of evolution.[32]

It seems we are asked to find, in the discoveries of Copernicus and Darwin, and Freud, Jung, and later psychologists, evidence for a successive "diminution" of humanity, the philosophy of ecocentrism taking its place as a sort of logical outcome of these discoveries. This particular "argument" from scientific empiricism is not, of course, deductive, but rests, rather shakily, on an inductive reasoning with very few premises.[33] Moreover, for

---

[32] Fox, *Toward a Transpersonal Ecology*, p. 14.

[33] The Copernican theory is unique here because it is a rediscovery of what can be plainly

science itself, the "discoveries," if sobering, have often been interpreted as proof of an ascendancy of humanity, thus *vindicating* an anthropocentric outlook. Therefore, to what extent can this alleged diminution be thought to have taken place?

Modern Science

To study any of the great minds of science is to encounter what seems almost paradoxical. For, on the surface, their particular perception often engenders a world or universe that is more extensive, detailed, and interconnected, even though this is achieved through a narrowing of focus, a reductionism and analysis. The resolution of the paradox, though, lies in seeing that the world has opened up in only one direction: "horizontally" towards materiality. To view the picture that science presents us with is to see only what can be measured, since all those qualities that cannot be measured are either not included, or have been concealed under the guise of quantity. Hence, mathematics and a few scientific instruments proved heliocentrism and removed the hierarchy of planetary "spheres" surrounding a fixed earth. And while this did not disprove the possibility of a non-material "vertical" ontological dimension, the belief that empiricism was defined by only the *measurable* aspects of what our senses revealed created the impression that it had undermined it.

Again, to study the purely material (measurable) aspect of life forms, as Charles Darwin (1809-1882) did, is to encounter all sorts of physiological and biological similarities and parallels between those life forms. Such a study had led, even before Darwin, to the view that an evolution of biological forms had occurred over time. Darwin's proposal of a mechanism—natural selection—by which the process of transformation might take place, tended to obscure once again an alternative that relied on the operation of more subtle realities. In suggesting a way by which living matter could over time be transformed, Darwin's theory provided circumstantial evidence, convincing to many[34], that a Creator of the sort

---

worked out using simple reasoning, and shown to be true. Other theories cannot be positively proven in the same way, since the facts they use do not discount alternative conclusions. Moreover, as we shall see, recourse to empirical evidence—which for science means, ultimately, what can be measured—can easily obscure other "facts" relating to both the world and to the human sphere.

[34] To ecophilosophers, it is perhaps the chief persuasion against an arrogant anthropo-

William Paley had envisaged,[35] was unnecessary to account for what we see in the world. Since life, now considered an epiphenomenon of matter, was compelled to react to the "forces of nature"—material forces—the idea that evolution is not teleological but random and directionless, took hold. Although nature was, in this way, capable of producing *Homo sapiens* from other species, it could as likely abandon that branching and produce very different alternatives.

After Darwin's revolution in thought, the separate areas of science—all based on measurement—were pieced together,[36] and it became clear that the concept of material evolution could be applied to the universe in its entirety. Studies in physics and chemistry combined to reveal a process of transformation from "singularity" to star-filled void, the creation of elements in the hydrogen-fuelled furnace of the stars, and the formation of planets. Geology described a process whereby compounds of the basic elements worked, with cataclysmic force, to manufacture, from lifeless rock, a world with spheres of air and water where life could take hold. Chemistry and biology described the emergence of life from simple chemical compounds, and traced its growing complexity over time. Such complexity as the outward form displayed was nevertheless "programmed" and driven by relatively simple instructions that were a particular arrangement of far simpler chemical bases. Indeed, not only life but also all of the subtler functions manifested within life forms—including high levels of consciousness—could be reduced to the movement and interaction over time of much simpler components: molecules, elements, and atoms, which respond to innate tendencies or "laws of nature." Parallels between the hu-

centrism. For Roderick Nash, "The evolutionary explanation of the proliferation of life on earth undermined dualistic philosophies at least two thousand years old. . . . No more special creation in the image of God, no more immortal 'soul,' and, it followed, no more dominion or expectation that the rest of nature existed to serve one precocious primate" (Roderick Nash, "Aldo Leopold's Intellectual Heritage," in *Companion to A Sand County Almanac*, ed. J. Baird Callicott [Wisconsin: University of Wisconsin, 1987], p. 67).

[35] In his well-known argument from design, the philosopher William Paley (1743-1805) considers the countless examples of the precise fit of biological forms to their environment or, in the case of organs, to their purpose. To find this sort of precision is, in the famous analogy, equivalent to finding a working watch; one readily concludes the existence of a watchmaker.

[36] *Neo-Darwinism* was a synthesis of the data and theories of such disciplines as biology, taxonomy, embryology, paleontology and genetics made during the 1930s and 1940s by Julian Huxley, Ernst Mayr, George Simpson and others.

man and animal psyche could be made because both had the same origins and cause. Considering that today, almost without exception, the various fields of human endeavour endorse this particular evolutionary view of the universe, and that it stands in contradistinction to all earlier worldviews, the designation "evolutionism" used by traditionalist writers is not inappropriate.[37]

ECOLOGY

Ecology, a scientific discipline the concepts, theories, and insights of which most clearly influence ecophilosophy, can be conceived as a synthesis of these varied branches of knowledge. As such, its inheritance is the view of the fundamentally material nature of the world, the concept of the evolution of matter, and a concern with outer material form.

---

[37] Precarious from its inception, despite the confident defence of its supporters, it seems only a matter of time before even science will be forced to redefine transformist theory. There are now many books and articles (some more astute than others) which argue that the basic assumptions of evolutionary theory are, at the least, flawed because the facts no longer support them. They include: Douglas Dewar, *The Transformist Illusion* (Ghent NY: Sophia Perennis et Universalis, 1995); Evan Shute, *Flaws in the Theory of Evolution* (Nutley NJ: Craig Press, 1961); Michael Denton, *Evolution: A Theory in Crisis* (London: Burnett, 1985); G. Sermonti and R. Fondi, *Dopo Darwin: Critica all' evoluzionismo* (Milan: Rusconi, 1980); W. Kuhn, *Stolpersteine des Darwinismus* (Berneck: Schwengeler-Verlag, 1985); Philip Johnson, *Darwin on Trial* (Downers Grove, Illinois: Intervarsity Press, 1993); Michael Behe, *Darwin's Black Box* (New York: The Free Press, 1996); and Osman Bakar, *Critique of Evolutionary Theory* (Kuala Lumpur: Islamic Academy of Science and Nurin Enterprise, 1987), a collection of essays by traditionalist writers as well as the biologists W.R. Thompson and Giuseppe Sermonti. In one of the most penetrating analyses, Titus Burckhardt draws our attention to science's failure to distinguish between qualitative form and quantitative substance. Under the heading "Evolutionism," he writes: "classical hylomorphism . . . distinguishes the 'form' of a thing or being—the seal of its essential unity—from its 'matter', namely the plastic substance which receives this seal and furnishes it with a concrete and limited existence. No modern theory has ever been able to replace this ancient theory, for the fact of reducing the whole plenitude of the real to one or other of its 'dimensions' hardly amounts to an explanation of it. Modern science is ignorant above all of what the Ancients designated by the term 'form', precisely because it is here a question of a non-quantitative aspect of things, and this ignorance is not unconnected with the fact that modern science sees no criterion in the beauty or ugliness of a phenomenon: the beauty of a thing is the sign of its internal unity, its conformity with an indivisible essence, and thus with a reality that will not let itself be counted or measured. . . . In a word, evolutionism results from an incapacity—peculiar to modern science—to conceive 'dimensions' of reality other than purely physical ones" (Titus Burckhardt, *The Mirror of the Intellect* [Cambridge: Quinta Essentia, 1987], pp. 33 and 40).

During the latter part of the nineteenth century and throughout the twentieth, the study of the interactions and interrelationships of individual organisms provided increasingly detailed and elaborate theoretical constructs of the way nature operates. The study began with plants, and then incorporated animal ecology. The concept of the *ecosystem*—an arbitrary whole made up of a number of species together with their environment—showed how a system depended on the interaction of its components in order to function. Any ecosystem could always be subsumed into a larger one, and, although the idea of "human disturbance" and "management" tended to perpetuate the distinction between nature and its observer, eventually it was suggested that humans and the total environment formed a single whole.[38] In Gaia theory[39] a very comprehensive level of interaction and interdependence was identified; all of the biosphere, geosphere, and atmosphere could be considered to operate as a single entity. The sun provides energy to run the system, but life and "non-living" matter operates in such a way as to keep temperatures within a specific range suitable for life, even though the sun's thermal output rises over time.[40]As the ecologist, Stephan Harding, makes clear, this global ecosystem need not be expressive of consciousness or teleology, but operates in accordance with Darwinian principles of selection.[41] Nevertheless, life no longer just reacts

---

[38] For example, see F.E. Egler, *The Way of Science: A Philosophy of Ecology for the Layman* (New York: Hafner, 1970), p. 126. Egler calls the whole the "Total Human Ecosystem." McKibben is suggesting the same idea in *The End of Nature.*

[39] See Lovelock, *Gaia, A New Look at Life on Earth.*

[40] It should be noted that this understanding of everything—life, air, oceans, and rocks—doing the regulating is somewhat more subtle than Lovelock's original conception, which was that life modified the atmosphere and geosphere to create conditions comfortable for itself. See the original 1979 edition of *Gaia: A New Look at Life on Earth.*

[41] Early critics saw "Gaia" as demonstrating altruism and therefore being incompatible with natural selection. However, according to Harding, "Key Gaian organisms hugely influence the global commons as a side-effect of pursuing their own individual well-being. Rainforest trees emit cloud-seeding chemicals which stimulate rain and scavenge nutrients from the air. Trees, lichens and bacteria weather rocks to find nutrients. Marine algae make the precursor of their cloud-seeding gas in order to deal with the salt stress they encounter in the ocean, and . . . they do so to promote dispersal by hoisting themselves aloft in the updrafts of air generated by cloud condensation. Gaia theory proposes that many such local effects weave and link together into an awesome and unexpected emergent property: the life-like ability of the Earth as a whole to regulate key variables essential for life. Gaia theory thus

to outside forces; in large part, it accounts for these forces. The whole is so tightly bound together that to extract from this whole two different things—life and an external environment—has become largely meaning-less.

Now, when Gaia is conceived as the overall operation of life over eons, then not all species can be essential or even necessary to Gaia's ongoing functioning. Ironically, those species commonly considered nearly insignifi-cant become, in this outlook, of paramount importance. The early links in a "food chain," such as phytoplankton in the oceans, are examples. But Lovelock sees the "non-living" anaerobic muds of the continental shelves as possibly indispensable to the functioning of Gaia.[42] A Gaian perspective thus provides a view of the world that supports the ecocentric outlook and, it might be thought, is conclusive proof of the diminution of human-ity.

However, it needs to be remembered that Lovelock, as any "ecolo-gist," is working within the parameters laid down by science and as such is obliged to see in nature only data that can be quantified. Ecology, careful to avoid "value" judgements, observes, measures, categorizes, and catalogues, the separate forms, outward movements, activities, and processes within ecosystems. The workings of nature—the interactions between individu-als, species, populations, communities, and ecosystems—are studied as if they were a machine of many moving parts, and in fact have often been compared to such.[43] Although most ecologists may well be aware of val-ues that cannot easily be quantified—such as life[44] and consciousness—and may, like anyone else, be overcome at times by a sense of the beauty and profundity of what they study, and suspect that the meaning or significance

---

extends natural selection to include the evolution of organisms and their physical environ-ment as a tightly coupled whole" (Stephan Harding, "Exploring Gaia," *Resurgence* January/February [2001]).

[42] Lovelock writes: "It is through the burial of carbon in the anaerobic muds of the sea-bed that a net increment of oxygen in the atmosphere is ensured. . . . Oxygen regulation is a key Gaian process and the fact that it occurs on the continental shelves of the Earth emphasizes their singular importance" (Lovelock, *Gaia, A New Look at Life on Earth,* pp. 112-113).

[43] For example, in Paul Ehrlich, *The Machinery of Nature* (London: Collins, 1986).

[44] Lovelock concedes that the "state of matter" known as life "has so far resisted all at-tempts at a formal physical definition" (Lovelock, *Gaia: A New Look at Life on Earth,* p. 144).

of the several parts of nature, or of nature as a whole, lies elsewhere than in what can be measured, in the end these aspects or "feelings" are not actually relevant to ecology; they are not what is being studied and they cannot be incorporated into the strictly scientific discipline that is ecology.[45] And this underscores the point made by Leopold: the ecologist "may become as callous as an undertaker to the mysteries at which he officiates."[46]

To this day, the willingness to explain the staggering complexity, intricacy, subtlety, precision, diversity, purposiveness, dynamism, consciousness, and awe-inspiring beauty of the universe by reference to a few laws and the innate nature of constituent components of an unconscious materiality, remains part of mainstream science, and can border on the complacent:

> Once one has become adjusted to the idea that we are here because we have evolved from simple chemical compounds by a process of natural selection, it is remarkable how many of the problems of the modern world take on a completely new light.[47]

Many leading scientists continue to express exasperation in the face of colleagues who make such claims.[48] Unfortunately, a mind committed to

---

[45] Hence Lovelock, after initial criticism of his theory, has reluctantly conceded that "To establish Gaia as fact I must take the . . . path . . . of science. . . . [And] the new science of Gaia, geophysiology, must be purged of all reference to mystical notions of Gaia the Earth Mother." Accordingly, he has gone to great lengths to demonstrate that Gaia theory conforms to a strictly quantitative analysis by resorting to the increasingly sophisticated computer modelling of "daisy world" (Lovelock, preface to *Gaia, A New Look at Life on Earth* [1995 edition], pp. ix and xi).

[46] Leopold, *A Sand County Almanac*, p. 174.

[47] Francis Crick, *Of Molecules and Men* (Washington: University of Washington, 1966), p. 87. Elsewhere Crick writes: "The astonishing hypothesis is that 'You', your joys and sorrows, your memories and your ambitions, your sense of personal identity and free will, are in fact no more than the behaviour of a vast assembly of nerve cells and their associated molecules" (Francis Crick, *The Astonishing Hypothesis* [New York: Simon & Schuster, 1995]). In the same vein, Carl Sagan writes: "The entire recent history of biology shows that we are, to a remarkable degree, the results of the interactions of an extremely complex array of molecules" (Sagan, *The Dragons of Eden*, p. 7).

[48] For example, the mathematician Roger Penrose, faced with the overwhelming difficulty of defining human consciousness or intelligence, confesses: "Perhaps we should seri-

mathematical empiricism or reductionism becomes so used to restricting its vision in order to deal with the world in a particular way, it often imagines not just that an underlying structure has been explained, but that the ultimate nature of reality—the essence of what the human being or the world is—has also been demonstrated with this method.

THE FALLACY OF DIMINUTION

When ecophilosophy utilizes the meta-narrative of science—the concluding phrases of which now describe a Gaian ecological perspective—to support ecocentrism, it is choosing, for the sake of a particular end, just this restriction of vision. In the manner of a mathematical equation, the preservation of the life of the world (or the ecosphere) is made to equate with the equal regard for the rights of all components of that world. In the "equation," we find that only the quantitative aspects are written in. If the other aspects common to a traditional hierarchical perspective are noticed, they are not deemed relevant to the sum. If humans, as the species *Homo sapiens,* are no more important to the functioning of the global ecosystem than any number of other species, then they have no right to claim ethical pre-eminence over those others. Thus, an ethical equivalence is made from a material equivalence, and is bought at the expense of all the rest. Is the diminution in question, then, something of a sleight-of-hand?

Firstly, it should be made clear that the merits of something like an ecocentric approach—that is, an approach that does not only see things in terms of their instrumental value, is not anthropocentric, and respects the contribution which all life makes to the whole—is not the point of dispute. However worthy the *underlying spirit* of ecocentrism, the need here is to see that, when it is arrived at through recourse to the findings of scientific reductionism and measurement, a number of qualities will be put to one side. Clearly, ecocentrism does not set out to discount all the special capacities of humans *that it can envisage.* Its aim, rather, is to disallow that these capacities make a difference to ethical considerability. However, it must be asked whether the adoption of a scientific perspective does not itself engender a limited apprehension of what those capacities might be,

---

ously consider the possibility that our intelligence might indeed require some kind of act of God—and that it cannot be explained in terms of that science which has become so successful in the description of the inanimate world" (Roger Penrose, *Shadows of the Mind* [Oxford: Oxford University Press, 1994], p. 144).

and thus in turn influence ecophilosophers to downplay our difference in relation to other species and so reach the conclusions they do.

Because scientific empiricism or reductionism shifts our focus to the quantifiable aspects of things, the successive *discoveries* of science (by which the nature of "matter" is thought to be revealed) may be seen to be just as much *veilings;* they do not just uncover other realities, but obscure whatever else might be there. By concentrating only on what is measurable, one of two things happen to the non-measurable qualities of the world: they are either denied altogether, or they are relegated to a more nebulous existence within individual consciousness; they become *psychic* states. Having grown used to the distinction between material things and the things of the mind, we have forgotten that the distinction is actually artificial. The "matter" which science talks of is in fact not a thing that exists *independently* of science. Science has not discovered what matter *is;* nor does it study a reality that can be termed "matter." Rather, science has *defined what matter is* through the measuring or mathematical approach it takes. To look at only quantifiable data is, as it were, to begin wearing lenses that allow only vision in shades of grey, and to eventually claim that colour is not real but imaginary. It is thus that, historically, the more subtle ontological states—acknowledged by philosophers prior to the advent of modern science—progressively "disappear" from the world, and begin to inhabit an interior, "psychic" domain. Divinity—once the ultimate ground of being—has been removed, as has the subtle element beauty, while the corresponding feelings they inspire—wonder, awe, love, joy, serenity, humility, a sense of sacredness—are no longer believed to arise in response to our *perception* of these things, but to have their origin in human consciousness. The neat division between an exterior world and an interior one might seem plausible, and it lends credence to a classification system in which some things are believed less real than others. But it persists, and is made coherent, only so long as our faith in measurement persists.

Even the grand narrative of science that posits the evolutionary unfolding of the universe does not so much demonstrate the validity of the duality, but itself hinges upon it. In this model, the simplicity of hydrogen "evolves"—in the nuclear furnace it creates when subjected to gravity—to helium and then progressively each of the other elements up to iron. The process of elemental creation is completed in the outpouring of supernovae. A solar system with an earth-like planet develops, after which comes the complex cycling of molecules in gaseous, liquid, and solid forms. Life manifests, and then increasingly complex and subtle sensory systems. Finally, within suitably complex organisms, consciousness emerges and is manifested in ever more subtle ways. The final stages of this ascending order seem to be expressed most fully in humans.

From one point of view, then, we *are* presented with a hierarchically structured ontology that attests to the pre-eminence of humanity. Yet, ecophilosophy is right to sense that this "pre-eminence" is granted little significance while it rests on the primacy of matter. When the immaterial qualities—which are categorized in terms of aspects of consciousness—appear to be no more than a prolongation of the ascending movement found in the material realm, then the argument for the essential equivalence of things appears reasonable. However, the now familiar cosmology used to support this argument *is itself underpinned by the supposition that measurable qualities are more real;* a world wherein matter produces consciousness is built out of the belief that matter is defined by measurable characteristics. Thus, a type of circular reinforcement has been set up, which creates the illusion of a valid worldview. Its collapse is prevented only as long as we believe in the legitimacy of the premise of measurement. No logic requires this of us, and our intuition—justifiably outraged by the diminished and seemingly back to front world this premise implies—must seek the ruin of such a system.

The pre-scientific tradition of the *hierarchy of Being,* which in one form or another found expression in the world's metaphysical traditions, not only classes as objective all the non-measurable qualities known to consciousness, but, because it is based on emanations from Oneness or Divinity, exactly reverses the order imposed by scientific knowledge. Instead of the hierarchy being assembled from material components upon a foundation of materiality, it relies on an emergence from the top down, as it were. To imagine this traditional account of ontological hierarchy to be founded on little more than wishful thinking is to hold far more store in the scientific method than is justified. Those who insist on conceiving the "upper" realms in terms of the materiality to which science subscribes, and then foolishly claim lack of evidence for their objective existence, display an ignorance of ontological possibility and a failure to recognize the limitations of scientific method. This alternative structure remains hidden to science only—and precisely—because it is inaccessible to scientific measurement. It is not the fault of science that the hierarchy of Being may not be encompassed by recourse to its method, but it is wrong to presume that it must be.

REASON AND PERCEPTION

To abandon the traditional outlook, as philosophy under the influence of modern science has been constrained to do, in favour of a scientific outlook that believes many aspects of the world to have their *origin* and *location* in the individual consciousness, is to *inevitably* conclude that Leopold was mistaken in his view, and that beauty is subjective. This is just the position ecophilosophy has been obliged to hold: the beauty Leopold attested is either dismissed because it is not measurable in the way "integrity" and "stability" might be, or it is treated *as if* it were real. Thus Callicott, in his appraisal of Leopold's land aesthetic, rightly extends the aesthetic experience beyond the visual:

> The appreciation of an environment's natural beauty can involve the ears (the sounds of rain, insects, birds, or silence itself), the surface of the skin (the warmth of the sun, the chill of the wind, the texture of grass, rock, sand), the nose and tongue (the fragrance of flowers, the odor of decay, the taste of saps and waters).[49]

"But," he says, "it is not enough simply to open the senses to natural stimuli and enjoy."[50] Since the appreciation of beauty "can involve the mind, the faculty of cognition . . . [then] ecology, history, paleontology, geology, biogeography—each a form of knowledge or cognition—penetrate the surface provided by direct sensory experience and supply substance to 'scenery.'" Callicotts's claim is that the land aesthetic "involves a subtle interplay between conceptual schemata and sensuous experience."[51] In other words, thought informs experience so that "what one experiences is as much a product of how one thinks as it is the condition of one's senses and the specific content of one's environment."[52] In Callicott's own experience, beauty in nature "is a function of the palpable organization and closure of the interconnected living components." However, "these connections and relations are not directly sensed in the aesthetic moment, they are *known*

---

[49] J. Baird Callicott, "The Land Aesthetic," in *Companion to A Sand County Almanac*, p. 161.

[50] Callicott, "The Land Aesthetic," p. 164.

[51] Callicott, "The Land Aesthetic," pp. 161 and 163.

[52] Callicott, "The Land Aesthetic," p. 164.

and *projected.* . . . It is this conceptual act that completes the sensory experience and causes it to be distinctly aesthetic."[53]

Callicott resists the disclaimer that beauty is not actually part of nature. Nevertheless, for him the higher levels of aesthetic appreciation are dependent on our own particular *conceptual* appraisal of the forms of nature. But, as we have seen, for Leopold beauty is an aspect of the world, and there is no necessary concordance between beauty and conceptual knowledge. Beauty is seen as perceptual, not rational; as such, if there is a hierarchy involved it is a hierarchy of *perception*, or *non*-rational consciousness, corresponding to an ontological hierarchy.

In a world where the mind or reason—held to be paramount—is taken to be the mediator of perception, the idea of a *direct perception of the world as it is*, independent of the reason, sounds anachronistic. Western philosophy has lived with the idea of both sensory and rational limits ever since Kant, who showed that the rational mind, imposing its *a priori* assumptions upon the sensory impressions, inevitably modifies them. Although prepared to imagine the *noumenon* (*Ding an sich*, the "thing-in-itself"), he believed there was no faculty adequate to its perception. This conclusion seems inevitable, though, considering it is reached, precisely, through an engagement with rational processes. An inordinate faith in the rational mode of consciousness was, as previously noted, not the original intention of philosophy. As Frithjof Schuon observes,

> Reason is formal by its nature and formalistic in its operations; it proceeds by coagulations, by alternatives and by exclusions—or, it can be said, by partial truths . . . it touches on essences only through drawing conclusions, not by direct vision; it is indispensable for verbal formulations but it does not involve immediate knowledge.[54]

By this account, virtually all post-Renaissance philosophy is questionable precisely because of its preoccupation with the rational faculty as a means to knowledge and by its failure to either discern or incorporate the nonrational or perceptive element it lacks. To coherently reinstate the hierarchy of beauty that Leopold considers to be in nature requires the reinstatement of a mode of consciousness, or perceptive faculty, adequate to the task of perceiving all that beauty *is*.

---

[53] Callicott, "The Land Aesthetic," pp. 165-166.

[54] Frithjof Schuon, *Understanding Islam* (Bloomington: World Wisdom, 1994), p. 15.

CHAPTER FOUR
Ecophilosophy in the Light of Tradition

While the science of ecology may be used to support a comprehensive environmental ethic like ecocentrism, the tenets of religion, which treat as objective that which science takes to be unreal, are found wanting in just this regard. Religion, because it deals primarily with the relationship of people with a Divinity or their higher Self, too easily falls prey to the perceived shortcomings of a "humanistic" or "anthropocentric" outlook; it cannot easily resist the tendency to bear our own interests in mind before that of other species (if not disregard their interests altogether). Ecophilosophers are often passionately concerned to distance themselves from a style of thinking that either takes no account of the interests of nature *in toto*, or downgrades those interests. However, in attempting to divest itself of a humanistic or anthropocentric framework, ecophilosophy has relinquished not only any allegiance it might have had to human priority over other creatures but, by association, allegiance to those very human qualities that religion sees as part of our nature and *which create for us our position in respect to nature.*

The polymath Jacob Bronowski once made an important observation about human uniqueness. "Man," he said, "is not a figure in the landscape—he is a shaper of the landscape. . . . [He] is distinguished from other animals by his imaginative gifts" and his reason.[1] It is in exercising those faculties that we stand apart from, and objectify nature. But this is only half the story. The senses, by contrast, bring nature *to* us; they are a means by which nature—the environment—communicates with us and we become, in a way, nature's subject. The senses bring form, texture, colour, sound and so on; they also channel more subtle perceptions like those of beauty or the sacred. If it is our nature to harbour such perceptions, then they are also a part of what distinguishes our humanity—no less a part of our nature than the faculties that give us the power to break nature apart and put it back together in new ways. To conceptually remove us, therefore, from

---

[1] Jacob Bronowski, *The Ascent of Man* (London: BBC, 1976), pp. 19-20. All the research into animal behaviour in the last three decades has not fundamentally changed this reality.

our position of observer, assessor, manipulator, or recipient of the world's properties, and then place us into nature as beings similar to all others, is to divest us of the very attributes that form a part of *our* nature, and which, in the context of environmentalism, lend wings to the passionate and voluntary involvement in, and compassion for, the state of the natural world. Although the science of ecology has *conceptually* removed us from a position of centrality, this alone does not entail an ecological *worldview*.[2] Equally, there is no evidence that instilling an ecocentric outlook will foster a feeling of identity with nature.

Interestingly, and in contradistinction, it is precisely *feeling,* resulting from the operation of just those perceptions that are part of our nature, that is (as we saw in part one) of the greatest importance. Our unique sense of beauty, and the sense of the sacred into which it extends, is indeed what engages us in our concern and love for the world. If it is impossible to be moved by evidence that we are a species like any other, it *is* possible, through an engagement with those higher, human, faculties to be moved by the sense of the significance and value of other beings and the world in general. When, therefore, it is suggested that we need a completely new paradigm to inform our interaction with the environment, the assumption seems to be that, unless the outlook is broadly *eco*centric, there exists the danger of attempting to marry a less than appropriate philosophy to a movement that asks only that all of the world's life be worthy of consideration. Yet this assumption is fallacious. It can be demonstrated empirically that a non-ecocentric approach is not at odds with suitable environmental practice. A tendency to minimize impact and destruction, to seek to repair what has been damaged, and to care for nature as well as human life, is to be found no less in "anthropocentric" philosophy. The older Leopold's outlook is a classic response in this mould, as too is the lifestyle and pragmatic ethics of Albert Schweitzer.[3] Nor need we exclude many of the Eastern religious traditions, which are easily able to balance a metaphysics that includes the supranatural and human pre-eminence with an ethical

---

[2] Bertrand Russell, responding to what science had revealed, could even express a moral superiority to the Universe: "In the world we know, there are many things that would be better otherwise, and the ideals to which we do and must adhere are not realized in the realm of matter" (Bertrand Russell, "A Free Man's Worship," in Why I Am Not A Christian [New York: Simon and Schuster, 1957], p. 16).

[3] See Albert Schweitzer, *My Life and Thought* (London: Unwin, 1966).

and compassionate concern for all life that minimizes environmental impact through a general philosophy of detachment from the world.[4] Nor, as we shall see shortly, need we exclude even the Abrahamic religions. It may appear contradictory, but a genuinely lived philosophy of this type—that is, one that directs consciousness *away* from a preoccupation with the world—can be environmentally sensitive and conserving of resources. This is because, as Nasr says, traditional "man,"

> who over the ages lived for the most part in harmony with nature, viewed himself, not so much as what he "was" but as what he should be . . . before the modern period, when man came to be seen as having ascended from the ape with no spiritual and ethically significant prototype, traditions all over the world envisaged man as having a spiritual archetype from which he had fallen or descended, and that archetype remained as the goal of perfection to be reached.[5]

In the Middle Ages, humanity's position in the hierarchy of Being was considered to lie between the phenomenal world and the "noumenal" one, and was likened to a bridge connecting the two.[6] Humanity was

---

[4] To take just the example of Hinduism, as well as incorporating the idea of the Divinity as immanent, the Yogic ethics of *Yama* and *Niyama* carry the ideals of *Ahimsa*, and *Aparigraha*—that is, non-violence whenever possible, and the minimization of material possessions. In this regard John Chryssavgis reminds us that "the present ecological crisis is a result precisely of our action—of considerable human effort and success to 'change' or 'better' the world—and not only of our greed or covetousness. The primary cause of our devastation and destruction is the relentless pursuit of what many people consider a good or desirable thing—namely, the modern, industrial-technological model of development" (John Chryssavgis, "The World of the Icon and Creation," in *Seeing God Everywhere*, p. 263).

[5] S.H. Nasr, "Man and Nature: Quest for Renewed Understanding," p. 8.

[6] Interestingly, and ironically for ecophilosophy, our position in the hierarchy, and the hierarchy in general, was not conducive to hubris. For while we may have been "bold" enough to conjecture that we expressed something more in the way of perception and consciousness than the plants and animals around us, we did not claim for ourselves a pre-eminence of the sort often made by science. The ascending ladder of creation continued on above us into "angelic" realms of being. This meant a psyche held in check and often a reverence for Earth as creation. In contrast, it can be argued that humanism and the discoveries of science actually elevated humanity's status, and that ego-consciousness, having become preeminent, promoted a hubristic belief in "man" as lord of creation, with the sanction to treat

pontifex (Lat. "bridge-maker") by virtue of the operation of the "faculty" known as Intellect (Lat. *Intellectus*, "perception" or "comprehension") which makes known that which belongs to an essential realm. When this realm is considered to be distinct from the world, it is natural to represent the Intellect as superior to or "above" the reason, "closer" to the transcendence of Divinity. But alternatively, from a perspective that acknowledges immanence, the Intellect may be conceived as lying *between* the senses and reason, unveiling divine qualities in nature by pre-empting the rational mode of consciousness. In this traditional metaphysics, then, the Intellect allows two things: a transcendence of the rational or discursive mind, and through this an *Intellective intuition* of the "underlying" substance or essence of nature.

By virtue of being the link or bridge between earth and heaven, the human being "bears responsibility to both the Divine Principle and to nature and is not free to do with the created world simply what he wills." Rather, freedom can be "realized fully only inwardly by reaching the Divine Realm, which is infinite and beyond all constraint."[7] By contrast, a secular philosophy applied to the world is no guarantee of ecologically sound practice, probably because its usually materialist view works against any motivation towards such practice. As Nasr explains:

> Paradoxically, those who have denied that man has any mode of existence beyond that of the earth have helped to turn the powerful forces within the soul solely *towards* the earth resulting in its degradation. Men have come to seek the Infinite in our finite earthly home with devastating consequences for that home. The fact that traditionally man was seen as a being made for the spiritual realm, but living in this world, served to emphasize the sacred quality of nature and man's responsibility towards it. The reduction of man to a merely terrestrial being with merely earthly needs and desires, but earthly needs and desires without limits, cannot but lead to the destruction of the terrestrial environment itself.[8]

nature—no longer sacred—as he willed.

[7] Nasr, "Man and Nature: Quest for Renewed Understanding," p. 8.

[8] Nasr, "Man and Nature: Quest for Renewed Understanding," p. 9.

Ecophilosophy can hardly be unaware of the paradox at the heart of an environmental ideology. Certainly, it is precisely because modern science is neutral about how one should respond ethically to its worldview that ecophilosophy has sought an ideology that might affect behaviour. Accordingly, it has been obliged to take into account the philosophies and religions which *do* apparently influence human behaviour—examining, for instance, the practices of Taoism, Buddhism, and Hinduism.[9] But in turning hence, what do we find? That the *fundamental concern* is for awakening or developing the very faculty within ourselves of which science is ignorant, but which is believed to define for us our humanity, our difference, and *allow us* to appreciate the sacredness of the natural world, thus diverting attention from the primacy of the material. Since modern science is at a disadvantage when talking about non-material aspects and the faculty that relates to these things, it might be expected that it would be deemed deficient, and religion correspondingly valued. Yet ecophilosophy, now reliant on the principles that underpin an ecological understanding, must acquiesce to certain "inarguable facts" such as modern cosmogony and cosmology, or the transformation of species through natural selection. Hence, only those aspects of religious belief that are suitably ambiguous towards this scientific knowledge are permitted a precarious foothold, while in the background hovers science's judgement that these things have their basis in the psyche, which is itself ultimately tied to the material realm.

"TRANSPERSONAL ECOLOGY"

The conception we now have of *psyche* stems from a belief in the illusory

---

[9] See, for example, for Hinduism: L. Gupta, "Purity, Pollution and Hinduism," in *Ecofeminism and the Sacred*, ed. C.J. Adams (New York: Continuum, 1993), pp. 99-116; K.A. Jacobsen, "The Institutionalization of the Ethics of 'Non-Injury' toward all 'Beings' in Ancient India," *Environmental Ethics* 16 (1994): pp. 287-302; and E. Deutsch, "A Metaphysical Grounding for Nature Reverence: East-West," *Environmental Ethics* 8 (1986): pp. 293-299. For Taoism see R.T. Ames, "Taoism and the Nature of Nature," *Environmental Ethics* 8 (1986): pp. 317-350; C-Y. Cheng, "On the Environmental Ethics of the Tao and the Ch'i," *Environmental Ethics* 8 (1986): pp. 351-370; and P. Marshall, *Nature's Web: An Exploration of Ecological Thinking* (London: Simon & Schuster, 1992). For Buddhism see K.K. Inada, "Environmental Problematics in the Buddhist Context," *Philosophy East and West* 37 (1987): pp. 135-149; P. Billimoria, "Indian Religious Traditions," in *Spirit of the Environment: Religion, Value and Environmental Concern*, eds. D.E. Cooper and J.A. Palmer (London: Routledge, 1998), pp. 1-14; and P. de Silva, *Environmental Philosophy and Ethics in Buddhism* (London: Macmillan, 1998).

nature of the higher element, the Intellect. The psyche, now an autonomous, localized entity (often correlated with the brain), is deemed not to have the capacity for any *real* connection with that which lies beyond its small sphere; its ability to "transcend" itself and "connect" with the environment around it being termed "identification," a process limited by imagination and empathy.

It is now usual to consider some form of identification or communication as an obvious corollary to the ecocentric position.[10] However, the restricted view of the psyche—the nature and potential of which is effectively a two-dimensional parody of the traditional view of the human being—is reflected in a readiness by some ecophilosophers to re-conceive the traditional view of *Self-realization* (the replacement, or subsuming, of the "self" by the "Self") as a matter of identification. Arne Naess, the originator of the "deep" ecological approach to environmentalism,[11] begins with the pronouncement that all beings should be permitted to self-realize—that is, realize their full potential.[12] For humanity, the term means an invitation to expand the sense of self to include nature as a whole. For Fox, who applied the term "transpersonal ecology" to this process, self-realization becomes "a this-worldly realization of as expansive a sense of self as possible."[13] He isolates three different types of identification,[14] one of which, as mentioned earlier, relies on the modern scientific narrative of the "creation"

[10] For instance, Freya Mathews' panpsychist view, which ascribes "a 'psychist' or mentalistic dimension to all matter, or to the physical realm generally . . . renders [the world] an arena not merely for causality but for communication" (Freya Mathews, *Reinhabiting Reality: Towards a Recovery of Culture* [Albany: SUNY, 2005], p. 14).

[11] Naess, whose philosophy is characterized by the attempt to uncover and then promote the most profound reasons for why the environment should be protected, utilized the terms "identification" and "self-realization" in several papers. See, for example, Arne Naess, "Identification as a Source of Deep Ecological Attitudes," in *Deep Ecology*, ed. Michael Tobias (San Diego: Avant Books, 1995), pp. 256-70; and, "Self-Realization: An Ecological Approach to Being in the World," *The Trumpeter* 4(3) (1987): pp. 35-42.

[12] In Naess's normative system, "Ecosophy T," the foundation of deep ecology, his first norm is "Self-realization!" and his second, "Self-realization for all living beings!" (Naess quoted in Fox, *Toward a Transpersonal Ecology*, p. 103).

[13] Warwick Fox, "The Meanings of Deep Ecology," *Island* 35 (1988): p. 34.

[14] They are the "personal," "ontological," and "cosmological" bases of identification. See Fox, *Toward a Transpersonal Ecology*, p. 249.

and evolution of the universe. In a sense it is a persuasion that, faced with the modern account of science that demonstrates the inextricable connection of all things, we should feel a relationship to everything. Not only are we composed of star stuff, but the cycling of virtually indestructible atoms throughout the planet also means that we all contain thousands of the atoms that previously went to make up any historical personage we care to imagine, or, indeed any other being at all.[15]

Now, given the concerns of environmentalism, which focus on the preservation of the natural world, deep ecology's suggestion might seem to answer well. Yet the foremost concern of philosophy *per se* should be to ascertain the truth, not to serve a particular doctrine. The world does not obviously demand identification, and, deprived of this request, we have no more than a decision to accept the promptings of an ecological understanding and claim identification as a laudatory act. More importantly, in this regard, if the nature of humanity is not defined completely by modern psychology, or the world by ecology, then the urging of humanity in the direction suggested will be in conflict with nature, not in harmony with it.

The Self-realization that is a familiar theme in traditional metaphysics is a lessening, even dissolving of the self, to be replaced by a Self which in no way consists of an individuated consciousness, but is rather the withdrawal of that consciousness in favour of the expression of a Unity. Much sacred literature (as we shall see in part four) makes this clear. For example, the process is described in a *hadith qudsi* thus: "When I love him, I am the Hearing wherewith he heareth and the Sight wherewith he seeth and the Hand wherewith he graspeth and the Foot whereon he walketh."[16] Regardless of this profound "psychology," and to suit the particular purposes of environmentalism, deep ecology is apparently advocating the expansion of the sense of individual selfhood, a very different thing. Isolated from a metaphysical framework that describes and guides the process of transformation, this might well be a prescription for either delusion or disaster. Identification becomes very much like the attempt to swallow the sea rather than be part of it. In a "this-worldly" expansion of self, it is hard not to see an expansion rather than diminishment of the ego.

---

[15] An observation made by Bill Bryson in *A Short History of Nearly Everything* (London: Doubleday, 2003), p. 120.

[16] Bukhari, *Riqaq*, 37; quoted in Martin Lings, *A Sufi Saint of the Twentieth Century* (Cambridge: The Islamic Texts Society, 1993), p. 37.

Ecocentrism, although it may be equated with ethics, is foremost a *descriptive* term derived from ecological information. Prompted by ecological insights we may think of ourselves as "one knot in the biospherical web," but this conceptualization does not in itself offer any great insight into appropriate behaviour. Deep ecology suggests a supporting non-prescriptive "ethics" of identification, so that "care flows naturally."[17] But, in practice, identification would not allow any of the destruction essential to live.[18] Remove identification, as we must to be practical, and we have to fall back on *decisions.* And here we reach a turning point, for identification and ethical considerations in general are subtle ideas that belong in the first place to an area of reality beyond the scope of modern science. Their origin is consciousness itself, and seemingly only our own—no other species demonstrates consideration for the ongoing working of the ecosphere. It is by virtue of our consciousness that ideas like "ethical considerability" and "intrinsic value" have their existence. And, significantly, it is through our consciousness that knowledge of how Gaia operates and what its aims are, exists. It is *we* who decide to preserve the Gaian ecosystem, and *we* who then decide on a management strategy. Given our unique standing in this regard, ecocentrism is impossible in any practical sense. Realistically, we can hardly place ourselves other than in the role of managers or, better, guardians of the system of which we are aware. We always *have* needed to make the decisions of stewardship, and there seems no choice—especially now that our adverse impact has become so apparent—but to continue in this vein. In this respect, the only relevant question is *how to be* wise stewards.

To be wise in the original sense of *sophia* would be to understand the nature of nature and, especially, our own nature. The ecocentrism of ecophilosophy subtly undermines the foundations of the human *qua* human by suggesting that human nature has no bearing on moral considerability. The empiricism of ecology is linked to a non-empirical axiological system to create a new paradigm. Fundamentally, this is to make a

---

[17] Naess writes: "Care flows naturally if the self is widened so that the protection of free nature is felt and conceived as protection of ourselves" (Naess quoted in Fox, "The Meanings of Deep Ecology," p. 34).

[18] Both introspection and experience shows that the cutting of trees, the destruction of soil life in order to grow food, and many other activities depend on deliberately *not* identifying with life.

prescription for a particular mode of thought, then dismiss as irrelevant anything that does not fall into that pattern of thought, even though it might be true, and might be a reason for altering that thought. Unwittingly, ecophilosophy, through recourse to the scientific disciplines of ecology and psychology, has forestalled any further consideration of the human being as standing apart from the world, or our need to stand apart to be truly human. A basic tenet of ecocentrism is that we should not deny the rights of other species to be truly what *they* are—Naess's philosophy is founded on this belief. Logically, then, we should apply this principle to ourselves, and be willing to carry Naess's policy of asking "deeper" questions[19] into the arena of metaphysics.

ORIGINS OF THE ENVIRONMENT MOVEMENT

It is no coincidence that the "worship of nature" began at a time when Christianity in Europe was in decline.[20] In fact, the Romantic Movement of the late eighteenth and early nineteenth centuries can be partially defined by just this turning away from a centuries-long preoccupation with "another" world and a re-orientation towards "this" one. In the shift of focus, the world of nature suddenly appeared very differently. The historian Kenneth Clark, quoting Thomas Gray, identifies the beginning of the change in sentiment: "Not a precipice, not a torrent, not a cliff, but is pregnant with religion and poetry."[21] So began an attraction or devotion to the majesty, the beauty, the sublimity and the sacredness of nature, expressed in painting, poetry and prose.[22] In 1798, Wordsworth could write of his youthful experience:

---

[19] The "deep" of deep ecology derives from Naess's injunction to always ask "progressively deeper questions about the ecological relationships of which we are a part" (Fox, *Toward a Transpersonal Ecology*, p. 92).

[20] Kenneth Clark's account of the collapse of religious faith and its resurrection as the spirit within Romanticism remains one of the most perceptive. See Kenneth Clark, *Civilisation* (London: BBC, 1969), chapter 11.

[21] Clark, *Civilisation*, p. 271.

[22] The major writers in England were the Lake Poets, and Blake, Scott, Byron, and Shelley; in France: Rousseau, Lamartine, Hugo, and Chateaubriand; and in Germany, the Schlegel brothers, Novalis, and Jean Paul Richter.

For nature then
To me was all in all. — I cannot paint
What then I was. The sounding cataract
Haunted me like a passion: the tall rock,
The mountain, and the deep and gloomy wood,
Their colours and their forms, were then to me
An appetite; a feeling and a love,
That had no need of a remoter charm,
By thought supplied, nor any interest
Unborrowed from the eye.[23]

The conviction expressed here, that a profound quality resides within nature and that its unveiling occurs through a pre-rational mode of consciousness, is typical of the Romantic temperament. For Coleridge, this inner essence far transcends what is normally perceived or believed to be there, and its deep intuition corresponds with the abeyance of ordinary thought:

> O dread and silent mount! I gazed upon thee,
> Till thou, still present to the bodily sense,
> Didst vanish from my thought: entranced in prayer
> I worshipped the Invisible alone.[24]

Rousseau, alone upon the shore of "his" island on Lake Bienne, describes a similar experience where absorption in nature induces the cessation of the sense of individual identity:

> I liked then to go and sit on the shingle in some secluded spot by the edge of the lake; there the noise of the waves and the movement of the water, taking hold of my senses and driving all other agitation from my soul, would plunge it into a delicious reverie in which night often stole upon me unawares. The ebb and flow of the water, its continuous yet undulating noise, kept lapping against my ears and my eyes, taking the place of all the inward movements which my reverie had calmed within me, and it was enough to

---

[23] William Wordsworth, "Lines Composed A Few Miles Above Tintern Abbey" (1798).

[24] Samuel Taylor Coleridge, "Hymn Before Sun-rise, in the Vale of Chamouni" (1802).

make me pleasurably aware of my existence, without troubling myself with thought.[25]

In these experiences, we have the distilled essence of today's environment movement: the natural world is the embodiment of a significance that far surpasses its outer form; at the same time, it mysteriously harbours a means of transcending the narrow confines of the individuated consciousness. Seen as a response to the goodness, beauty, and meaning in nature, "Romanticism" has always been with us; its seemingly dramatic historical appearance is a function of its antithetical status: in an age of reason and science, it attracts our attention as would a bright flower in a desert.

As the Enlightenment faltered, the *conception* of a transcendent Divinity which had occupied post-Renaissance Europe—the remote, but almost human Creator, the "father in heaven" Michelangelo had painted[26]—began to be replaced for some by a renewed subtlety of *perception*; a departure from the humanist stance—where man, "the measure of all things," had defined nature and God in terms of his own conceptions—towards a witnessing of realities within nature that vastly transcend such conceptions, and are testimony to the validity of direct experience. The beautiful and the sacred were found to be immanent, a "discovery" that has its prolongation in the perspective identified in part one. The associated word *sublime*[27] described that aspect of nature with the power to effect a change in ordinary consciousness. Nature must always defy humanism, however heroic;

---

[25] Jean-Jacques Rousseau, *Reveries of the Solitary Walker*, trans. Peter France (Harmondsworth: Penguin, 1979), pp. 86-87.

[26] Philip Sherrard refers to the "tendency within the post-mediaeval Christian world to look upon creation as the artifact of a Maker who as it were has produced it from without. This has provided us with a picture of a God in heaven who, having set the cosmic process in motion and having left it to run more or less on its own and according to its own laws, now interferes directly on but rare occasions. . . . The result is that the relation between God and creation tends to be seen predominantly as one of cause and effect: God is a world cause, a supreme or first cause or principle of being; and the world and its laws are what He has produced" (Philip Sherrard, "The Desanctification of Nature," in *Seeing God Everywhere*, p. 110).

[27] The word was first used by Longinus in about 200 CE. *On the Sublime*, translated into English in 1712, was just one book that helped to define the "new" outlook. Edmund Burke, in *A Philosophical Enquiry into the Origins of our Ideas of the Sublime and Beautiful*, defined the sublime in terms of nature's overwhelming power.

against the power and majesty of nature the self is diminished, and this may become the prelude to the dissolution of the rational, or egoic, consciousness, and the emergence of another mode of consciousness responsible for the perception of a deeper beauty.

Two reasons for the change in outlook regarding nature may be identified: modern science itself, and the introduction of an Eastern mysticism. Clearly, the catalyst which produced a reaction as potent as the decline of one form of religion and the consequent redirecting of human consciousness, must be singular. Indeed, the scientific revolution, that in only two hundred years had both instilled a mechanistic view of the world and been responsible for a vigorous new age of the machine, had severely eroded the conventional conception of God's creation as something to be revered. By the beginning of the nineteenth century, Wordsworth could write, "I now affirm of Nature and of Truth . . . that their Divinity Revolts, offended at the ways of men."[28] The spirit that rallies to the perceived oppression of people under the tyranny of the machine is the same one that responds to the subjugation of nature itself. And the adverse treatment of both must stem from a machine-like mentality:

> For Bacon and Newton, sheath'd in dismal steel, their terrors hang
> Like iron scourges over Albion: Reasonings like vast Serpents
> Infold around my limbs, bruising my minute articulations.
> I turn my eyes to the Schools & Universities of Europe
> And there behold the Loom of Locke whose Woof rages dire,
> Wash'd by the Water-wheels of Newton: black the cloth
> In heavy wreathes folds over every nation: cruel Works
> Of many Wheels I view, wheel without wheel, with cogs tyrannic
> Moving by compulsion each other, not as those in Eden, which,
> Wheel within Wheel, in freedom revolve in harmony & peace.[29]

Blake's Eden reminds us of a nature free of the strictures of Enlightenment science, and of the "paradise" of an alternative perception of nature that existed prior to this new thought. Blake, though, was not pointing in the direction of an already enfeebled exoterism, but to an earlier age still

---

[28] William Wordsworth, "The Excursion" (1814) I, 983-985.

[29] William Blake, "A Vision of Albion," in *Jerusalem: The Emanation of the Giant Albion* (1820).

cognizant of the inner dimension of religion; towards that state of consciousness capable of discerning the error of rationalism and materialism, and where they would lead. It is no small irony that the eventual inheritors (in the twentieth century) of this first—and ultimately unsuccessful—defence of nature would initially be prepared to overlook the decisive role of the scientific mentality in the environmental crisis, and instead attack that which, for Blake, held a remedy for the spreading malady of this "scientism." In "The Historical Roots of Our Ecological Crisis,"[30] Lynn White rounded upon the already recognized adversary of modern science—religion—delivering a putative *coup de grace*. Drawing attention to various biblical passages (and, it must be said, ignoring others) White believed he had identified key inducements to a pattern of thought that had motivated a harmful response to nature for upwards of two thousand years. As Nash observes, "this exposure of the shortcomings of Western religious tradition . . . [was] taken for granted by environmentalists after the 1960s."[31]

The validity of White's thesis has been challenged many times since its first publication, often by apologists who claim that it is always possible to read scripture more sympathetically. However, it cannot be seriously denied that almost from the beginning in Christianity there were corruptions of the original teaching that came about due to its impact with temporal powers.[32] Nor can it be denied that this "weakness" provided an opening for the development of a secular science, even though, as Nasr points out, this "paradigm . . . was created from many strands during the Renaissance, the 17th century and the Age of Enlightenment, often in opposition to Christianity whose teachings on nature became ever more eclipsed and marginalized."[33]

---

[30] Lynn White Jr., "The Historical Roots of Our Ecological Crisis," in *Western Man and Environmental Ethics: Attitudes Toward Nature and Technology*, ed. Ian G. Barbour (Reading, Massachusetts: Adison-Wesley, 1973), pp. 18-30.

[31] Roderick Nash, "Aldo Leopold's Intellectual Heritage," in *Companion to A Sand County Almanac*, p. 70.

[32] For Sherrard, when Christianity "became the religion of a civilization it was forced to incorporate Roman and even common law into its structure. . . . This has meant that it has always been more easy to detach . . . the political, social and economic sphere of human life from the framework of the Christian revelation and so to leave it exposed to domination by purely secular interests and influences" (Sherrard, "The Desanctification of Nature," pp. 121-122).

[33] Nasr, "Man and Nature: Quest for Renewed Understanding," p. 7.

Notwithstanding the above, White's thesis remains spurious because it encourages an *exoteric* understanding of religion. By creating for us an association between the written word and the consequences of applying it straightforwardly to the world, White gives us an image which we inevitably project upon the past, thus blinding ourselves to the clear distinction that should be made between the way scripture *may* be interpreted and the way it *was* interpreted. To reason as White does is to infer that the consciousness of the past was sufficiently like the present so that scripture would have been always and everywhere interpreted in the same way.[34] It is to propagate a view which cannot but hide for us a religion's *esoteric* side. Clearly, the interpretation of any written material will mainly depend on the preconceptions, beliefs and perspectives that form the *Weltanschauung* of the times. While "dominion" (or any similar term) would mean one thing to a culture which believes the world to be mechanistic, to a culture that already saw the world in terms of sacred presence, it would mean something else entirely. Sensitivity to this distinction is vital. The fact that Judaism or Christianity is capable of being read in the way White reads it, implicates not religion as such but rather the decline of an esoteric element which in turn led to the modernist state of mind—*the platform from which White now speaks.* If modernist ears are sensitive to the biblical terms and phrases that suggest control, it may be because they are no longer sensitive to the deeper dimension of religion. The failure to find in scripture a clearly stipulated environmental ethic of the sort we now ask for can just as easily suggest that this missing ingredient was once too well understood to warrant enunciation.

For traditionalists, the decline in question amounts to an increasing inability to distinguish between two modes of consciousness, the rational and the Intellective. Effectively this means that over time there are fewer and fewer individuals within a religious tradition who, by virtue of the inner dimension of consciousness, are responsive to the inner dimension of the world. The course of Christianity bears witness to this, the early centuries standing in some contrast with what Christianity would later become.

---

[34] Wendell Berry makes the same point when he says that to read and understand the Bible "entails . . . the making of very precise distinctions between biblical instruction and the behaviour of those peoples supposed to have been biblically instructed" (Wendell Berry, "Christianity and the Survival of Creation," in *Seeing God Everywhere*, p. 54).

For the first Christians, and many of the Church fathers, the teachings of Christ contained a complete message pertaining to "inner" knowledge, summarized in his affirmation that "The Kingdom of Heaven is within you." Expressed in parable and symbol this knowledge was recognized to be compatible with the metaphysical inheritance from the Greek world.[35] Thus, St Dionysius the Areopagite forged a link between Christianity and Plato,[36] who spoke of the same potentialities of human consciousness and the same spiritual underpinning to the world to which that consciousness was open.

Following Christ's death there were, for the evangelists, inevitable political exigencies to deal with in their encounter with other cultures.[37] Consequently, their writings contain a mixture of the profound and the mundane; the Pauline letters illuminate both a consciousness in touch with deeper realities, and a mind attempting to confront the temporal power of the Greek and Roman world. Later Christian writers of mystical bent—more or less removed from worldly affairs—equally well understood and expressed the Intellective consciousness and the mystical quality of the world. They include the saints, Thomas, Irenaeus, Clement of Alexandria, Athanasius, Gregory of Nazianzus, Isaac of Nineveh, and Maximus the Confessor.[38]

---

[35] The compatibility of the esoteric teachings of any of the great metaphysical traditions is accepted by traditionalist authors, whose writings endeavour to reveal the parallels. See, for example, Frithjof Schuon's classic work *The Transcendent Unity of Religions* (Wheaton, Illinois: Quest Books, 1984), and Whitall Perry's *A Treasury of Traditional Wisdom* (Cambridge: Quinta Essentia, 1991).

[36] See *On the Divine Names* and *The Mystical Theology*, trans. C.E. Rolt (London: Society for Promoting Christian Knowledge, 1920-1940).

[37] To take one example, an early controversy hinged upon whether the Gentile converts could be exempt from traditional Mosaic Law (such as circumcision, or the ban on the eating of pork) but still achieve equal status with the Jewish converts. See Henry Chadwick, *The Early Church* (Harmondsworth: Penguin, 1990). Paul, cognizant of the way the esoteric teachings of Christ had attempted to cut through such outer detail, had to remain mindful of those for whom the deeper truth was opaque. A controversy such as this one, well represents the inevitable and endless clash between the exoterist and the esoterist.

[38] The Gospel of St Thomas is a Coptic manuscript of the fourth century CE from Egypt, probably adapted from an earlier Greek work. St Irenaeus (130-202) was a theologian and Bishop of Lyon. Clement (150?-220?), a Greek theologian, flourished in Alexandria as head of the catechetical school. Athanasius (293?-373) was Patriarch of Alexandria. St Gregory

After an authoritarian Roman Empire absorbed Christianity in the fourth century, intellectuals like Augustine developed from Plato and the neo-Platonists an elaborate doctrine compatible with scripture. But over time, Plato's and Plotinus' original sense of *nous* (the Greek term corresponding to *Intellectus*) became hazy. The incorporation of Aristotelian thought into medieval Scholasticism[39] meant an increasingly rational doctrine. In the thirteenth century, Thomas Aquinas could still judge that "if God's essence is to be seen at all, it must be that the intellect sees it through the divine essence itself."[40] However, the attempt by the rational faculty to provide a fixed and coherent rational basis for belief meant the marginalization, and eventual eclipse, of Intellective consciousness. Esoterism resists being institutionalized within a dogma. Nor can it be wholly captured or objectified by discursive thought or reasoning; "The letter killeth, but the spirit giveth life," St Paul had said.[41] As a bridge, the Intellect—which, above all, defines esoterism—exists as the only pathway to the indwelling Spirit in both nature and "in" our consciousness. The Church, as a vehicle for preserving Christ's teaching, may offer scripture, sacred ritual, and other sacred forms such as art and architecture,[42] to support or be a reminder of this other knowing. But when these things are taken to exist in and for themselves, a definite bifurcation ensues, and the esoteric dimension, although never absent, is no longer recognized. Within an ever more confining framework of orthodoxy, the early teachings, and later ones like those of Saint Francis[43] or Meister Eckhart, were increasingly misunderstood as unorthodox or even heretical.

(325-389) was Archbishop of Constantinople. St Isaac, mentioned in the *Philokalia*, flourished in the sixth century, and St Maximus (580-662), a theologian, was abbot of Chrysopolis.

[39] Chief among the Scholastics were Albert the Great (1200-1280), Thomas Aquinas (1225-74), Bonaventura (1221-74), and Duns Scotus (1264-1308).

[40] Aquinas, *Summa Contra Gentiles,* III. li.

[41] 2 Corinthians, 3: 6.

[42] Among medieval cathedrals, for example, Chartres may be counted a supreme crystallization of the subtleties of Western Christianity. See Titus Burckhardt, *Chartres and the Birth of the Cathedral* (Ipswich: Golgonooza Press, 1995).

[43] The life of St Francis (1182?-1226) epitomizes the respect and reverence for nature that results from the vision of God within. It is recognized by White as a pre-eminent example of a wise stewardship. See White, "The Historical Roots of our Ecological Crisis."

After the centuries following Aquinas, then, during which time an outer carapace of rationalism closed over and concealed the inner essence of Christianity, the sudden arrival, in the eighteenth century, of translated scriptural texts from the East—especially India—represented nothing less than the irruption of the undisguised esoteric doctrine into the European consciousness.[44] "Hinduism," it is recognized, never encountered the need to conceal the inner teaching of religion—something almost mandatory in the West to counter charges of heresy and a persecution wrought by the rigid and literal-minded.[45] The *Vedas, Upanishads,* and *Bhagavad Gita*[46] revealed to the German, French, and English poets and philosophers of the nineteenth century the relationship between the consciousness of the perceiver and the world that is perceived. "What cannot be thought with the mind, but that whereby the mind can think: Know that alone to be *Brahman,* the Spirit," says the *Kena Upanishad.*[47] And, in the *Isa Upanishad,* we are told: "The Spirit . . . is incorporeal and invulnerable, pure and untouched by evil. He is the supreme seer and thinker, immanent and transcendent."[48] These scriptures also revealed the relationship of the Divinity to the world. In the *Katha Upanishad,* it is said of the Supreme Spirit, "In space he is the sun, and he is the wind and the sky. . . . He dwells

---

[44] One can speak of *the* esoteric doctrine because the esoteric is the common essence of all religions. Hence, the Indian texts, although first and foremost introducing the doctrine of the Vedanta to the West, actually served to disclose inner meaning in the Christian writings, now largely forgotten. Oldmeadow, commenting on Friedrich Schlegel's adoption of Catholicism, says, "[an] immersion in Eastern thought and spirituality [is often] followed by a return to one's own religious tradition" (Harry Oldmeadow, *Journeys East* [Bloomington: World Wisdom, 2004], p. 21).

[45] Martin Lings writes: "the Advaita Vedanta has the advantage, shown by its altogether direct manner of expression, of never having had to speak in veiled terms in order to avoid a conflict with the limitations of exoterism" (Martin Lings, *The Eleventh Hour* [Cambridge: Quinta Essentia, 1987], p. 79).

[46] The *Vedas* are the oldest sacred writings, and comprise The *Rig-Veda,* the *Yajur-Veda,* the *Sama-Veda,* and the *Atharva-Veda.* The *Upanishads,* philosophical treatises, were composed between 400BCE and 1500CE. The *Bhagavad Gita,* c. 500 BCE, forms part of the Indian epic the *Mahabharata.*

[47] Juan Mascaró, trans., *The Upanishads* (Harmondsworth: Penguin, 1975), p. 51.

[48] Mascaró, *The Upanishads,* p. 49

in men and in gods, in righteousness and in the vast heavens. He is in the earth and the waters and in the rocks of the mountains."[49]

In one burst of light from the East, a world that had been darkened and drained of life and soul by modern science was renewed and sanctified by a vision of God within. As J.J. Clarke has said,

> the Hinduism of the Upanishads offered an exalted metaphysical system which resonated with [the Romantic philosophers'] . . . own idealist assumptions, and which provided a counterblast to the materialistic and mechanistic philosophy that had come to dominate the Enlightenment period.[50]

Far from being a lifeless mechanical contrivance wound like a clock at the beginning of time (as it had come to be viewed by the science of Isaac Newton's day) or even a living creation brought forth *ex nihilo* by the Creator, the world was affirmed as a manifestation of Divinity. In the *Bhagavad Gita*,[51] its essential oneness is revealed to Arjuna:

> I am the soul . . . which dwells in the heart of all things. I am the beginning, the middle, and the end of all that lives. . . . I am the beauty of all things beautiful. . . . Know . . . that I am the seed of all things that are; and that no being that moves or moves not can ever be without me. . . . Know that with one single fraction of my Being I pervade and support the Universe, and know that I AM.[52]

Unsurprisingly, the most affected were those of poetic sensibility. Yet, while the German Romantics—notably Schelling, Goethe, and Schopenhauer—were profoundly moved by the "music" of the Orient, their influence in the English-speaking world has remained limited. Instead, we find that the chord struck in the hearts and minds of the English Romantic poets is what reverberates today:

[49] Mascaró, *The Upanishads*, p. 63

[50] J.J. Clarke, *Oriental Enlightenment: The Encounter between Asian and Western Thought* (London: Routledge, 1997), p. 61.

[51] This text, first translated into English in 1785 by Charles Wilkins, was familiar to Blake.

[52] *The Bhagavad Gita*, trans. Juan Mascaró (Harmondsworth: Penguin, 1975), pp. 85-88. Unless otherwise noted, all subsequent citations are from this text.

To see a World in a Grain of Sand
And a Heaven in a Wild Flower
Hold Infinity in the palm of your hand
And Eternity in an hour.[53]

And I have felt
A presence that disturbs me with the joy
Of elevated thoughts; a sense sublime
Of something far more deeply interfused,
Whose dwelling is the light of setting suns,
and the round ocean and the living air,
And the blue sky, and in the mind of man:
A motion and a spirit, that impels
All thinking things, all objects of all thought,
And rolls through all things.[54]

The idea of the presence of the Spirit in nature and in humanity created a clearly distinct and alternative avenue of thought from the one science was taking. Those who subsequently encountered this new path, including the American transcendentalists Emerson, Whitman, and, especially, Thoreau[55] (whose classic, *Walden*, is now recognized as a significant influence in environmental thought), Spinoza, Schopenhauer, and, more latterly, T.S. Eliot and W.B. Yeats, have all espoused a philosophy that is deeply mistrustful of the direction of modern Western thought. Carl Jung, on encountering the Eastern tradition, was even moved to wonder whether all Western knowledge was not just abstraction.[56]

METAPHYSICS

Indian metaphysics stands as counterpoint to modernist thought because it affirms the "faculty" of perception adequate to the realizing of the na-

---

[53] William Blake, "Auguries of Innocence" (1803).

[54] Wordsworth, "Lines Composed A Few Miles Above Tintern Abbey."

[55] The influence of an Eastern metaphysical tradition is apparent in Emerson's "Brahma" and "Hamatreya"; in Whitman's "Leaves of Grass"; and in Thoreau's *Walden*.

[56] C.G. Jung, "The Dreamlike World of India," in *Collected Works* Vol. 10 (London: Routledge, 1969), p. 518.

ture of nature, while relegating reason to a secondary position. "Beyond the senses is the mind, and beyond the mind is reason, its essence. Beyond reason is the Spirit in man," (Skt. *Buddhi*, Intellect) says the *Katha Upanishad*.[57] In contrast, by assuming the absence of just this dimension to ontology—as Enlightenment philosophers did—an artificial discontinuity between the mind (perception) and nature (the perceived) was established. The two are now sustained as separate things, so that, rather than engagement with nature, there is study of it. Moreover, this *objectification* of nature through the use of reason acts to maintain the duality; while "knower" and "known" persist, identity is not possible. Reason and the senses prove to be poor collaborators in finding Truth. Nature comes to seem more and more elusive, and what at first seemed objective reality begins to look more like a construct of the mind itself. Hence, by the time Kant suspected the limitations of reason, and declared that the true nature of nature could not *be* known, the Western philosopher had become as a man confirmed in the practice of swimming, who claims that the other shore of a river is unreachable because he can no longer see the bridge that spans it. The fate of philosophy has been to remain spellbound by Kant's view ever since. The discoveries of science—even the science of the twentieth century— were taken to confirm the finality of this view. The assumption that there is no state, or form of consciousness, that definitely subsumes the apparent duality of observer and observed, has meant an entrenched dualism. It is no help, existentially, if quantum physics describes an interactive relationship between mind and world, or even postulates a ground of existence that subsumes the two, for the *conceptualization* of such a process or state, itself confirms the separation of psyche and world.

To identify Divinity within nature is to re-establish a non-material (that is, non-measurable) essence to nature. Nature is then more than outer, or material, form because it is composed of qualities that belong to the reality that is God. One way to interpret this insight would be *pantheistically*: nature, being the sum of those qualities, is what the Divine is. Alternatively, the *panentheistic* outlook—that nature is God but does not exhaust what God is—reverses the image: now nature, in Schuon's words, "is mysteriously plunged in God."[58] The panentheistic outlook—the only legitimate

---

[57] Mascaró, *The Upanishads*, p. 65.

[58] Frithjof Schuon, "Apercus sur la Tradition des Indiens de l'Amerique du Nord," *Etudes Traditionnelles* (Paris: Chacornac, 1949), p. 164.

one from the traditionalist point of view—implies several things. Because nature includes many of the attributes of God, a reductionist approach to nature, which uses empiricism and reasoning to remove many of these qualities, cannot result in finding out what nature (or God) is, and is therefore inappropriate.[59] Instead, a holistic approach, which seeks a means by which all the attributes of nature may be known, is essential. Now, since we are a part of nature—immersed in the Being of God—a clue to what these attributes are is provided by our own consciousness. An ultimate ground of being must subsume the apparent distinction between our consciousness and an "outer world" of nature—of perceiver and perceived.[60] It is our *perception* of qualities, precisely, that indicates their objectivity. If a consciousness that has beauty as its perception is part of a greater whole, then beauty suggests itself to be no less a part of that whole. Beauty *is* in nature only because it cannot be anywhere else.

We know that perceptions of beauty vary. But to acknowledge this is only to acknowledge the relative persistence of an illusory duality, wherein an understanding of beauty (or any quality) in depth must remain limited. Bridging the gap between the two "realities"—the self and the Self—is to bridge the gap between a limited perception of beauty and its full reality. Crucially, if God and God's attributes are "in" the world, then the aspirations of the self to transcend its limited view, realize the state of non-duality, and so become aware of all that beauty is, need not be aimed wholly towards a *transcendent* reality, but may be helped by recourse to the "natural world."

To recognize that the Eastern view of immanence is not unique but is just the clear exposition of a doctrine at the heart of all religions, is to see that what White had struck at was really only an outer shell formed

---

[59] The Christian concept of creation *ex nihilo* led to what is almost a cliché in physics: God as supreme mathematician. Once mathematics was conceived of as a description of the objective truth of things—the innate structure of nature—it implied that the creative element of God's mind must take the form of mathematical propositions. Entertained by Newton, Einstein, and some more recent physicists, it is perpetuated today by Hawking, although in a "tongue-in-cheek" way—mathematics has long since become transcendent itself, not to be contradicted even by "God." For a discussion of these ideas, see the chapter "The Fetish of Mathematics and the Iconoclasm of Modern Science," in Philip Sherrard, *Human Image: World Image* (Ipswich, England: Golgonooza Press, 1992).

[60] This, as we will see in the next part, is similar to, but not the same as, one interpretation of quantum physics.

by centuries of humanistic thought and scientific rationalism. Since Blake's day, the march of science has tended to further obscure the true dimensions of religion, while at the same time lending credence to the legitimacy of science. The deep misgivings Blake had for the overall benefit of science and for the ethos of science have largely dissipated. Because of this, the chasm that actually separates religion and science appears less wide and even bridgeable. In the Christian West, which has born the full brunt of science's impact, we find that the Church—failing to defend a dimension no longer apprehended[61]—has slowly acquiesced to science and seen the necessity of modifying its doctrine to suit "unquestionable" truth.[62] Thus, the Church's position today often reflects some version of Teilhardism.[63] Here, the traditional metaphysics accepted by the Church up until the Renaissance (wherein the *ultimate* origin of outer manifestation is a pre-existing essence or archetype), is abandoned in favour of the speculations of a modern mind (Darwin), uniquely—and surprisingly—favoured by God

---

[61] Ananda Coomaraswamy writes: "[Christianity's] intellectual aspects have been submerged, and it has become a code of ethics rather than a doctrine from which all other applications can and should be derived; hardly two consecutive sentences of some of Meister Eckhart's sermons would be intelligible to an average modern congregation, which does not expect doctrine, and only expects to be told how to behave" (Coomaraswamy quoted in Brian Keeble, "Ananda K. Coomaraswamy: Scholar of the Spirit," *Sophia* Vol. 2, No. 1 [1996]: p. 82).

[62] Paul VI, responding to one of the moon landings (perhaps the pre-eminent achievement of science to date) manages, in one telling statement, to express an anti-traditional humanism and scientific hubris: "Honour to Man, honour to thought, honour to science, honour to technique, honour to work, honour to the boldness of man, honour to the synthesis of scientific and organizing ability of man who unlike other animals, knows how to give his spirit and his manual dexterity these instruments of conquest. Honour to man, king of the earth, and today Prince of heaven" (Paul VI, *Doct. Cath.* No. 1580, January 21, 1971, quoted in Rama Coomaraswamy, *The Destruction of the Christian Tradition* [London: Perennial Books, 1981], p. 95).

[63] See Pierre Teilhard de Chardin, *The Future of Man* (London: Collins, 1973). Teilhard combines the Christian religion with evolutionary theory to posit the continuing emergence over time of more subtle levels of consciousness. From a traditional perspective, the "evolution" of consciousness for a person is an always-existing potential taking place in a non-temporal dimension. The desire to reconcile religion and science generally involves, says Sherrard, "an attempt to adapt the principles of religion—transcendent and immutable—to the latest findings of science, and so to make religion 'reasonable' or in keeping with the 'spirit of the age' by appearing 'scientific'" (Sherrard, "The Desanctification of Nature," pp. 119-20).

to comprehend His real manner of working. Science, for its part, when it *is* willing to approach religion, does so only with *its* mode of thinking, and wielding its own terminology. Thus, in the present day, Fritjof Capra, seemingly without any sense of irony, confidently assesses Eastern religious traditions dating back thousands of years in the light of the latest physics and believes there are parallels to be made.[64]

Both these approaches obscure the fact that the fundamental nature of religion is not being truly represented, and make too much of a relatively recent mode of thought, or consciousness, peculiar to modern science. The fundamental nature of religion is suggested by the word itself. In the Latin *religio* (from *religare*, to "bind back"), we have reference to the element capable of re-establishing a connection between our own consciousness and a more comprehensive reality. It is the Intellect or Intellective faculty—once orthodoxy—that fulfils the essential function of religion. However, in the glare of modern science it has become part of an invisible esoteric dimension. Having first reduced the world to material and psychic components, and more latterly to the material alone,[65] science cannot recognize this other, vertical, dimension. Implacably pressured, as it were, to remain "reasonable" and "objective"—to in fact *align ourselves with a particular mode of consciousness*—there is little chance to see that this mode, valid within its own sphere, might be justly suspect when it shines its light at religion and pronounces: "nothing found." Yet the traditional perspective (no less valid simply because science repudiates it), which posits an alternative mode of consciousness, stands always ready to be vindicated by contemplating the very quality that cannot be tackled by science—beauty.

THE PERCEPTION OF BEAUTY

Enclosed within the sphere of scientistic thought, there may be fewer times than once there were, when the mystery, miracle, and beauty of the world impinges, and allows insight into "another" nature. But there are occasions. To wake in the early hours and, as the darkness slowly fades, to be drawn into the song of birds greeting the dawn, their melodies rising and

---

[64] See Fritjof Capra, *The Tao of Physics* (London: Fontana, 1983). Most of the suggested similarities are spurious, however, as chapter 6 should make clear.

[65] The psychic, whether conceived of as independent of its physical matrix or not, is nevertheless individual and subjective.

falling; to stand under the unfathomable and still canopy of night awash with stars, and then turn to glimpse the full and silent moon edge over nearby hills; to experience the piercing light of a thunderstorm alive upon the glowing backdrop of clouds while the roaring wind is heard but not yet felt. A cascading stream in a forest glade; the unexpected scent of a single rose, breathed in; the white foaming surf collapsing forever on a lonely shore—events such as these are without number. They move the soul in ways that challenge the outlook of the rationalistic mode of consciousness. They evoke the sense that the beautiful and the sacred do not just reflect a way of perceiving but are qualities that belong to nature. Crucially, since it is a pre-rational and contemplative mind that first becomes aware of beauty, it is only the same mind that will endorse this perspective. In analysis, in reasoning, in discursive thought, much of the substance of beauty disappears. Under the scrutiny of science, beauty becomes a disembodied entity, destined to haunt the landscape of our mind as a ghostly remnant of its true self, either existing tenuously in the "eye of the beholder," or, worse, not seen at all.

Rational consciousness is not perceptive; rather it *interprets* sensory data. Only a consciousness that is non-discriminatory, impartial and passive when it comes to that which the senses bring to it—that evaluates holistically so to speak—could rightly be termed perceptive. Thus, beauty is given back life only when the pre-rational intuitive consciousness is granted legitimacy as a faculty of perception. In this regard, it must be seen as of the highest significance that the traditional understanding of human knowing included a faculty adequate to the perception of the subtler aspects of the world. If we were to look for a remnant expression of this faculty "beneath" the now dominant rational consciousness, we would surely fix upon the perception of beauty. The subtle but profound and indubitable character of this perception (before it has been subjected to the pronouncements of reason) seems to confirm the reality of the Intellect. By virtue of these linkages, beauty's reality is upheld and the common thread uniting environmentalism and religion is made more evident. Beauty's inextricable association with religion makes uncompromising the distinction that is often made between science and religion. The attempt to bring together what are, at root, two ways of seeing, is not possible without either drastically weakening religion or making more claims for science than can be substantiated. The question that beauty poses for ecophilosophy is whether it will resist the momentum it has gained from a materialistic science and move instead to realign itself with a tradition of *sophia* that is adequate to an understanding of the nature of nature. Only by studying the key philosophical developments that shaped modern science and led to the demise of the *sophia* in Western civilization and the demise of beauty, do we begin to appreciate what this choice involves.

Part Three

THROUGH A GLASS DARKLY

CHAPTER FIVE
Reductionism

Whenever we trace the origin of the particular spirit that is modern science, it is not uncommon to look towards those individuals in the classical Greek world engaged in speculation about what underlies the world of appearance—philosophers like Thales, Anaximander, and Democritus, whose theories, absent from the European consciousness for centuries, were brought to light during the Renaissance. The word *underlie* is significant because it points to an embarkation, over two thousand years ago, upon a singular imaginative venture, and the abandonment of a more holistic outlook—that of the philosophical giants, Socrates and Plato. It is to first conceive, and eventually put into practice, the basic principle that the process of looking "within," by dividing, analyzing, reducing, and measuring the perceptive world through the application of reason and mathematics, is legitimate in the quest for substance or essence in nature.

Because the reductionist theories of these early philosophers remained largely speculative, they were not a challenge for those who also looked towards the world, but whose more expansive vision led in an "upward" direction. The first tentative steps towards what today we might term a *non-religious* view of the nature of the essence or substance of the world relied on deductive reasoning and "self evident" knowledge rather than experiment. Consequently, the first attempts to uncover underlying structure are viewed today as the naive blundering of those who have not the requisite light to shine where it is needed. Their form of "science" seems a poor match to the power of *inductive* reasoning based solely on recourse to sensory data, which developed fully in the scientific revolution of the seventeenth century.

The process of reduction, both theoretical and practical, would not have been successful beyond a certain point without the tool of mathematics, and once again the origin of the application of this to the world may be found in Greek thought. The curious and compelling relationship between our perceptions, the world, and mathematics has been an enduring one, and, with the development of modern science, it became an ineluctable one. Although reductionist thought would eventually lead mathematics elsewhere, its initial association with beauty was strong. For example, Pythagoras showed that the musical notes which are thought to sound harmonious or beautiful together were correlatable (on a stringed instrument) with an exact mathematical sequence. When geometry—an artificial mathematical world of form in one, two, or three dimensions— was invented and promoted by Pythagoras, Euclid and others, beauty was abstracted from the perceptive world into this other one by the "discovery" that pleasing proportions in art and architecture were at least partially quantifiable—for example in the "golden section" (or *phi*, a ratio of 1:1.618).[1] The adoption of measure—the comparing of the natural world with an artificial one—began a centuries-long belief that the world was somehow describable in the language of mathematics.

Contained within the belief in a sensory world that can be taken apart, lay the dormant seed of a particular duality set to dominate every aspect of what would become modern thought. Because if, in our encounter with the world, there is not an *experienced* correlation between perception and that which is perceived; no longer the experience that *our* nature and the *world's* nature are actually only different aspects of the same thing, then a bifurcation results. There originates, in the analytical mode of awareness, the conception that there is a thing, "the world" or the observed, and an entity that is different from it: an observer. Following on from this duality is the conviction that what is being found out about the world is not *influenced* by the particular consciousness that is being brought to bear, but is, instead, a correct description of the world.

Although the Greek mind did not make the radical distinction between observer and observed that we do, or confuse the mental construct with the reality[2], we can nevertheless say that its use of *measure* started

---

[1] The golden section may be derived from a mathematical sequence (beginning: 1, 1, 2, 3, 5, 8, in which each number is generated by adding the preceding two) "discovered" by Fibonacci during the Renaissance. The Fibonacci Series "underlies many features of the natural world: it determines the number of leaves grown and extended by any plant for optimum chlorophyll production. It also governs the spiral seed display on pineapples, the spirals generated by snail shells and the chambered nautilus; the horn configuration of deer and antelopes; and the mating patterns and number of generational descendents of bees, rabbits and other small mammals, even insects" (Lane, *Timeless Beauty*, p. 60).

[2] For the Greeks, says Richard Tarnas, there was "implicit emphasis on an integrated multiplicity of cognitive modes." Furthermore, the cosmos was a "transcendent and pervasive unitary order informing both inner mind and outer world, in which recognition of the one necessarily signified knowledge of the other" (Richard Tarnas, *The Passion of the Western*

the process that would lead to this state of extreme duality. We may locate in this early thought the precursor to *our* mode of science, the basic premises of which are, firstly, that substance is to be found through reductionism—that is, through a reasoned analysis and measuring of the material world; and, secondly, that the reasoning process allows a faithful description of reality because it operates independently of the world. Despite recent developments, modern science still imagines that the essential nature of what exists is to be found through an investigation by reduction, using an empirical method and mathematical analysis. Either through imaginative speculation or in a practical way only dreamt of two thousand years ago, we take nature apart to find smaller and more elementary components. Indeed, reductionism has come to seem the *only* means by which knowledge of substance or essence can be had. Having invested so much faith in reductionist thought, we find ourselves unable to conceive of an alternative. We extol the early manifestations of this approach, and tend to marginalize thought which seems at odds with it. Thus, a prominent philosopher of the twentieth century, Bertrand Russell, could confidently oppose the *definite* knowledge of science with the *dogma* of theology.[3] For Russell, "self-evident" knowledge belonged to the latter, and its origin was the brain of the philosopher. In consequence, "traditional religious beliefs . . . are felt to need justification, and are modified wherever science seems to make this imperative."[4]

Permitting scientific method to have such decisive influence is, for Lord Northbourne,

> to consign to the waste-paper basket, metaphorically or otherwise, the whole of the 'perennial philosophy' that is enshrined in the sacred Scriptures of the world, all the exposition and exemplification of that philosophy given by the saints and sages whom the world has revered from time immemorial, all religion, all tradition, in short, all that has hitherto given meaning to human life.[5]

Mind [New York: Ballantine, 1991], pp. 287 and 286).

[3] Bertrand Russell, *A History of Western Philosophy* (London: Unwin, 1984), p. 13.

[4] Russell, *A History of Western Philosophy*, pp. 14-15.

[5] Lord Northbourne, "The Beauty of Flowers," in *Looking Back on Progress* (Ghent, NY: Sophia Perennis, 1995), p. 45.

The dimension of "height" (in both the perceptive world and in perception itself), to which the perennial philosophy—or *sophia*—attests, defies the simplifying categories of Russell. As the very antithesis of reductionism, reductionist thought cannot be applied to the vertical dimension without the danger that it will be lost to any meaningful understanding. If Plato has not the same association with science (although he influenced the way science would develop because of his "search for perfect timeless mathematical forms that underlay the phenomenal world"[6]), it is because he accepted that the structure of reality meant a correspondence between our nature and that of the world; a greater understanding of the world requiring only a greater engagement with our nature. The supra-sensory, transcendent, essential, or vertical dimension to reality was not open to investigation using analytical reason, but was known by means of the "faculty" of perception, originating prior to reason, that partook of the nature of this transcendence—the *nous* (Intellect).

Significantly, the movement in science towards a fully inductive empirical system corresponds to a steady decline by the expositors of such a system in the belief or acceptance of the alternative means of knowing. While Plato's doctrine was kept alive within certain schools in the Christian West throughout subsequent centuries (from Neo-Platonism and the early Scholastics, to the traditionalists of today), those who drove science forward in the seventeenth and eighteenth centuries became increasingly suspicious of this alternative as representing anything other than a delusionary way of thinking.[7] Natural philosophers, often having a close affiliation with the Church, retained, in principle, access to the esoteric teachings via the Church's founding fathers. In reality, however, a general understanding of this esoteric dimension was in strong decline after the Renaissance, which drew more from the secular humanistic side of Greek thought than from the "theological" or esoteric side. Moreover, the critical confrontation between scientific endeavour and the Church at the time of Galileo

---

[6] Tarnas, *The Passion of the Western Mind,* p. 292.

[7] The origin of this view, Sherrard says, can be traced at least as far back as the late Middle Ages, and Aquinas' claim that "the only knowledge which man as a rational creature could effectively obtain was . . . that which he could derive from the observation of phenomena through the senses—a proposition which is at the very basis of the later scientific attitude to knowledge" (Sherrard, "The Desanctification of Nature," in *Seeing God Everywhere,* p. 126).

meant that the chance for a valuable interchange was effectively ended. This led eventually to an outright rejection of the reality of the Intellect.

In relation to our own times, it is significant that a consciousness that has been "trained," as it were, in the ways of the scientific method, and has learnt to view it as the only valid one, would be biased when faced with the suggestion of another way of knowing. Its condition would now be such as to dismiss or fail to appreciate an alternative, only because to it the alternative is not there. This predisposition is indeed part of the scientific worldview, and has worked to prevent a re-assimilation of the idea of the existence of a more comprehensive knowledge, one not allied to the reductive method, but gained by way of adding to or unveiling the initial sensory impressions through the operation of a subtler perception. Thus Plato, in asserting the True, Good and Beautiful—realities apprehensible by this more subtle perception—is admired for imaginative genius, but no longer for accuracy of thought. And, to compound an injustice, since Plato frequently framed metaphysical concepts in a "non-theological" language, terms such as "idea" and "form" (Gr. *eidos*) were more open to being adapted and manipulated by a secular science.

The reductionist method of science cannot be called subtle. Inherent is a confining quality that consciously restricts the boundary of the acceptable. Today, many of the popularizers of science hold so strongly to the conviction that their method works, that it reveals what is true, and that there is no other method, they are sometimes openly hostile towards the suggestion of an alternative.[8] This serves to reinforce the legitimacy of the reductive method amongst those who practice science, and to hold the layperson, who is usually not familiar with the epistemological assumptions and uncertainties inherent within science, in thrall. Within the closed house that is science, even the light of history is allowed to penetrate only dimly. The Intellect, no longer thought of as "perception," lives on in corrupted form, as a subtlety of ordinary thinking. The rational mind has not only successfully usurped the throne but now claims that it was always sovereign. In the words of historian Richard Tarnas,

---

[8] Several of the books of Richard Dawkins or Carl Sagan, which marshal the "facts" of science to expose the "unreasonableness" of religious beliefs, could be cited in this regard. See, for example, Sagan's *The Demon Haunted World*, and Dawkins' *The River Out of Eden* and *The God Delusion* (London: Bantam, 2006).

having extracted whatever was useful for its present needs, the modern mind reconceived classical culture in terms respectful of its literary and humanistic accomplishments, while generally dismissing the ancients' cosmology, epistemology, and metaphysics as naive and scientifically erroneous.[9]

LANDMARKS IN A NEW "METAPHYSICS"

Charting the development of the current assumptions of modern science and exposing their detrimental outcomes is a common theme in the writings of both ecophilosophers and traditionalists. The difference between the two lies in the extent of the criticism meted out. As we have seen, ecophilosophers are more likely to sympathize with some of the findings of scientific empiricism because they provide a platform for their outlook. Traditionalists, mindful of all that remains lost due to the influence exerted by science, are less accommodating. By looking in some detail at the origins of our present worldview, this section offers a chance to understand such criticism by bringing into relief the distinction between the two modes of approach to essence which science and religion express.

If we take metaphysics to consist of three aspects—cosmology, ontology, and epistemology—then the figures of Nicolaus Copernicus (1473-1543), Galileo Galilei (1564-1642) and René Descartes (1596-1650) stand as clear landmarks that signal three drastic changes in course that would steer us towards the modernist outlook. These three men provided the essential elements for a new vision of reality. While there were those who opposed the new direction taken,[10] those who supported it were the more persuasive and the legacy of their endeavours is the particular sea in which we now travel. In a search for the origin of beauty, it is important to mentally retrace this course if we are ever to discern the nature of the harbour from which we have sailed. Beauty is woven of the very fabric of an earlier metaphysics in that far off place, and its rich and colourful threads have been made pale and thin by travel. In abandoning that distant shore, in our

---

[9] Tarnas, *The Passion of the Western Mind*, p. 294.

[10] For example, the philosopher and mathematician, Nicholas de Cusa (1401-1464); the humanist philosopher and Neo-Platonist, Marsilio Ficino (1433-1499); the Christian mystic, Jacob Boehme (1575-1624); William Blake; and the English Platonist Thomas Taylor (1758-1835). Their voices, if increasingly ignored, were not wholly silenced, evidenced today by the resurgence in the exposition of the *sophia*.

determination to explore an uncharted territory, we have become mesmerised by a vast and lonely seascape. We no longer accurately remember why we once viewed the world the way we did, or what we could know without voyaging at all. We live, as Philip Sherrard says, in an "industrial and technological inferno," a nightmarish world of our own making, content to criticize the knowledge of the past despite "our fall to a level of ignorance and stupidity that threatens the survival of our race."[11]

COSMOLOGY

The basic facts of Copernicus' heliocentric system are well known. But it is not always remembered that the system was initially advanced more in the manner of a theory,[12] and, at first, sat relatively comfortably with the Church as an abstract and mathematical description of the heavens. Slowly gaining credibility within the universities and amongst the more scientifically minded of the time, however, meant that its defence as truth was inevitable.

The clash between the "father of modern science" and the Catholic Church, upon the publication of *Dialogue on the Two Chief World Systems* in 1632, has often been enunciated, with the censure of the Church and the glorification of Galileo's courageous, if doomed, stance against it in mind. This might be unsurprising from the defenders of modern science. But an official "apology" from the Vatican in 1992[13] confirms the Inquisition's trial as a mistake, and—more significantly—suggests that the opposition to Galileo's assertions was always indefensible.

What, if anything, might be said in defence of the Church's initial stance? Granted, many of the reasons for holding it may have been politi-

---

[11] Philip Sherrard, *Human Image: World Image*, (Ipswich, England: Golgonooza Press, 1992), p. 3.

[12] The first edition of *Revolutionibus Orbicum Coelestium* (*On the Revolutions of the Heavenly Spheres*) even contained an unauthorized preface by Andreas Osiander, which described the book as hypothesis only. See Colin Wilson, *Starseekers* (London: Granada, 1982), pp. 105-106.

[13] In 1979, Pope John Paul II officially re-opened the case against Galileo. "Four years later, the commission reported that Galileo should not have been condemned, and the church published all the documents relevant to his trial. In 1992, the pope endorsed the commission's conclusion" (Stephen Hawking, *On the Shoulders of Giants* [London: Penguin, 2002], p. 398).

cally motivated. But if we discount the likelihood that Galileo's treatment came mainly as a result of the continued Counter Reformation strategy to rein in "heretical" ideas that would add to the already existing threats to the established position of the Church,[14] can there be extracted a more legitimate, if more subtle, reason for the opposition to Galileo's geokinetic system?

One does not lightly criticize the imaginative insight that saw the use to which invention could be put to confirm the conclusions of Copernicus. Galileo trained his own telescopes on planetary bodies like Jupiter, and discovered unknown worlds revolving there, proving that there are some things that do not go round the earth. He noted that Venus showed phases, indicating that it went round the sun, and that bodies like the moon are not perfect spheres but actually betray the same irregularities as the earthly realm. It is indeed to be abhorred that in the face of such revelations came the threat of torture. Considering that the contrasting geocentric system of Ptolemy—a pagan idea itself—had once been adopted by the Church, could not the new ideas have been allowed also without much damage? We feel that religion does itself a disservice whenever ideas are defended so vehemently. It seems to bespeak a foolish fundamentalism at odds with a genuinely wise handling of both established religious principles and new findings. We now defend Galileo who was definitely right, and believe the Church was defending what was definitely wrong. Yet to posit the question, "Was it wrong in all ways?" is to embark upon a path leading to the possibility of synthesis where there seems at first only irreconcilable difference.

By way of starting on that path it might be said that from a phenomenological point of view (and, curiously, an empirical one) the observable facts do not support an earth that moves. Even the effect of hundreds of years of knowing the heliocentric system makes little difference. To the "untrained" eye the sun still rises and sets, the earth appears at rest. For

---

[14] The idea of a movable Earth, which was contrary to a literal interpretation of certain scriptural passages, might have been accommodated in an age with less need for caution. However, the Church was under attack by a Protestantism critical of just this sort of divergence from Biblical "truth." Tarnas states: "While in an earlier century, Aquinas or the ancient Church fathers might have readily considered a metaphorical interpretation of the scriptural passages in question, thereby eliminating the apparent contradiction with science, the emphatic literalism of Luther and his followers had activated a similar attitude in the Catholic Church" (Tarnas, *The Passion of the Western Mind*, p. 252).

virtually all practical purposes, the heliocentric system does not seem to count in the world of experience; it does not seem true. Indeed, the sky that turns around us—especially the night sky—has existed in the human imagination as a perfect, unchanging, *spiritual* realm because that is how it presents itself. Its sacred nature relied on its being set apart from the world we inhabit. In whatever way *this* world might be thought subject to decay and corruption or gross in substance, the world above, unreachable, showed evidence of the never-changing, sacred and eternal aspect of reality. Hence, it became variously the abode of the gods or a peoples' ancestors, the several heavens or, in Greek mythology or Christian cosmology, the "crystalline spheres" which surround our earthly home and are where divine Forms or forms of the Divine rest. The journey of a human soul beautifully unfolds in Dante's *Divine Comedy* within this matrix.

Yet, to dwell upon the literal here would be to miss what is relevant. For only in an appreciation of symbol is seen the true importance of the traditional view. The geocentric system, as an intellectual construct paralleling the observational evidence, meant that the world above us provided an initial image which, embellished by imagination, operated to provide a symbol for the hierarchical or vertical dimension understood to exist in the realm of the human soul. The withdrawal of just this symbol meant the withdrawal of a dynamic that could lend wings to the imagination. In advancing the idea that the earth and planets orbit the sun, Copernicus was complicit in removing from the European consciousness symbolic support for a vertical dimension in the human sphere. It is the *journey* of Dante's protagonist that is significant, because it classically represents the hierarchy of states to which the human being might aspire.

If this *inner* verticality is not recognized—and increasingly, as science moved forward, it was not—the tragic quality of the imposition of the heliocentric system hardly registers. Yet, if it *is* recognized, then the removal of that imaginal support, seen to weaken awareness of that dimension, becomes significant. This is not at all the same thing as lamenting the weakening of a view that is merely incorrect.

All cosmologies, including the modern one, might be said to support a particular view of ourselves, a particular human image. The difference between modern civilization and all others is that it declines to allow that a cosmology could be anything but an attempt to describe an empirical reality. In the emergent West, Charles Le Gai Eaton says,

It was assumed by people who had completely lost the capacity for analogical and symbolic thinking that the myths . . . were meant to be taken quite literally and represented no more than the first gropings of the rational animal towards a scientific explanation of the universe.[15]

Yet, this does not represent the working of the pre-scientific mind. Instead, in all cultures prior to our own, the vertical dimension—an experiential realm no less significant than the realm of the outer senses—found expression in particular cosmologies, whether those of the primal peoples like the Australian Aborigines or American Indians, the Oriental religions, or the finely-wrought cosmologies of Classical Islam and the Christian Middle Ages.

The "correctness" of the geocentric system then, could be seen in its symbolic suitability. The outwardly observed structure of the world was in harmony with an inner structure; therefore, the outer world of the senses could be used to direct the consciousness towards what is not clearly seen by allowing it to represent the inner dimension. Hence, it is not the cosmology itself that is the significant thing or that might need to be defended, but rather that which it supports and defines.

In the Islamic world, in contrast with what happened in the Christian one, this inner hierarchical dimension remained uppermost in the awareness of those who conducted the science of the times. Moreover, as Nasr explains,

as long as . . . *scientia* continued to be cultivated in the bosom of *sapientia*, a certain "limitation" in the physical domain was accepted in order to preserve the freedom of expansion and realization in the spiritual domain. The wall of the cosmos was preserved, in order to guard the symbolic meaning which such a walled-in vision of the cosmos presented to most of mankind.[16]

While heliocentrism remained only a theory, however credible, it could not supplant the old cosmology. The danger lay rather in the prom-

---

[15] Charles Le Gai Eaton, *King of the Castle* (Cambridge: Islamic Texts Society, 1990), p. 166.

[16] S.H. Nasr, *Science and Civilization* (Cambridge: The Islamic Texts Society, 1987), p. 174.

ulgation of the Copernican system as the *only* truth, for that *would* necessitate the abandonment of that cosmology. Whether the Christian clergy were aware of all the implications of Galileo's stance being adopted, in the way that Nasr suggests the Islamic scholars were, may never be known. But it is now a matter of historical fact that once the new system was in place[17] it did remove, from the collective imagination of the West, a cosmology which allowed the human mind to find symbols for higher or non-rational states, and the vision of the manifestation in nature of another, *non*-material realm. And there is an element of the doubly tragic since this loss of vision came with the breach of the new science with the Church and, by extension, *all* religion. For the Church, the forcefulness of Protestantism seemed to suggest the horns of a dilemma, the path of escape being either one way towards science or the other towards literalism. Lacking opportunity or insight meant a failure to "take the bull by the horns" and escape by the middle way. Ironically, religion could from then on be painted in terms of opposition to truth. The repercussions would extend into the area of philosophy, and so colour ecophilosophy too, which can least afford to reject that which might help to confront the ecological crisis. But the middle way—that of allowing the old to subsume the new in a synthesis that recognizes both fact and symbol—is a path still open to us.

The crucial point here is that the "facts" of modern cosmology remain not just unnecessary, but can even be a hindrance to an encounter with the essence of reality as it has been understood throughout history up until modern times. Old perceptions are denied, and the human gaze is turned "outward" or "downward" to the world of "matter." The heavens are apparently not perfect or unchanging. They do not have the form of "crystalline spheres." Along with the earth, they also are "corrupted" in the imagination—that is, subject to change and decay. Being of the same nature as the earth, they also are open to empirical investigation. The telescope is a typical tool for this, revealing further detail of outer form by magnifying the capacity of ordinary vision. Yet, while such instruments may reveal more things that are beautiful, they do not increase our *capacity* to perceive beauty. They cannot be a substitute for an "inward vision," which responds to the things of ordinary sensory experience and discovers, within

---

[17] Galileo promoted the system by the devious, and it might be said insulting, means of a polemical dialogue between two proponents of the new system and a third, *Simplicio*, who seemed to represent the Pope.

them, the levels of meaning that Leopold spoke of. On the contrary, a concentration on finding out more of the outward reality—a "horizontal" or "two-dimensional" awareness—can act to divert attention from a need for inward perception, which is that of seeing in the deeper or "vertical" sense.

Ontology

If Galileo had been responsible just for championing Copernicus' new description of the heavens, he might have remained guilty only of helping to remove one of the imaginative constructs that supported the philosophy of the Middle Ages. Moreover, since the reality to which an imaginative construct refers should be more resilient than the construct, it is likely it would have accommodated the new world system over time. A synthesis, in which both world systems are accepted as valid from their own point of view, might have been the outcome. However, a trend in modern science far more blameworthy—because of the direction in which it pushed European consciousness—had its origins in Galileo's own thought, and was to further undermine the conception of the vertical dimension in ways less subtle.

Copernicus had demonstrated the power of mathematics to reveal what was not apparent. Galileo had ascertained that the celestial realm was no different from the earthly one. Mathematics promised, therefore, to be a suitable tool for revealing hidden realities in the world around us. Hence, it seemed appropriate—in order to do science in the way Galileo wanted—to remove those fundamental qualities of nature which could not be quantified from the purview of science. Now, initially there may have been a certain nobility in this thinking. Plato, after all, had believed that mathematical patterns could be distinguished in the celestial realm. However, for Plato the nature of this realm was very different and its perfection was not in question. Since it was indicative of a numinous or divine level of being, mathematics by association could be considered correspondingly rarefied. With the destruction of this realm, mathematics became dissociated from its links to a mystical world—the vertical dimension relating to both the inner human world and the imaginal outer celestial one, considered to be reflections of each other—and associated instead with a gross or material realm.

Galileo's procedure, which we recognize today as the scientific method—that is, experimentation combining observation with mathematics—was to separate those qualities which could be quantified (*primary* qualities) from those which could not (*secondary* qualities). "Philosophy," said Galileo,

> is written in that great book which ever lies before your eyes; but we cannot understand it if we do not first learn the language and characters in which it is written. This language is mathematics, and the characters are triangles, circles, and other geometrical figures.[18]

He argued that

> to make accurate judgements concerning nature, scientists should consider only precisely measurable "objective" qualities (size, shape, number, weight, motion), while merely perceptible qualities . . . should be ignored as subjective and ephemeral.[19]

Consequently, as the psychologist R.D. Laing once observed,

> Out go sight, sound, taste, touch and smell and along with them has since gone aesthetics and ethical sensibility, values, quality, form; all feelings, motives, intentions, soul, consciousness, spirit. Experience as such is cast out of the realm of scientific discourse.[20]

Superficially, Galileo's categorization may seem to echo the Scholastics *materia prima* and *materia secunda*. But in Galileo everything is turned on its head, so that what is normally considered secondary substance has been promoted in importance, while essential quality has been relegated to an almost irrelevant lower level. Galileo's method more clearly than ever narrowed the focus of the search for essence to a pitifully small range. Henceforth, it was to be found only within the confines of the quantifiable and the analyzable.

Now, the idea of analysis of both space and time into units that can be measured leads, in the fields of mechanical engineering and kinematics (the

---

[18] Galileo quoted in John Herman Randall, *The Making of the Modern Mind* (New York: Columbia University Press, 1976), p. 237.

[19] Tarnas, *The Passion of the Western Mind*, p. 263.

[20] R.D. Laing quoted in Fritjof Capra, *The Turning Point* (London: Fontana, 1990), p. 40.

subject of Galileo's *Two New Sciences* published in 1638), to some useful knowledge concerning what could be built or not using certain specifications in materials, the motions of falling bodies and projectiles, the motion of pendulums and so on. But the notion that this approach should be the only legitimate one, and that unless the study is quantifiable it does not lead to certain knowledge, is a curious one to hold, and must be regarded as mistaken in the sense that being so restrictive it could not hope to reveal all of the nature of things. This is so for two reasons. Firstly, as the physicist David Bohm once pointed out, "the very word 'measure' . . . [denotes] mainly a process of comparison of something with an external standard."[21] In other words, when we assign mathematical labels to an object—magnitude, shape, number, and position—the object can only be talked about in this way because we have another object—a rule of some sort, a yardstick, an accurate timepiece—which we can apply to it. We are actually only *comparing* the first thing with the graduations on a measuring instrument. As René Guénon has perceptively noted, "despite certain prevalent misuses of ordinary language, quantity is never really that which is measured, it is on the contrary that by which things are measured."[22] Time itself, which is rarely *experienced* as uniform in flow,[23] must also be converted to a spatial thing in order for it to be measured, and Galileo's discovery of the isochronism of the pendulum enabled just such a correlation. Without the tools of measurement, we are unable to apply the mathematics of reduction to nature in the first place. The illusion that mathematics somehow explains what nature is, or that time possesses a regularity akin to geometry, or that nature possesses any of the precision or regularity of mathematics, disappears again. We are left where we started—face to face as it were with the whole, undivided, entity.

Secondly, our straightforward perception of nature is obviously not *reliant* on quantification. For example, we rarely even count the *number* of

[21] David Bohm, *Wholeness and the Implicate Order* (London: Routledge, 1983), p. 22.

[22] René Guénon, *The Reign of Quantity and the Signs of the Times* (New York: Sophia et Perennis, 1995), p. 36.

[23] For Guénon, "The truth is that time is not something that unrolls itself uniformly, and consequently the practice of representing it geometrically by a straight line, usual among modern mathematicians, conveys an idea of time which is wholly falsified by over-simplification. . . . The correct representation of time is to be found in the traditional conception of cycles" (Guénon, *The Reign of Quantity and the Signs of the Times*, p. 53).

birds on a pond, let alone begin to submit them or the trees or stones we encounter to measurements of a more detailed sort, unless we have some other purpose than perception. Intuitively, we are aware that an engagement in measurement proceeds only in the direction of analysis of time or space—towards a dissection of the immediately experienced outward form—and we tend not to consciously analyze. Normally perception is holistic and consists of a host of things that are even more obviously non-mathematical in nature, such as colour, sound, scent, warmth, or beauty. If these perceptions or qualities are taken away, or mentally subtracted, it cannot be then claimed that they no longer exist, or that they are uncertain, only that they are no longer the object of study.

Eventually, of course, even aspects like colour and sound were, like time, cleverly brought within the purview of measurement by once again reducing them to what could be measured. Thus, they were identified with the lengths of waves of electromagnetic radiation, or the wavelengths of compressed air in the case of sound. But the idea that a wavelength of, say, 475 nanometres is the same thing as the colour blue, must remain, to all but the most dyed-in-the-wool reductionist, absurd. All we have succeeded in doing is describing the perception of blue using certain arbitrary terms, which have no reality other than that given by us. The insight of Eddington's that we were only ever dealing with pointer readings on instruments is not always kept before us.[24]

For the same reason, beauty cannot be held to be described, other than superficially, by the discovery that the proportions between many of the elements in the living world correspond to *phi*. Clearly much of nature does not conform to this mathematical relationship, yet this does not bar it from being considered—or from being—beautiful. More importantly, though, the perception of beauty occurs irrespective of whether things conform, indicating once again that beauty cannot be tied to the realm of the measurable, but belongs to a realm that transcends quantification.

When the arbitrariness of the way *primary* quality is established is recognized, the so-called *secondary* qualities may be considered as at least as important as the "primary" ones, or even as more important, precisely *because* they resist the crude manipulation to which tangible form is susceptible. However, Galileo's ideas, subsequently taken up by thinkers like Descartes and Bacon, acted in a curious way on the human imagination.

---

[24] See Arthur Eddington, *The Nature of the Physical World* (New York: MacMillan, 1928).

Having once posited the validity of the mathematical method, idea and reality became confounded. The initial hypothesis that nature could be understood using mathematics became transposed slowly into the belief that the nature of nature *was* mathematical.

EMPIRICISM

Once the first breach in the wall of Church authority had been made, and the successful use of the scientific method demonstrated, confidence in the new science grew and it quickly worked as a flood might through this opening, to inundate and slowly submerge the great towers of medieval and Platonic thought that had seemed fixed forever. The metaphor seems right, for they were not destroyed in the sense of being lost to view or understanding, but rather overlaid by new thought which seemed, for more than three centuries, to be capable of supporting a new reality, but which latterly seems to possess the insubstantiality of water.

Nevertheless, in England at the beginning of the seventeenth century Bacon declared his confidence in the foundation being solid and unshakable. In Tarnas' words,

> through the careful observation of nature and the skillful devising of many and varied experiments, pursued in the context of organized cooperative research, the human mind could gradually elicit those laws and generalizations that would give man the understanding of nature necessary for its control.[25]

Faithful to the initial reasoning of Galileo, Bacon was committed to the observation of the natural world through the empirical method based on quantification and induction. By the time the atomistic theory, originally attributed to Democritus, resurfaced in Europe through translations from the Arabic, there existed, due to Galileo, a system ideally suited to its study. The conception of these constituent components of reality as having only quantitative characteristics, as Democritus had postulated, and not being possessed of other qualities like life or consciousness, meant the beginning of a long obsession with a mechanical and lifeless universe. Descartes, a contemporary of Galileo, suggested that individual atoms did not move randomly to form the aggregates they did, but obeyed mechanically

---

[25] Tarnas, *The Passion of the Western Mind*, p. 272.

certain—and discoverable—mathematical laws. Given the hypothesis that matter attracts matter, Newton showed that all of the motions observable in the heavens, together with terrestrial motion, could be explained by the operation of just a few of these laws. Thus a new mechanistic world quite different and non-intuitive—since it seemed not at all to fit the extravagantly alive, non-mathematical, purposive, intelligent, beautiful, world that ordinary perception revealed—was born. For Tarnas, "The Newtonian-Cartesian cosmology was . . . the foundation for a new world view . . . the heavens were composed of material substances . . . [and] their motions impelled by natural mechanical forces."[26]

For the contemporaries of Newton, and for the scientists of the next few centuries, the validity of what had been discovered was not questioned, despite the fact that the methods by which the discoveries had taken place had ignored most of the qualities to which our intelligence and senses normally ascribe importance. If the divine essences of Plato and the final causes of Aristotle had ever been anything more than abstract ideas, certainly they were considered unintelligible to Bacon and the new men of science. In Bacon's writings, we find the clearest evidence of the deliberate turning away from that which bespeaks transcendence both in the outer realm and in the realm of the human soul. Religion and natural philosophy, he said, should not be "commixed together." Religion "is grounded upon the Word and oracle of God," and therefore "out of the contemplation of nature, to induce any verity or persuasion concerning the points of faith is in my judgement not safe."[27] Bacon is effectively divorcing Divinity from the world. A faith in empiricism and inductive reasoning had convinced him that "To fill the world with . . . intelligible divine essences, as did Plato, was to obscure from man a genuine understanding of nature on its own terms."[28]

---

[26] Tarnas, *The Passion of the Western Mind*, pp. 270-271.

[27] Francis Bacon, *Advancement of Learning*, ed. W.A. Wright (Oxford: Oxford University Press, 1900), II,6,I and II,24,3. Sherrard comments: "The divorce between religion and philosophy is absolute: concern for the spiritual is banished from the study of physical phenomena and all scientific knowledge must be derived from the observation of a natural world regarded as a self-subsistent entity" (Sherrard, "The Desanctification of Nature," p. 114).

[28] Tarnas, *The Passion of the Western Mind*, p. 273.

The denial of a supra-sensory dimension, and the relinquishment of any recognition that reality might be structured to allow human perception to be adequate to the understanding of the essence of the world without the need for scientific investigation, and the concentration instead on a *material* world and its exclusively rational treatment, was an occurrence without precedent. Insensible to the handicap we have been given, we are liable to believe that, before the advent of scientific methods, much of what was termed knowledge had no basis in reality, but did indeed exist in the heads of the philosophers concerned. Were we to reflect on this presumption, though, we might, like Schuon, find reason to pause:

> If humanity has been stupid for thousands of years, one cannot explain how it could have ceased being so, all the more so as it occurred in a very short period of time; and one can explain it still less when one observes with what intelligence and heroism it has been stupid for so long and with what philosophic myopia . . . it finally became "lucid" and "adult."[29]

The mistake, of course, is to assume that the early philosophers were *depending* on belief without foundation. But for Schuon today, as for Plato over two thousand years ago, it is the Intellect that allows knowledge. Reason, standing below it on the hierarchy of human faculties, and not itself perceptive, is a means to enunciate and defend that knowledge as best as possible. Without the guiding light of the Intellect, reason is fallible and, as Plato understood, prone to lead thought in varied and opposing directions, into paradox and confusion, as the runaway horses of an uncontrolled chariot.

To the rational mind, the profound truths of Plato and Socrates, which have their origin in Intellective perception, become only axioms that cannot be substantiated, and the "definite" knowledge of science is contrasted with the "dogma" of theology. Ironically, from the perspective of Intellective knowing, it is the path based on reason that is fraught with uncertainty, while religion—because it harbours the doctrine of a more comprehensive knowledge—may more justifiably lay claim to certainty. However, once the empirical method is believed to lead to truth, then there seems no need for the non-empirical. Thus, science and religion diverged and grew

---

[29] Frithjof Schuon, *From the Divine to the Human* (Bloomington: World Wisdom, 1982), p. 12.

further apart. An increasing inability to see across the chasm that divided meant an increasing inability (for the scientifically minded) to distinguish between the two modes the "mind" was capable of, and to comprehend the state of consciousness alluded to by theology. The problem became exacerbated because over time the conviction of the scientist affected the vision of the theologian. Eventually, lacking clear insight itself, the Church would come to defer to science and so, unwittingly, fulfil its reputation as a repository of dogma and superstition.

EPISTEMOLOGY

Confronted with the "errors" of past "thinking," it is unsurprising that a general doubt and scepticism concerning all such thinking should begin to prevail within those of scientific bent. In hindsight, it seems it was only a matter of time before a Descartes would, in the interests of the new experimental approach, wish to formally renounce all earlier thought and attempt to construct an entirely new epistemology based on the reasoning faculty.

Descartes began by doubting everything he could. Since, however, for the doubter there remains one indubitable presence—the thinking self—it was this reality that became a new cornerstone upon which a more scientific philosophy was to be built. The idea that this approach was particularly original or profound would, of course, only occur to a mind cut adrift from the operation of the higher element of human perception. From the perspective of esoterism, this was to do no more than assert the pre-eminence of the discursive mind by removing the Intellect. In Plato's metaphor it was to toss out the rider in the chariot and look instead to just the horses and reins. Or, to use another Platonic metaphor, it was to perceive in the manner of the captives in the cave, deluded by phantasmata, unaware of the sun at the centre of their being which could provide the light to see clearly. Removal of the Intellect, the bridge between the "Self" and the "self," necessitates the ascendancy of the psyche, or "I-maker" (in Sanskrit, *ahamtattva*), to pre-eminence. Paradoxically, it also appears to the new consciousness as a *discovery;* clearly, Descartes perceived it as such, and was well pleased with what he had found. Today, although we continue to make adjustments and modifications, modernist thought has remained with this new system of consciousness—the individual psyche existing in isolation from a greater reality.[30]

---

[30] It is in Descartes' new epistemology that we find the origins of the present-day confusion

Since only the thinking substance, *res cogitans*, possessed the nature of certain truth, everything else, *res extensa*, the extended substance—what we would call the world—was of a different order. This subject-object dualism became another of the cornerstones of science; it is the understanding that it is possible to have a system composed of an isolated consciousness that is dissociated from—and therefore unaffected by and not affecting—the object that it studies. However, (as we saw in part two) according to esoterism, the self and the world both take part in the same reality: the Self, or Divinity. They appear as subject and object—as distinct—precisely because of the nature of the individuated self, an entity that might be defined by just this perception. It is the operation of the Intellect that confirms the ultimate illusion of this duality, and disallows the absoluteness of discontinuity that Descartes affirmed. The type of consciousness that can proclaim an unbridgeable gulf between the two is precisely that which believes itself to operate independently of the higher Self. Viewed from the esoteric point of view the duality is always only nominal, the reconciling of the apparent duality in the synthesis of unity made possible by the fact that the self and the world are in reality part of the same essence. Objections to the idea of essential unity, when looked at dispassionately, usually only relate to a reluctance of the self (the "I maker") to accept that it is not an autonomous entity and does not exist independently of a greater reality. The problem that the self has with this is compounded by the fact that the Intellect, precisely because its existence has been thrown into doubt and it has been treated as a mental construct, has come to seem *less* real than the individuated self, not more.

For ecophilosophy, the mind-world split affirmed by Descartes is significant because it was able to crystallize the conception of the world as a soulless machine. However, just as pertinent is the fundamental cause of Descartes' thought processes—the split between reason and Intellect. Since the Intellect is a perceptive faculty, the conjecture that perception might be mistrusted, not just superficially and occasionally, but in a fundamental manner, meant that Descartes' consciousness was not being influenced at all by this faculty. To think as he did necessitated the removal of any recognition that *res cogitans* was not the dominant player in the makeup of the human being. While Galileo had posited a method to be used if science

---

between "spirit" and "soul," the two quite separate entities being confounded in his philosophy. On this matter, see Guénon, *The Reign of Quantity and the Signs of the Times*, p. 283.

was to be successful in knowledge, Descartes had defined (constructed, as it were) a consciousness that from then on disallowed another way of knowing altogether. Descartes had "enthroned human reason as the supreme authority in matters of knowledge, capable of distinguishing certain metaphysical truth and of achieving certain scientific understanding of the material world."[31]

The dominance of reason would see the understanding of the nature of Intellective intuition consigned to an *esoteric* dimension of religion. Meanwhile, the exoteric framework of religion remained influential for some time, and reference continued to be made to a significant reality distinct from the material world that was being investigated. Although God was not considered immanent, and although the recognition of the higher faculty by which Divinity or essence could be known was gone, the acceptance of God's existence meant there was still some support for the direction of human consciousness towards a reality that was non-material and non-sensory in nature. In the early years of science, a sensitivity to the importance of theological matters still motivated men like Galileo, Descartes, and Newton (Newton, for instance, always believed that his scientific works were of little significance compared to the "esoteric" tradition to which he devoted the majority of his time). Nevertheless, although for Descartes there was still a relationship between his own mind and God, for later thinkers working with the methods pioneered by him, this correlation was less obvious. As Tarnas explains, "Descartes unintentionally began a theological Copernican revolution, for his mode of reasoning suggested that God's existence was established by human reason and not vice versa."[32] Inevitably, over time the idea that God and the various truths relating to the spiritual realm were somehow the invention of reason gained ascendancy. From the perspective of the most recent science, the prospect of the Divinity in the face of the material universe is doubtful at best, since science recognizes no vertical dimension to reality; Divinity has taken on the same quality of illusory reality that the new thinkers like Bacon thought they had seen in the minds of their predecessors.

---

[31] Tarnas, *The Passion of the Western Mind*, p. 279.

[32] Tarnas, *The Passion of the Western Mind*, p. 279.

Towards Modernism

If men like Descartes, Galileo and Bacon initiated the new voyage of science, the Enlightenment thinkers were responsible for ensuring that the heading was maintained. Rationality and empiricism combined to form a belief in the supremacy of the human mind over a world of materiality. The hegemony of rational empiricism, to the exclusion of another way of knowing must be thought to have reached its zenith in the writings of David Hume (1711-1766). In *An Enquiry Concerning Human Understanding,* we are presented with an extreme logical outcome:

> When we run over libraries, persuaded of these principles, what havoc must we make? If we take in our hand any volume; of divinity or school metaphysics, for instance; let us ask, *Does it contain any abstract reasoning concerning quantity or number?* No. *Does it contain any experimental reasoning concerning matter of fact and existence?* No. Commit it then to the flames: for it can contain nothing but sophistry and illusion.[33]

Hume, along with other philosophers such as John Locke (1632-1704), George Berkeley (1685-1753) and Immanuel Kant (1724-1804), would eventually become sceptical of the power of science to go beyond a certain point using the vessel of empirical method, but remained resolute in the conviction that there existed no alternative. Kant, in *The Critique of Pure Reason,* demonstrated that both *primary* and *secondary* qualities were subjective perceptions, and the ultimate nature of reality was unknowable,[34] thus drawing to a close—for philosophy at least—the long search for essence or substance using reason and measurement that had begun centuries earlier. By then, however, the pronouncements of philosophers had little impact upon the scientifically minded, and the quest of science continued unabated. Certain writings of Darwin further undermined the traditional metaphysics by bringing humans within the orbit of empirical investigation. "Darwinian" thought removed altogether the necessity for a supernatural agency, often invoked to uphold the structure of the world. As we

---

[33] David Hume, *An Enquiry Concerning Human Understanding* (Oxford: Oxford University Press, 1983), p. 165.

[34] See the synopsis in Russell, *A History of Western Philosophy,* p. 685.

saw, the processes within nature itself, largely random and purposeless, were held responsible for selecting all the forms of life, and could conceivably have driven the evolution of the universe. In correlating our humanness with other species, Darwinism further diminished any sense of the human being's transcendent qualities. It initiated, too, the process by which the mind itself was to become associated with the material realm, leading to the belief that it is an epiphenomenon of the brain.

CHAPTER SIX
The Crisis of Modern Science

It was not until the advent of quantum physics in the early twentieth century that the landscape that always seemed just ahead on the horizon began to shimmer and dissolve. To study the findings of quantum physics is to be made aware that the seemingly stable structure—the epistemology, ontology, and cosmology of science that has been built up over the preceding four hundred years—has already revealed a serious flaw. Yet, to examine the deep fissure that is quantum science closely is to see not only evidence for imminent collapse, but also an opening through which the light of a traditional metaphysics still penetrates.

A confidence in the power of reason to reveal what was true, along with the clear distinction between subject and object, had prevailed into the twentieth century despite the scepticism of philosophers, even within relativity theory. Although time and space seemed to display curious characteristics in defiance of the absolute qualities that Newtonian mechanics posited, Albert Einstein (1879-1955), one of the last prominent physicists to retain the belief that science was in some way seeking to fathom God's mind, was still confident that the new findings of physics could be squared with this belief. The quantum world of Werner Heisenberg (1901-1976) and Niels Bohr (1885-1962), though, seemed to do for physics what Darwin had done for evolution. It displayed a non-causal randomness so at odds with what had been expected that Einstein thought it absurd; "God is subtle," he protested, "but he is not malicious."

Bohr had begun by questioning Ernest Rutherford's (1871-1937) nuclear model of the atom, believing it unstable since the electrons should have fallen into the nucleus when they gave off energy. He theorized that the absorption and emission spectra (known of, but not explained) corresponded to the sudden release or absorption of quanta of energy in the form of photons by the electron when it jumped instantaneously between orbits or energy states. However, the "planetary orbit" view was thought unsatisfactory and unnecessary by Heisenberg, who developed a strictly abstract mathematical description of the spectra (a quantum or "matrix" mechanics). At the same time, Louis de Broglie (1892-1987), continuing with the older idea of light as wave rather than particle, proposed that particles (electrons), too, be thought of as waves. Erwin Schrödinger (1887-1961) showed that the electron could be conceived of (and visualized once again) as a "standing wave" whose frequencies corresponded to the "orbits" of Bohr, and the "energies" calculated by Heisenberg. However, although Schrödinger's mathematical solution (or "wave function") was equivalent to Heisenberg's, only the standing wave of *one* electron was conceivable in three-dimensional space; more waves required extra dimensions. Hence, for Max Born (1882-1970), the waves were only "waves of probability" in abstract space. The attraction for the intuitive clarity of "wave mechanics" over the abstraction of "matrix mechanics" seems to reflect a desire for the retention of certainty about the nature of the subatomic world—ultimately, the retention of a duality where the observer could know with certainty the nature of the observed. However, Heisenberg's mathematics showed that the value of some observables meant the uncertainty of others; the position and momentum of particles cannot *both* be established since the act of observation changed the properties of an object (a fact later demonstrated in the famous "microscope experiment"). Thus the resulting "indeterminacy principle" was a statement about the ineluctable connection between observer and observed. Bohr agreed about the uncertainty of accurate measurement, but not about there being existing properties within the atom that we were supposedly affecting by our measurements. In the 1927 "Copenhagen interpretation" of quantum theory, Bohr and Heisenberg agreed that the very fact of our interaction meant there could be no separate or independent "things" in the subatomic realm, but only "tendencies to exist"; cause-and-effect relationships are not tenable if reality is an indissoluble whole.

When it was realized that the new physics was showing that the constituents of matter demonstrated only probabilities of existence, atoms being neither discrete (particles) nor continuous (waves) but able to exhibit both characteristics; that the universe was not fundamentally mechanical or causal in nature; and that we could no longer claim to be able to study nature as discreet observers, but that we actually influence the outcome of an event, it should have prompted suspicion. Was the long-held assumption that substance or essence is to be found through reductionism mistaken? Was a coherent ontology possible, given the self-imposed restrictions on the gathering of data and the restrictions on what can be studied? Is the "metaphysics" of modern science true or only *relatively* true? Since *what* is examined, and *how* it is examined, can be traced to a conscious choice, to what extent is the consciousness of the perceiver involved in the outcome?

Indeed, *could the mode of consciousness operating while doing science be the reason for the particular answers that nature was giving?* This was not at all the conclusion reached. Bohr thought that if people were not deeply disturbed by the findings, they had not understood them. For him, there was no underlying reality that could explain what the instruments of detection were registering: "There is no quantum world. . . . There is only an abstract quantum description."[1] Heisenberg was almost in despair: "I repeated to myself again and again the question: Can nature possibly be so absurd as it seemed to us in these atomic experiments?"[2] Nevertheless, the particular reading of the quantum world fixed in the "Copenhagen interpretation," absurd though it might seem, was believed by Bohr to be what lay at the heart of things. By 1932, John von Neumann (1903-1957) had demonstrated mathematically the impossibility of physical reality consisting of "ordinary objects," thus vindicating quantum theory to most physicists.

Given that the universe was apparently very ordered and displayed at the macro level ample evidence of causation, there was good reason to doubt either the findings or the methodology. Einstein was passionate in his refusal to admit that the universe was as Bohr said: "That [God] plays dice . . . I cannot believe for a single moment," he declared.[3] But, continuing to work from the basis of mathematics, Einstein was unable to resolve the problem of an indeterminate world. And although some physicists believed that the equations did not actually describe how the world is, to save the methodology, as it were, others pointed to an inadequacy of human cognition—the world could not *be* known:

> the structure of nature may . . . be such that our processes of thought do not correspond to it sufficiently to permit us to think about it at all. . . . We have reached the limit of the vision of the great pioneers of science, the vision, namely, that we live in a sympathetic world in that it is comprehensible by our minds.[4]

---

[1] Bohr quoted in Wolfgang Smith, "Bell's Theorem and the Perennial Ontology," *Sophia* Vol. 3, No. 1 (1997): p. 23.

[2] Heisenberg quoted in Capra, *The Tao of Physics*, p. 58.

[3] Einstein quoted in Bryson, *A Short History of Nearly Everything*, p. 131.

[4] P.W. Bridgman quoted in Huston Smith, *Beyond the Post-Modern Mind* (Wheaton, Illinois: Quest, 1989), p. 8.

The conclusions of Kant and Hume had finally extended into the realm of science. At the same time, because, as Thomas Kuhn (1922-1996) recognized, there is always an unwillingness to break with a long-standing "paradigm," most physicists have continued to do science as if these findings were not applicable—as if hidden variables could re-instate and make valid the separation of observer and observed. Even when there is a willingness to admit of an alternative to scientific consciousness, when writing from the perspective of science there is retained something of the conviction of the scientific method. Hence, the "unreasonable," even paradoxical characteristics of the new physics have led some, like Capra, to suggest not a contrast, but a comparison with the subtleties of esoteric thought. Such musings are based on the assumption that the two are equally valid as ways of knowing. In *The Tao of Physics*, Capra writes:

> Whenever the essential nature of things is analysed by the intellect, it must seem absurd or paradoxical. This has always been recognized by the mystics, but has become a problem in science only very recently.[5]

Yet, for Capra, this "problem" does not lead to scepticism in regard to science, for he states: "Atomic physics provided the scientists with the first glimpses of the *essential nature* of things."[6] Capra is not seriously questioning the findings of quantum physics or the methods which science has practised since the days of Galileo. Instead, he sees a similarity between the failure of ordinary language to deal with the quantum world and the way that language fails to adequately describe the mystical one, resulting in the "paradoxes" of, say, Zen, Eckhart, Sufism, or the Vedanta. Yet the two cannot be considered at all alike unless one believes that reductionism is of equal validity to its opposite—holism; or that the analysis of science is somehow equivalent to that of the mystic's non-analysis; or that reason or discursive thought is of equal validity to Intellective intuition. Granted,

---

[5] Capra, *The Tao of Physics*, pp. 58-9.

[6] Capra, *The Tao of Physics*, p. 60, emphasis added. The attitude of ostensibly making room for religion while at the same time giving no ground, is nowhere better represented than in E.O. Wilson's *Consilience: the Unity of Knowledge* (New York: Vintage, 1999). See Wendell Berry's critique of this book in *Life is a Miracle: An Essay against Modern Superstition* (Washington DC: Counterpoint, 2000).

paradox often results upon translation of the mystical experience into ordinary language, but the initial perception is not based on reductionism, analysis or reason. The mystic would say that their perception is of how the world actually is, whereas science will tell us not how it is, but only how it appears, based on a more limited perception and approach.[7]

The movement towards a synthesis of Eastern thought with modern science that Capra attempts, then, is initiated not so much by a similarity in findings but by the failure of science to continue on the path of measurement by, and of, discreet entities. Quantum physics has in fact revealed an obstacle to the continuation of the methods of reductive science. Yet, until the obstacle is recognized as an insurmountable one, then no genuine movement in the direction indicated by mysticism is possible. So long as Capra and other scientists fail to tackle the question of the legitimacy of the scientific method, they must live with its claim to the uncertainty of knowledge—and thus, logically, a scepticism concerning the esoteric.

Yet, is the claim by science that knowledge is always uncertain legitimate? It must be remembered with what tools science works. Since the days of Galileo, we have remained committed to a singular quest. We have defined the parameters by which we will study reality, by insisting that we use quantifiable data; that we use only our senses combined with reasoning, both inductive and deductive; and that we fragment the world. As Sherrard makes clear:

> Having restricted the scope of scientific investigation to the rationally observable and purely quantitative aspects of what is changing and impermanent, and having adopted more or less exclusively a view of causality that takes into account merely efficient causes and ignores formal or spiritual causes, scientists are literally condemned to trying to explain things in terms of those meager interpretive possibilities which are all they can now envisage. In other

---

[7] For Nasr, "*The Tao of Physics* does not really speak of Hindu cosmology or Chinese physics, but only mentions certain comparisons between modern physics and Hindu and Taoist metaphysical ideas . . . there are many profound correlations and concordances to be found between certain aspects of biology, astronomy and quantum mechanics on the one hand and oriental doctrines of nature, of the cosmos, on the other. . . . But what has occurred for the most part is not . . . [a] profound comparison . . . but its parody, a kind of popularized version of a religious knowledge of nature" (Nasr, *The Spiritual and Religious Dimensions of the Environmental Crisis*, p. 16).

words, their theories or hypotheses do no more than reflect the limitations within which they operate and have no greater objectivity than the arbitrary and illusory assumptions which underlie them.[8]

Consequently, science is not in a position to confront an underlying qualitative essence simply because such a quality has been excluded from the world by the very methodology that science uses to study the world. Ironically,

> it is tacitly assumed that there is nothing else to know about [the objects science investigates] . . . except what can be observed by the so-called scientific method. . . . Having adopted a method of investigation which in its nature precludes the perception of spiritual qualities, it is gratuitous, to say the least, to pronounce that the object one investigates is to be explained in non-spiritual categories alone.[9]

Moreover, it is a mistake, logically, to now assume that because the method has failed to supply a coherent or exact knowledge, we are not in a position at all to understand reality. We may well have found the limits of the scientific method; this is quite different from finding the limits to knowledge.

Mathematics

The desire to make the world answer to mathematical description may be considered to lie at the heart of the quandary that besets the scientific paradigm, for it is in the application of mathematics to the world that reductionism finds its impetus. The human invention of mathematics worked well within the abstract and imaginal world of ideal proportions: exact mathematical values and exact mathematical figures in two or three dimensions may be conceived, and mathematical relationships, such as Pythagoras' theorem and *pi*, described. For a time it also worked well when applied to the celestial realms, which could, initially, withstand the application of abstract concepts because they themselves were not considered

---

[8] Sherrard, "The Desanctification of Nature," p. 117.

[9] Sherrard, "The Desanctification of Nature," pp. 116 and 117.

concrete. It worked reasonably well when applied to the human world of invention and artefact, but only because this world could be *made to conform* to mathematical principles; for instance buildings could be constructed in accordance with geometrical shapes and according to particular mathematical ratios. The mistake came with the attempt to apply mathematics to a world not of our making.

Nature, as it happened, was to demonstrate extreme reluctance to having the comparison made. It must always have been as clear as it is today that the natural world allows very few opportunities for this form of description. It contains virtually nothing that is exact. There are no truly straight lines or the equivalents of precise geometric shapes. Indeed the basic starting points for geometrical space are themselves illusory; the horizon is only apparently straight, while its perpendicular, provided by gravity, is not even visible. Crystals are rough approximations of the perfection that is mathematics. Exact circles do not exist in the real world, so the ratio *pi*—itself not even calculable—could never be applied exactly to anything in nature; the earth is not perfectly round, nor is the solar or lunar disc. And no two things, that might at first appear the same, actually *are* the same. This is as true of trees, leaves and flowers as it is of whirlpools, clouds or snowflakes. An almost infinite diversity, which extends into the microscopic level (and quite probably the "sub-atomic" level) as well as to the macroscopic, is evident. The attempt, then, to categorize what was observed meant it was necessary either to postulate that the realm which lay beyond reach *was* perfect, and conformed to mathematical and geometric exactness of form and motion, or to create—for the world that *was* open to investigation—some arbitrary measuring sticks which were themselves of the nature of exactness, and apply *them* to the world.

With regard to the non-earthly realm, the heavens refused to obey any such "perfect" motion. The difficulties which beset the Ptolemaic system (where a successive series of epicycles had to be introduced to overcome obvious discrepancies in the simplistic structure of "heavenly spheres") were only resolved with the less-than-perfect elliptical orbits of Johannes Kepler (1571-1630). Yet, even the ellipse we imagine as somehow "out there" is actually not anywhere; it is a representation in abstract form of what takes place in the heavens. Here, as elsewhere, mathematical entities have been given an ontological reality that is not justified.

Elegant and seemingly precise mathematical laws such as Newton's inverse square law of gravitational attraction contained hidden discrepancies, which meant they did not exactly fit the world. Newtonian calculations could not explain Mercury's perihelion, necessitating and prompting a revision based on the mathematics of relativity theory. Thus, the same reality was described in new ways by using new mathematical formulas; relativity theory subsumed Newtonian mechanics, which became a special instance of that theory. And although Einstein's equation $E=mc^2$ describes the existence of some equivalence between what we term matter and energy, its variables rely once again on the use of arbitrary measuring sticks to make the formula work.

Ironically, science, by choosing the methods of mathematics and reductionism to seek the essence of reality, has succeeded only in overlooking essence. This is because the essence of things, according to a traditional metaphysical perspective, is not to be found through stripping away the "unimportant" qualities (such as colour, sound, life, consciousness, and beauty) and substituting mathematically quantifiable characteristics. Nor, alternatively, does it lie in the retention of those qualities together with their perception by a subject consciousness. The essence cannot lie anywhere but in the unity of a whole that is both subject and object combined. This implies the re-assembling of just those elements that modern science has chosen to keep separate. "Overlaying" the outward form of a thing are its subtler aspects, and these subtler aspects have an ineradicable relationship with our own being because both they and the consciousness perceiving them belong to a more encompassing reality. This *re-assembly of reality* must involve the removal of the artificially imposed dualism that treats the realm of the mind as distinct from the realm of nature. Only then will those aspects, which for so long have been considered to reside in a realm dissociated from nature, have a chance to be incorporated back into the structure of nature. The perceptions, like that of beauty, which we believe are possessed by "us," are then seen to be intrinsic to the world. They are not "ours" if we do not, at a fundamental level, exist as separate entities. Rather, perception and the perceived are part of the same whole.

It is a mistake to imagine that the latest physics in some way describes the nature of ultimate reality and shows it to be insubstantial. Rather, the revelations of this physics are the extreme outcome of what happens when the non-quantifiable aspects are overlooked in favour of the quantifiable ones. The history of science may be seen as an attempt to come to grips with the essence of the world through an *objective* encounter with it. However, this process has produced an artificial construct, since the very element necessary for the revelation of nature's real nature has been divorced from it.

Faced with the uncertainty of "sure" knowledge coming from science it might be considered inevitable that we would attempt a reassessment of the metaphysics of the past; that, faced with a blind alley we would seek another avenue. Yet belief in the scientific method is so strong that we are extremely reluctant to abandon it as a means to gaining knowledge. Like Capra, we would like to incorporate its failures within the paradigm itself and view knowledge as having uncertainty built into it. Retaining its largely incomprehensible truths, we prefer to utilize a traditional metaphysics to vindicate those "truths," when we should, instead, be using the light of tradition to shine upon the desolate world that science conceives.

THE SCIENCE-ENVIRONMENT INTERFACE

For countless generations one could stand under the sky at night and quite naturally feel that, gazing upon this glory, one was looking up towards a reality that far transcended our life on earth; indeed, that the veil before the face of God had been lifted. And in that vertical stance and upward gaze we embodied, too, a symbol; we quite literally *stood* for an inner verticality, a path that leads "upward" from this phenomenal world to everything that lies beyond it.

In only a handful of generations, what have we been taught as counterpoint to this traditional view? That we look out upon the cold, and the lifeless, and the story of a stellar evolution. That we ourselves embody this evolution and, from our dust-mote perspective, are asked to contemplate a universe of matter, moving and turning mechanically through time at the behest of so many laws. How far removed from Dante's vision of heaven upon heaven, and an ascension to Divinity. Our gaze too readily falls away now in defeat before an unapproachable vastness, an ungraspable conception. Most in the West are now familiar with the grand story of "creation" offered by science, if not directly, by what they have been told, then indirectly by what they have *not* been told—what has been left *un*said. If the stars themselves mindlessly manufacture the materials that are destined, after uncountable eons, to form the chemistry of our bodies and brains—enabling the universe, at long last, to contemplate itself—then the cosmologies of old are only the fairy stories of childhood. We are assured by the popularizers of science that there is still wonder and awe in this new narrative, and that if God was always illusory then *we* at least retain significance by virtue of being the "most intelligent lifeform" we know, with the capacity to now understand the real workings of the universe.

There was a time when the men who stood for science also stood for something more; when a Newton could still acknowledge the Divinity standing behind phenomenal appearance or "nature and nature's laws." But the light of the Intellect was then little more than a memory. And that memory is now truly fading. Inexorably, rationality and an empiricism based on mathematics has gained the upper hand and these, coupled with an increasing belief that the real resides in materiality alone, has led, by way of evolutionary theory, to a present world view completely at odds with the traditional: that of man having ascended from an ignoble past and now well on the upward road, destined for a greater and greater view of the surrounding landscape. The adoption of this intoxicating vision has been, and is being, urged upon a larger and larger portion of humanity.

Prior to this, an acceptance of the Divinity, and our connection to it, had meant an acceptance of a sacred creation. If there was not exactly a prohibition on the utilization of the world for need, there was restraint. We did not, as Sherrard says, "deliberately blast its guts out . . . or rape it in any of the thousands of ways in which we are now raping it."[10] But the world stripped of its sacredness as either divine manifestation or creation, and humanity stripped of *its* sacredness, its higher potentialities, meant "free" beings destined to utilize a now wholly material world for material benefit. The "desolation" referred to above is far more than conceptual. The tenets of science—its epistemology and ontology—which provide the particular image we have of the world and of ourselves, inevitably extend their influence into the phenomenal world. From the very beginning, science's approach to nature and its life encouraged a level of abuse that had not existed in all the preceding centuries. In Bacon's view of nature as the feminine needing to be "hounded," and in the Cartesian experiments on live animals, we can witness the beginning of what would become a sustained destruction and pillage, still reflected today in the belief that we have the right, in the name of science, to experiment or tamper with any lifeform. Even so, the detrimental impact could be largely overlooked until the technological inventions of the nineteenth and twentieth centuries (their use sanctioned by a belief in the world as a soulless mechanism) made it impossible not to draw a parallel between the scientific paradigm and its effect on the world.

---

[10] Sherrard, *Human Image: World Image*, p. 5.

An "environmental" awareness, beginning in the nineteenth century and extending into the next two, made it apparent to many people that the beauty of the natural world was disappearing, stripped away and converted into the things which technology—a product of science—could create out of it. The advent of the materialist view seemed to promote the removal of everything that bespoke a pre-scientific, pre-materialistic outlook. The natural world had stood as counterbalance to the world of human culture, offering a reminder of all that lay beyond that sphere. Now the "death of nature" looms on the horizon, the conversion of the planet into a human ecosystem of drastically impoverished proportions signalling, perhaps, the breakdown of the entire Gaian system. The products of science are tearing "Gaia's" face; the black dust of nuclear war could obscure it completely. If these potentialities are not thought the worst indictment of science, it is only because science itself has helped to foster a mentality of detachment from the world it has brought forth.

Bronowski once passionately expressed his defence of science. In one of the most powerful moments in film, he is seen to walk fully clothed into a shallow pool at one of the Nazi death camps, and, crouching, take up a handful of the mud there:

> It is said that science will dehumanise people and turn them into numbers. That is false, tragically false. . . . The concentration camp and crematorium at Auschwitz . . . is where people were turned into numbers. Into this pond were flushed the ashes of some four million people. And that was not done by gas. It was done by arrogance. . . . When people believe that they have absolute knowledge, with no test in reality, this is how they behave.[11]

But it is scientists who have treated the world as a machine. It is science that has measured most of the world out of existence, and has progressively stripped away the subtler attributes of humanity, substituting instead a being with the nature of a mechanism. It is science that has claimed the authority to describe what the world is and what we are. If humanism or spirituality still survives, if a love of the world's beauty, its life, still moves the human imagination, it is not to the credit of science that it does so, but to those who refuse to acquiesce to the inhuman world that science often

[11] Bronowski, *The Ascent of Man*, p. 374.

imposes by virtue of the way it perceives. Those—many of whom are to be found in the environment movement—who intuitively rail against the diminished self and world and reach back to a dim memory of what was, must reject much of what science has taught and continues to teach.

What is under question here is not so much the right of an empirical method to establish a *relative* truth. It is the tragic assumption that the old truth is to be judged in the light of the new, and the terrible injustice of often propagating a view—quite untenable—that science deals with *all* of reality. Through this, a deception is foisted on humanity; faced with seemingly only one truth, what choice can then be made?

It is always tempting to question the legitimacy of earlier beliefs—it is what science does best. Today the scientific outlook is so pervasive in academic circles that it is increasingly difficult to talk, other than defensively, of Divinity or a Truth independent of scientific knowledge. Proponents of the scientific enterprise point to the obvious credibility the modern outlook has, by virtue of the very fact that it has triumphed over what went before; that a return to a previous thinking would be somehow impossible because of what we now know; that we must not give up a system that seems to work, and so on. Yet, is it not easy to discern here the defence of a new absolute?

Leaving aside the near impossibility of convincing the rational sceptic of the reality of what cannot be studied with the methodology of science, two observations may be made here. Firstly, there is the somewhat sobering point that much of humanity is not persuaded by the secular beliefs of the modern world, and does not subscribe to the answers of science in matters of metaphysics, but retains the remnants of a more traditional perspective. Secondly, there need be no fear of a return to an "age of ignorance," since a return in that sense has been made impossible anyway. Because of all we have experienced at the hands of science, and because of all we have lost thereby, the wisdom of our age must lie in encompassing more and more of what has gone before. Precisely by virtue of the times in which we live, traditionalists have been compelled towards what in a sense *is* new: a synthesis of thought, where the relevance of our metaphysical heritage is made cogent not just by the comparing of various religious traditions but by its contrast with the limitations and failings of scientific knowledge. We may choose to stand now as one in old age who, with hindsight, sees where they went astray; knowing the mistakes that were made, but determined not to repeat them; remembering the truths learnt in childhood, and honouring the legacy of the past.

It is often claimed that it is not the scientific paradigm—itself supposedly neutral—that is bad, but the products of the scientific vision—that is, technology. Yet this view fails completely to take into account the working out of the underlying assumptions of science. It cannot be neutral since it is based on premises which themselves cannot be proven, for example that only quantifiable sense data is the true measure of what is real, or that reason is the best, or only, interpreter of that data. These premises must by their inherent logic deny, often actively oppose, a view which suggests that there is more to the world, and to ourselves, than meets the eye. Thus, setting itself up as the sole arbiter of what is acceptable, it must be implicated in the ongoing production of a host of evils which, no longer having any counter-knowledge to oppose them, are indeed accepted without much fuss. We have only to think of the wholesale and systematic destruction of plant and animal life across the globe; the manufacture of deadly chemicals that we pour with seeming abandon over our land, that poison crops, rivers, seas, the animals, the birds, and ourselves; the use of more chemicals to adulterate our food, and in drugs which often deplete and ultimately breakdown our bodies; the relegation of our animals to no more than machines in factory farms; the relegation of ourselves to a similar fate in the cities—lives lived without real purpose or beauty; the storage of spent nuclear fuels, or their deliberate release in the wars we wage, that can only promise a nightmarish outcome sometime in the future. The list is not exhaustive. In reference to the subject at hand though, we might ask how long the practices of that latest product of the scientific paradigm, genetic engineering, would last if the traditional view of life as representing a divine handiwork were seriously entertained once more.

When the underlying assumptions of science are found to have such devastating consequences, we are right to criticize. And since any philosophy that does not recognize the purely relative nature of the epistemology and ontology of science can never be wholly free of the stain of these consequences, it also must be challenged. "A totalitarian rationalism," says Schuon,

> that eliminates both Revelation and Intellect, and at the same time a totalitarian materialism that ignores the metaphysical relativity . . . of matter and of the world . . . does not know that the suprasensible, situated as it is beyond space and time, is the concrete principle of the world, and that it is consequently also at the origin of that contingent and changeable coagulation we call "matter."

A science that is called "exact" is in fact an "intelligence without wisdom", just as post-scholastic philosophy is inversely a "wisdom without intelligence".[12]

REDUCTIONISM AND BEAUTY

Almost without exception modern ideas concerning beauty have been placed precariously upon a foundation of thought that is dualistic, reductionist, and materialistic; and the seeming solidity of the quantifiable or measurable cannot but contrast with that which eludes measurement. While the view that there was a correspondence between the world's nature and our own perception of it prevailed, there remained a sense in which non-measurable things were still real, even though they could not be studied using the methods of science. But when Descartes postulated the radical dualism of mind and world, he effectively removed that connection, and the so-called *secondary* qualities were fully identified with *res cogitans*, or the psyche. Descartes himself believed the mind to be the more significant of the two. Hence, apart from a brief period in the eighteenth century when empiricists such as Joseph Addison (1672-1719) and Francis Hutcheson (1694-1746) saw nature as worthy of aesthetic appreciation, this general belief affected the philosophical approach to beauty well into the twentieth century. Beauty in nature was largely ignored in favour of art; indeed, aesthetics was considered to be the philosophy of art.[13] Meanwhile, the ascendancy of science tended towards a reversal of Descartes' view, and today it is far more likely that those qualities taken to belong to the mind, and called "subjective," will be thought *less* important, because less real. The subjectiveness of beauty is now a commonplace, reflected above all in the relinquishment of objective standards in art. The twentieth century movements in art were not just a response to the turmoil that scientific endeavour had brought to both the phenomenal world and the conceptual one, they also reflected a movement towards the total expression of individualism, a belief that because beauty was subjective anyway, anyone's view of beauty was valid.

Aesthetic appreciation of nature reappeared in philosophy in the second half of the twentieth century. Regard for the beauty of nature had

---

[12] Frithjof Schuon, *Light on the Ancient Worlds* (Bloomington: World Wisdom, 1984), p. 117.

[13] See Allen Carlson, *Aesthetics and the Environment* (London: Routledge, 2000), pp. 3-5.

existed as an undercurrent within the North American nature writers of the nineteenth century. John Muir, especially, equated beauty with wild nature, and, since he also saw ugliness wherever the human world impacted, the clear association between an "integral" wilderness and beauty was made. Muir influenced the particular view now common among environmentalists that nature which bears no discernible human imprint is unquestionably beautiful. This "positive aesthetics" which Allen Carlson has enunciated[14] readily acquiesces to the two aspects—"stability" and "integrity"—which Leopold propounds, and views the third—"beauty"—as a natural concomitance.

A significant point to make in regard to this modern view, though, is that under the influence of science the appreciation of nature can easily tend towards the rationalistic; that is, the view that if we are aware of the aspects in nature that are objective or measurable, then our appreciation of its beauty will be increased. Callicott's "environmental aesthetics" (referred to in chapter 3) is a case in point. Here the perception of beauty is steered towards intellectual constructs and away from what is, otherwise, taken to be a purely sensory experience. Thus, consciousness is held in thrall to reason and not permitted to expand in the direction of pre-rational awareness, or encouraged towards the awareness that there is more in nature than science allows. More significantly, through the influence of a scientifically underpinned modernism, natural beauty goes unrecognized as a reality that could extend the range of consciousness so that more of what nature is could be known (a logical outcome of the traditionalist perspective). Instead, the scientific paradigm, with its singular understanding of our limits and of nature's limits, looms in the background ready to redirect the consciousness of those who are at all versed in a scientific knowledge of things.

In *The Abolition of Man*, C.S. Lewis brings to mind the story of Coleridge who overhears two people discussing a nearby waterfall; one calls it "pretty," the other "sublime." The poet mentally endorses the second assertion and rejects the first. However, a school textbook of Lewis's day concludes of this aesthetic experience:

When the man said *This is sublime*, he appeared to be making a remark about the waterfall. . . . Actually . . . he was not making a

---

[14] See Allen Carlson, "Nature and Positive Aesthetics," *Environmental Ethics* Vol. 6 (1984): pp. 5-34.

remark about the waterfall, but a remark about his own feelings. What he was saying was really *I have feelings associated in my mind with the word "Sublime"*, or shortly, *I have sublime feelings.*[15]

Such sentiments have changed little; but one senses that the outrage Lewis felt on reading this has diminished considerably in the sixty years since, along with our inclination to defend beauty's objectivity as passionately. When we say beauty is in the eye of the beholder, we do not mean by this that a special way of seeing is needed in order to perceive it. An aesthetic text may well discuss beauty as though it were in the world, but if pressed the role of *reification* is readily acknowledged: the abstract is being treated *as if* it were concrete.[16]

The tenets of science—reason, empiricism, reductionism, and dualism—are both pervasive and persuasive. However, since science itself has revealed that the application of such tenets is incapable of providing certainty or revealing the nature of nature, and that it is not even legitimate to maintain a dualistic perspective, we are, if we are to be faithful to philosophy, obliged to confront both an alternative metaphysics and the question of consciousness itself.

In support of this urgent requirement, it is to a fuller treatment of traditional thought that we turn in the following chapters. A study of consciousness becomes the means by which to draw together and augment what so far have been isolated strands of esoteric thought. In this way we may hope to reweave the tapestry of nature, presenting it once more with the dimension of depth and resplendent through and through with the threads of beauty.

---

[15] Quoted in C.S. Lewis, *The Abolition of Man* (Glasgow: Fount Paperbacks, 1978), p. 7.

[16] For example, Elaine Scarry can write, "the claim . . . that beauty and truth are allied is not a claim that the two are identical. It is not that a poem or a painting or a palm tree or a person is "true," but rather that it ignites the desire for truth by giving us, with an electric brightness shared by no other uninvited, freely arriving perceptual event, the experience of conviction and the experience, as well, of error. This liability to error, contestation, and plurality—for which "beauty" over the centuries has so often been belittled—has sometimes been cited as evidence of its falsehood and distance from "truth," when it is instead the case that our very aspiration for truth is its legacy. It creates, without itself fulfilling, the aspiration for enduring certitude" (Elaine Scarry, *On Beauty and Being Just* [Princeton, NJ: Princeton University Press, 1999], p. 53).

Part Four

THE VERTICAL DIMENSION

CHAPTER SEVEN
Descent

Quantum physics brought to a close the centuries-long search for the underlying substance or essence of nature through the application of the scientific method. Until the advent of the new physics, it was assumed that the measurements being made of the world always correlated with some actual thing or substance that, if not seen, could nevertheless be imagined. From the indivisible atoms of Democritus to the miniature solar system of particle theory, an image of the world we could not immediately perceive perpetuated a belief in a coherent reality. But quantum science did not so much paint a world, as blank the canvas. The subatomic realm was not a thing, but a "tendency to exist." In the "Copenhagen interpretation," only the mathematics used to describe that world were relevant; the true nature of what was being described could no longer be known. Sub-atomic particles were mathematical abstractions; they depended, for their existence, on the collapse of the "wave function" brought about by the mathematician's own action. Thus, the observer was intimately connected with the observation made. Indeed, the two could no longer meaningfully be separated; the knower and what was known were indissolubly linked. Our theories and observations in one sense create the universe we perceive; at any one time, the universe and our perceptions of it are the same. This is not to say we create an objective universe independent of our perceptions of it, only that what is known by us is always dependent on our perception or consciousness.

For Kuhn, the apparatus, theory and observer are all part of a particular, highly subjective "paradigm," or point of view.[1] Kuhn reasoned that there is no definite progress in science, only changes in this point of view. Now, it would be a superficial reading of this insight to imagine that a shifting of the scientific outlook takes place against the background of a more or less stable subjective consciousness; that consciousness could be treated as largely independent of the ideas that it adopts. The intuition

---

[1] See Thomas Kuhn, *The Structure of Scientific Revolutions* (Chicago: University of Chicago Press, 1977).

that there is a more subtle two-way interaction between consciousness and paradigm is an ineluctable component of both Kuhn's observations and of quantum science itself. Consciousness must itself be structured by the ideas that compose it.

Ironically, a key indicator for the truth of this subtle idea is the strength of resistance to its assimilation. For, in the face of the extraordinary conclusions of quantum science, there has been a continuation of the conventional way of doing science, as though the rules science has applied all along to conduct its investigations still hold good. Nearly a hundred years after the "Copenhagen interpretation," ever larger super-colliders reveal ever more "particles" that cannot be described other than mathematically, while prominent physicists like Stephen Hawking continue to make claims for a grand unified theory as though we were really able to describe what reality is, and not just our own perceptions of it.[2] Admittedly, the belief that old "paradigms" are subsumed by newer ones, and the general belief in progress, helps to explain the momentum of science. However, one could as easily say that it was as though the implications of the more recent discoveries have not been *able* to impinge. Clearly, implicit within the findings of quantum physics is not just the issue of the relationship between a consciousness and reality, but the *type* of consciousness. Those who set aside the more profound implications of quantum physics for the sake of a continuity of ordinary dualistic science are effectively choosing to ignore this question of consciousness. To assume the standard approach to doing science is to fix as it were a *particular* consciousness of the observer, to crystallize the self into a particular pattern, a mathematical, rationalistic, dualistic pattern, which cannot but produce a corresponding pattern of "reality."

Bohm

To turn to the speculations of the remarkable twentieth century physicist David Bohm (1917-1992)[3] is to encounter an intellectual approach more

---

[2] "I think," says Hawking, "that there is a good chance that the study of the early universe and the requirements of mathematical consistency will lead us to a complete unified theory within the lifetime of some of us who are around today" (Stephen Hawking, *A Brief History of Time* [London: Bantam, 1988], p. 167).

[3] Bohm, a theoretical physicist and philosopher, developed ideas too speculative to be accepted by mainstream physics. Yet, as one of the "maverick" scientists who departed

consistent with the findings of quantum physics, and one that engages more fully with this question of consciousness. By 1952, Bohm had successfully countered von Neumann's proof with one of his own, re-establishing an objective model of the electron. His theory was confirmed when, in 1964, John Stewart Bell (1928-1990) showed that von Neumann's assumption that "ordinary objects" were local entities (that is, restricted to communicating through known forces at the speed of light) was unwarranted. Instead, Bell's theorem showed that reality must be *non-local*; events are not localized but actually extend their influence across the entire universe. The atomic world was like "a poorly defined cloud, dependent for its particular form on the whole environment, including the observing instrument."[4] Interpreting the clearly ambiguous nature of the experimental findings of quantum physics to mean that "nature will respond in accordance with the theory with which it is approached,"[5] Bohm concluded, like Kuhn, that "all theories are insights, which are neither true nor false but, rather, clear in certain domains, and unclear when extended beyond these domains."[6] Thus, for example, Newtonian mechanics, which works very adequately when it comes to computing the manoeuvres and orbits of spacecraft, is unworkable at velocities close to *c*, where relativity theory must operate. Because, as Bohm says, "a theory is . . . *a way of looking at the world*, and not a form of knowledge of how the world is,"[7] the despair Heisenberg felt when confronted with the "absurdity" of nature arose from a misunderstanding. While he believed quantum physics had uncovered the true nature of reality, all along its answers were only relatively true and contingent upon the particular method chosen to approach nature—the method itself based on prior beliefs. Like earlier scientific worldviews, the worldview of quantum physics is evidently a reflection of a *state of consciousness*.

For Bohm it is only to be expected that all theories are eventually falsified and none positively affirmed, as the philosopher Karl Popper had

---

from orthodoxy in order to forge links between modern science and metaphysics, Bohm represents a necessary movement away from the (still largely unrecognized) impasse that science has reached.

[4] David Bohm, *Wholeness and the Implicate Order*, p. 9.

[5] Bohm, *Wholeness and the Implicate Order*, p. 6.

[6] Bohm, *Wholeness and the Implicate Order*, p. 4.

[7] Bohm, *Wholeness and the Implicate Order*, p. 4, emphasis added.

suggested.[8] Yet, significantly, "The fact that our vision of the world can be falsified as a result of further movement, observation, probing, etc., implies that there is more in the world than what we have perceived and known."[9] Thus, "all our different ways of thinking are to be considered as different ways of looking at the one reality."[10] Bohm saw that we have always attempted to understand the world by first hypothesizing about it—forming a mental construct or image of it—and then approaching the world with just this idea of what it might be. Ever since the days of the rationally oriented Greek philosophers, we—as the subject consciousness—have attempted to develop theories about this whole—the ultimate nature of reality—and not realized that the very process of creating this mental construct meant not only creating a fragment of the whole, but possibly confusing the constructed fragment with the world as it is. Put another way, we first create a theory that delimits or fragments the world and then, armed with our delimited view, begin to believe that it and the world are one and the same. Reciprocally, "fragmentation is continually being brought about by the almost universal habit of taking the content of our thought for 'a description of the world as it is.'"[11]

For Bohm, the real significance of quantum physics lies not in the value of its method or worldview but in its ability to make clear the limitations built into conceptual systems as such, and so provide the impulse to step outside the scientific paradigm altogether. The evidence of quantum physics suggests that reality consists not of separate and distinct entities that interact with each other; these are our ideas of what is, based on the belief that we are entities that exist apart from everything else, and on our mental constructs regarding the world. The reality that quantum physics points to is an undivided whole without boundaries in time or space. It is an "undivided wholeness in flowing movement,"[12] so that what are taken to be separate entities appear as such only in the way vortexes in a stream might be treated as distinct for a while before they either change their

---

[8] See Karl Popper, *The Logic of Scientific Discovery* (New York: Harper and Row, 1959).

[9] Bohm quoted in John P. Briggs and F. David Peat, *Looking Glass Universe* (Glasgow: Fontana, 1984), p. 104.

[10] Bohm, *Wholeness and the Implicate Order*, pp. 7-8, emphasis added.

[11] Bohm, *Wholeness and the Implicate Order*, p. 3.

[12] Bohm, *Wholeness and the Implicate Order*, p. 11.

character or disappear once more into the overall flow. Therefore, "what is needed," says Bohm,

> is to give up altogether the notion that the world is constituted of basic objects or 'building blocks'. Rather, one has to view the world in terms of universal flux of events and processes. . . . [The universal flux] cannot be defined explicitly but . . . can be known only implicitly, as indicated by the explicitly definable forms and shapes, some stable and some unstable, that can be abstracted from the universal flux. In this flow, mind and matter are not separate substances. Rather, they are different aspects of one whole and unbroken movement.[13]

Bohm's account of mind as being no different to matter confronts the dualism Descartes promoted, Hume retained, and Kant partially attenuated.[14] But since the dualism is essential to the process of reasoning itself,

---

[13] Bohm, *Wholeness and the Implicate Order*, pp. 9 and 11.

[14] When Kant claimed that "all human cognition of the world is channelled through the human mind's categories" (Tarnas, *The Passion of the Western Mind*, p. 343), he prophetically pre-empted the eventual conclusion of science. Yet the bleak prospect, in which we are forever unable to experience reality as it is, because we are dogged by the necessarily human and therefore limited mental construct we take to the world, stems from a belief in reason being the pre-eminent human faculty. To the reasoning mind, metaphysics seems speculative; its pronouncements take on the appearance of propositions that can as easily be negated as affirmed.

For Hume the only certain propositions were those of a non-sensory nature, and they were, anyway, deductive, necessary and tautological. *Inductive* propositions, those related to phenomenal experience, may not provide *certain* knowledge (since causality could not be proved), yet the empirical method as undertaken by the thinking subject seemed to be the only legitimate means to approach reality. Kant agreed that phenomenal experience provided the only legitimate knowledge, but re-imposed a form of certainty by working past supposed "naive" realism (which accepts that the perception of phenomena corresponds to the phenomenal world), and producing the idea of *a priori* categories, or predispositions of the mind. The perception of the structure of the world is then explained by the structure of the mind. But this structure does not necessarily have any ultimate relation to the world. Thus, "Kant had rejoined the knower to the known, but not the knower to any objective reality, to the object in itself. Knower and known were united, as it were, in a solipsistic prison" (Tarnas, *The Passion of the Western Mind*, p. 348). An escape from this prison relies on recognizing that this very process of reasoning is itself operating like a conscious category, imposing its own outlook on the mind itself, and sets up a type of

Bohm, who now manages to throw into doubt the legitimacy of the separate self and its conceptualizations, is immediately caught in a complex paradox which always faces those who confront the unreality of the isolated self by means of that very self. Although we can superficially take a "God's eye" view, our very thinking process invalidates that possibility. The dualism in question resists disruption since Bohm's own theorizing falls within the set of all possible conceptualizations. For this reason the question, "What is the nature of the implicate order, the unity, the stable entity which is a composite of the thinking subject and all else?" can only be solved at a level beyond the ordinary consciousness—that is, beyond the discursive or rational mind which deals with concepts.[15]

Poised, then, upon the elevated platform that Bohm provides us with, we may glimpse a *vertical* dimension to consciousness opening up before us, where the self, by escaping its own conceptions—its own rationality—might take wing. Yet we are pinioned. Clearly, we are not in need of further theories for the rational mind to entertain regarding itself (more measurements of the mental landscape now before us) but the means to fly within this space of consciousness. Indeed, so long as we attempt to come to grips with consciousness by applying a conceptual methodology to it, by studying it as if it were an object, so long do we fail completely to appreciate what Bohm was hinting at. Consciousness cannot be studied as object. To *study* consciousness is not to know consciousness at all.

---

circular reinforcement of its own validity. If Kant's logic is itself restricted to the sphere of this method, any conclusion necessarily pertains only within this sphere, not outside it.

Kant was satisfied he had disposed of various theological proofs. But, for Schuon, "the ideas of [the] 'Great Spirit' and of the primacy of the Invisible are natural to man. . . . What is natural to human consciousness proves *ipso facto* its essential truth, the reason for the existence of intelligence being adequation to the real. . . . We have heard someone say that the wings of birds prove the existence of air, and that in the same way the religious phenomenon, common *a priori* to all peoples, proves the existence of its content, namely God and the after-life; which is to the point if one takes the trouble to examine the argument in depth" (Schuon, *From the Divine to the Human*, p. 6).

[15] It is evident that Bohm was aware of both the paradox and the need to transcend it in some way. In his latter years, he promoted a particular form of "dialogue"—the exchange of thoughts and ideas free of judgments or defensiveness—to help break through the paradox. "Dialogue" can be seen as an exercise in heightening conscious awareness of the processes of consciousness itself, an attempt to free us from a rigidity of thinking, even escape the net of conceptualizations altogether.

SHERRARD

There may be no better contemporary demonstration of this insight than the following one by Philip Sherrard, written as a letter declining an invitation to attend an International Symposium on the theme "Science of Consciousness." Both a critique of science and a defence of traditional metaphysics, it has the virtue, while seemingly applying the rules that rationality itself would respect, of speaking for a form of consciousness that transcends the purely rational:

On why a knowledge of the nature of consciousness does not lie within the competence of the modern scientist.

1. It is with my consciousness that I perceive whatever I do perceive.

2. Thus, how something *appears* to me depends on the mode of my consciousness.

3. I can perceive only what I am capable of perceiving, observe only what I am capable of observing, understand only what I am capable of understanding.

4. Hence my understanding of the nature of something can only be according to the mode of consciousness that I possess; and this means that the true nature of what I perceive may be very different from that which I perceive it to be.

5. A higher mode of consciousness than mine will be capable of perceiving the true nature of something more clearly than I can perceive it; and so on, up to the highest mode of consciousness.

6. These same propositions apply also to a knowledge of the nature of consciousness itself; my understanding of the nature of consciousness can only be according to the mode of consciousness that I possess.

7. Nothing can be known except according to the mode of the knower.

8. A higher consciousness than mine will be capable of a higher understanding of the nature of consciousness than that of which I am capable.

9. Ultimately, to know what the nature of consciousness is in itself I must have attained the highest mode of consciousness that it is possible to attain, namely, that which is one with consciousness itself.

10. Only such a mode of consciousness can experience and in this way verify a knowledge of the nature of consciousness.

11. Only my experience of the nature of consciousness in itself can constitute knowledge of and evidence for it.

12. Short of that my understanding of the nature of consciousness can be but hypothetical, mere opinion tailored according to the limitations of my particular mode of consciousness, vitiated by the ignorance which these limitations impose, and totally inaccessible to verification through experience. In such circumstances, how consciousness *appears* to me will be very different from what it actually is.

13. The highest mode of consciousness, or consciousness in itself, is that in which there is no dualism between knower and what is to be known, observer and what is to be observed, consciousness and that of which consciousness is conscious.

14. This means that so long as there is in my own consciousness any dualism of this kind I can be sure that I have not attained the highest mode of consciousness that it is possible to attain. Hence my conception of the nature of consciousness can be but a hypothesis or opinion, distorted by the ignorance that pertains to any consciousness still in the thrall of the dualism in question. In the nature of things such hypothesis, or opinion, cannot constitute knowledge.

15. As the mode of consciousness effective for the modern scientist is one that is still in the thrall of such a dualism—for if this

were not the case he could not be a modern scientist—it is only too clear that a knowledge of the nature of consciousness does not lie within his competence. His competence, in this respect as well as in other respects, is necessarily limited to hypothesis, opinion, speculation, and none of these can be said to constitute knowledge.

16. By definition, any attempt to understand the nature of consciousness that is not based on the experience and knowledge of those whose consciousness has transcended every form of dualism is doomed to futility. There is no point in wasting time on enterprises that *a priori* are doomed to futility.

17. Moreover, to proceed to an investigation of the nature of consciousness otherwise than through the study of the testimonials of those—divinely inspired metaphysicians, mystics, seers, prophets—who through direct experience have attained a knowledge of the nature of consciousness would be a manifestation of extreme arrogance, not to say sheer impudence; for to proceed otherwise than through such study would be to assume the possession of a degree of understanding and insight superior to those possessed by the finest intelligence known to the human race. It would in fact be an unexpected bonus to find at a conference such as the one proposed even a single scientist who has studied in depth—that is, with at least the same diligence and dedication as he has studied his own discipline—the writings of such people. Yet unless he has studied these writings in this way, what qualifications does he possess that entitle him to speak to any purpose on the theme under discussion? The blind cannot lead the blind.

18. And if in response to this last question it is claimed that the question itself is irrelevant because consciousness continually evolves and therefore our understanding of consciousness is in a continual state of evolution, what additional evidence is needed in order to demonstrate both the bankruptcy of the mind that can make such a claim and the pointlessness of any further discussion?[16]

---

[16] Philip Sherrard, "The Science of Consciousness," *The Scientific and Medical Network Newsletter* 48 (1992): pp. 5-7.

Forceful as Sherrard's argument is to an intelligence not bowed by the dictates of rational empiricism, to the scientific consciousness it *will* inevitably appear flawed. For, despite Sherrard's invitation to think or see things outside the reference point that is ordinary or scientific consciousness, that consciousness, if it is to be applied at all (and not remain mute), will inevitably approach the problem strictly on its own terms. Sherrard, although framing his argument in the rational terms respected by science, must step away from this point of reference in order to advance a thesis about the limits of the very mode of consciousness that science expresses. Scientific consciousness, true to its nature, knows, and so can make, no such movement.

To engage with Sherrard's vision of consciousness is not just to appreciate the reality of a vertical dimension, but to see also the indicators of "up" and "down." His appeal to the mystical and metaphysical tradition prepares us for the direction his writings take (and the movement within this section), while the abrupt and only quasi-logical manner of this appeal may be seen as an address to an intuitive mode of consciousness, still the preserve of such tradition. Sherrard makes clear what Bohm mooted: since consciousness is itself the faculty of perception, it cannot be studied from "outside," it cannot be made an object of observation in the way all else can. To treat it as such is to remain static before the view of this vertical dimension. The knowledge of what consciousness is comes through the experience that consciousness provides. Likewise, knowledge of the vertical dimension comes through the experience of movement in this realm—that is, through "flight."

Although, for Sherrard, consciousness is seen as hierarchical in nature, it is adequate to his purposes to speak of the extremes: of a consciousness either "egoic" or "angelic" in nature. To invoke the term *angelic* is to be reminded not only of a heavenly realm but of the aspect of life pertaining to goodness or, in modern parlance, ethics, and in *Human Image: World Image*, which confronts the errors of modern science, it is made clear that in scientific consciousness we are dealing with a form of consciousness at the opposite extreme from the angelic. To allow ourselves to be persuaded by the mentality of quantification—which (as we saw in part three) epitomizes this consciousness—is, from Sherrard's perspective, to descend within an ever more confining chasm of thought, where the true dimensions of the "sky" of consciousness above are hidden from view.

To see modern science in terms of a "descent" of consciousness is, of course, to exactly reverse the conventional image. Yet even if we suspected this conventional image to be not the truth of the matter, but one of the outcomes of being entrapped by a paradigm of thought, this does not itself provide the means of escape from either the image or the paradigm. Two possible ways of affecting an escape present themselves. One is to take Sherrard's approach and allow the mind's eye to gaze as far into the "angelic" realm as is possible. Such a metaphysical exposition is the subject of the following chapter. Another, is to illumine our own "dark" condition of egoic consciousness with the "light" that our sense of beauty and ethics still gives, and this will be the task taken up now.

The following two extracts from *Human Image: World Image* in one sense recapitulate a key finding of part three. For Sherrard, what defines the downward movement more than anything is the "fetish" for mathematics that the progenitors of modern science displayed:

> Although ... [these men] were responsible for accomplishing what amounted to a philosophical revolution, they were not themselves philosophers. ... [To] delineate the main features of their philosophy does not mean, therefore, that we have to explore a complex, finely-wrought tapestry of wisdom. ... We have only to try to bring into focus the few 'clear' and 'distinct' notions to which they gave single-minded adherence and which constituted the mainsprings of their activities. The clue to the nature of these few uncomplicated notions ... is provided for us if we remember that ... these men were brilliant mathematicians.[17]

> The *a priori* assumption that the structure of the universe is mathematical means that physical reality is mathematical and that what is real in nature is only that which can be expressed in terms of strict mathematical laws. The real world is a world of mathematically measurable motions in time and space. If God created the world according to strict mathematical principles, it must follow that the whole realm of physics is reducible to mathematical qualities alone. And the corollary to this is that the only way in which it is possible for us to know objects in nature—to know natural phenomena—is through knowing their mathematical qualities, for it is these qualities alone that constitute their reality. What

---

[17] Sherrard, *Human Image: World Image*, p. 35.

is ultimately real in nature is only that which can be expressed mathematically and of which mathematical knowledge is possible. Everything else—every non-mathematical quality—is irrelevant.[18]

Applying this philosophy to the world requires that the world be broken into quantifiable "constituents," not in the abstract way of the Greeks, but literally. The suicidal assaults on our environment and upon ourselves remain mysterious only so long as we ignore this process of quantification by which all the negative traits of a purely egoic consciousness form:

> The industrial and technological inferno we have produced around us, and by means of which we are now devastating our world, is not something that has come about accidentally. On the contrary, it is the direct consequence of our allowing ourselves to be dominated by a certain paradigm of thought—embracing a certain human image and a certain world image—to such a degree that it now determines virtually all our mental attitudes and all our actions, public and private.
>
> It is a paradigm of thought that impels us to look upon ourselves as little more than two-legged animals whose destiny and needs can best be fulfilled through the pursuit of social, political and economic self-interest. And to correspond with this self-image we have invented a world-view in which nature is seen as an impersonal commodity, a soulless source of food, raw materials, wealth, power and so on, which we think we are quite entitled to experiment with, exploit, remodel and generally abuse by means of any scientific and mechanical technique we can devise and produce, in order to satisfy and deploy this self-interest. Having in our minds desanctified ourselves, we have desanctified nature, too, in our minds: we have removed it from the suzerainty of the divine and have assumed that we are its overlords, and that it is our thrall, subject to our will. In short, under the aegis of this self-image and world-view we have succeeded in converting ourselves into the most depraved and depraving of all creatures upon the earth.[19]

[18] Sherrard, *Human Image: World Image*, p. 36.

[19] Sherrard, *Human Image: World Image*, p. 3.

If, within the scientific community itself, it is too easily forgotten that modern science is always impinging upon the field of ethics, for ecophilosophy this correlation is clear. From a study of the seemingly endless list of detrimental outcomes of the workings of modern science it is but a small step to conclude, as does Sherrard, that modern science reflects a particular mindset that is itself often dangerous and working counter to the interests of human life and planetary welfare; that the whole scientific venture is not just ethically neutral but *un*ethical in nature. Yet time and again, the temptation is to excuse the scientific process *itself* of culpability, to imagine a certain innocuous neutrality in the experimental procedures that precede any "real world" applications.[20]

Although already refuted in previous chapters, two more things may be said in response to this position. Firstly, the *process itself* is not beyond criticism. Long before we are ready to apply the findings of science, we are already engaged in suspect actions. Environmental philosophy can be credited with bringing to light long-standing but hitherto "invisible" unethical procedures. Ever since the days of Descartes, animal experimentation in the laboratory and in the "field" has been a common element in many areas of research and has led to the systematic abuse, torture, and death of untold numbers of individuals. Sometimes this is in the name of possible "benefits" to our own state; more often just curiosity to determine how nature functions. Nor, as ecophilosophy justifiably claims, need ethical concern be restricted to sentient creatures. Yet the rights, or the infringement of the rights, of "inanimate" nature to be free of unnecessary experimentation are rarely perceived even to exist. If we also include what amounts to an experimental exposure of the human organism to a barrage of synthetic chemicals and radiation with partially unknown effects, or experimental medicine and surgery, or the exposure of millions to the risk of injury and death through large-scale electromagnetic experiments that test our capacity to disrupt normal atmospheric states, it is clear that the very *attempt* to do science is often ethically dubious.[21]

---

[20] For Nasr, "One of the great tragedies of the modern world is that the dominant paradigm . . . has divorced ethics from metaphysics and cosmology so that, within its framework, to speak of the sanctity of life and the ethically immoral character of the destruction of the sacred is viewed as mere sentimentality, subjectivism or poetry—not as a position grounded in objective knowledge" (Nasr, "Man and Nature: Quest for Renewed Understanding," p. 10).

[21] It is worth reminding ourselves that it was not so long ago that the sacredness of even

Secondly, in the rare cases when the practice of science can be thought initially free of obvious ethical concerns, we find that a faith in the overall positive outcome of science expresses itself as a hubris that often leads, while it lasts, to heedlessness, blindness, or disregard for the consequences. This mindset acts to lead along a particularly destructive path, and the supposed neutrality is exposed as imaginary. Here, there may be no clearer example, or one that remains potentially more hazardous, than that of the development of nuclear weaponry.

It will be recalled that it was Einstein who was responsible for the mathematics that revealed the equivalence of mass and energy, and so the colossal destructive forces contained in a given mass. As a theoretical physicist, Einstein *could* be thought exempt from culpability in the use to which his work was put—the development of the atomic bomb.[22] It is far less certain, however, that the Los Alamos team under the leadership of Robert Oppenheimer (who, in the first trial of the bomb, was prepared to risk igniting the atmosphere of the planet) was as innocent. Oppenheimer's own confession, after witnessing the destruction of Hiroshima and Nagasaki, that "the physicists have known sin; and this is a knowledge which they cannot lose,"[23] may be the strongest ever indictment of the scientific enterprise by a scientist. His declaration might have been regarded as cautionary: science, through its unleashing of extraordinary energies of destruction, could never again be seen as just a way to describe the world, and must now be mindful of its ethical responsibilities.

Nevertheless, any concerns that existed had little impact upon future nuclear policy, as atmospheric and underground nuclear tests continued in Australia, the continental United States, and the Pacific islands. By the

---

the human corpse meant the prohibition of its dissection. Because of this, the Renaissance artists, Leonardo and Michelangelo, were forced into a cautious and secretive study of human anatomy. By contrast, the routine modern autopsy can involve the removal or re-use of, even experimenting with, bodily organs. In connection with the potentially devastating Earth-scale weather modification experimentation by civil and military organizations, see, for example, Rosalie Bertell, *Planet Earth: The Latest Weapon of War* (London: Women's Press, 2000).

[22] Einstein clearly felt anguish over its use, though, once proclaiming: "If only I had known I should have become a watchmaker" (*New Statesman*, April 16, 1965).

[23] J. Robert Oppenheimer, in a lecture at Massachusetts Institute of Technology, November 25, 1947.

last decade of the twentieth century, French Polynesia—once a paradise on earth—had been converted into a high-level nuclear waste dump. It has been claimed that a devastating plutonium leak from one of the many spheres of detonation beneath the seabed of Mururoa atoll is possible within 10-20 years, and certain in 500-1000 years.[24] The fact that we have now "learned to live with" these outcomes, does nothing to change their unethical nature. More significantly, in the context of the "vertical dimension," complacency and an expectation of tragedy, suggest more than just the existence of a particular pattern of thought or mindset; they suggest the downward movement of consciousness that will lead to ever-greater tragedies.

EHRENFELD

To illustrate this notion more fully we could do no better than refer to David Ehrenfeld's *The Arrogance of Humanism*.[25] Part of the book's format echoes the two-fold nature of applied science that seems destined to repeat itself time and again: a confident outlook at the beginning is followed by "unforeseen," often disastrous, consequences, demonstrating that science's self-view is fallacious. Ehrenfeld examines three different areas—mind, body, and environment—in which the application of science promises future improvement. In his analysis, it can be seen how the strands of ethics and beauty intertwine, both affected by a consciousness arrogant in its faith in the methodology of quantification.

In the first section we are shown how the application of this methodology to the identification and categorization of personality traits, beginning at birth and extending through youth to maturity, would assist in detecting "disabilities" and enable suitable behaviour modification to achieve "normality." And, on a larger scale, we are shown how mathematical modelling, applied to past social events like the American system of slavery, could objectively determine historical conditions. The same procedure applied to current events like prison riots could be used to predict their future occurrence and therefore allow for a behavioural engineering of large groups.

---

[24] Peter Davies, "Mururoa: How Safe are the French Tests?" (*Quantum* television documentary, Australian Broadcasting Corporation, August 23, 1995).

[25] David Ehrenfeld, *The Arrogance of Humanism* (New York: Oxford University Press, 1981).

Next, we see that the innate desire of humanity to transcend its own limitations has been transferred from its long association with the *soul's* development, and re-conceived in largely material terms. Thus, the ideal of the "superman" might now be realized through the remodelling of the human organism, making it free of sickness, ageing, and even death—bionics, drugs, and genetic engineering being useful techniques here.

Finally, we encounter the desire to perfect the environment to match our *own* coming "perfection." The problems of drought, flood, fire, disease, infertility of soils, and limited solar energy, may all be overcome by the mobilization of technological power against natural forces. And, if even the alteration of a "less-than-adequate" planet does not fulfil our dreams, we could build an ideal habitat in earth orbit, or even re-design whole worlds.

For Ehrenfeld, this is the myth. The reality, which he proceeds to unfold in the second section, brings these fantasies to ruin. The attempt to apply mathematical systems to history or to human behaviour always entails a simplification of what goes to make up events or human personalities:

> Which numbers do we choose from among the millions that are available? . . . Which of an infinity of possible questions do we ask of our numbers, and how do we know that our numerical manipulations really do ask the questions that we are trying to have answered? How can we know whether the forms of our equations are automatically biasing and limiting the ranges of possible solutions?[26]

Mathematics deals with quantities. Its use in relation to people, who define themselves and their environment in terms of imprecise *qualities*, can therefore never be objective:

> For real objectivity, we must increase our perspective and broaden our view, and to do this it is often necessary to ignore claims and counter-claims concerning methods, intermediate goals, and theoretical objectives, and look exclusively at the *final results* of a technology or a set of humanistic beliefs.[27]

---

[26] Ehrenfeld, *The Arrogance of Humanism*, pp. 69-70.

[27] Ehrenfeld, *The Arrogance of Humanism*, p. 59, emphasis added.

Lake Pedder, Tasmania

Lake Pedder from
Frankland Range, Tasmania

Showers, Frankland Range, Tasmania

Weld River, Southern Tasmania

Morning light on Little Horn, Cradle Mountain, Tasmania

Trisul, Himalaya, India

Two birds, copper rendition of 16th-17th century ceramic tilework,
Hotel dû Grand Monarque, Chartres, France

Mihrab, Persian, 14th century

Cosmic wheel from the solar chariot, Sun Temple, Konarak, India

Christ Pantocrator, Sancta Sophia, Istanbul, Turkey

Blue Virgin Window, Chartres Cathedral, France

Shiva as Nataraja,
Sri Lanka, 11th century

Gautama Buddha, Sarnath, near
Varanasi, India, 5th century

Mountain landscape, Taoist painting
attributed to Fan K'uan, Sung Dynasty

Patio de la Acequia, Generalife Gardens,
Alhambra, Spain

Mirador de Lindaraja, Alhambra, Spain

For this "end-product analysis," mathematics or quantification is of no avail. Instead, "The basic requirement for such an analysis is the ability to distinguish short-term effects and objectives from long-term ones,"[28] a task "more intuitive than formal . . . [which] does not demand the services of an expert."[29] Since these long-term effects often impinge upon the indefinable qualities by which we live, the criterion for the ultimate success or worth of any scientific procedure is whether these qualities have been either eroded or destroyed, or retained and embellished. Thus, before assessing and remodelling "aberrant" behaviour in the young, we should ask:

What are "hyperactive" and "minimally brain damaged" children like when they are allowed to grow up without stigmatization or specific treatment—not just at age twenty, but until death? Do they share any distinctive personality traits, do they have the same sorts of failures and achievements, are they different from other people? What is their net effect, as adults, on society? For example, do they promote war or peace? . . . Is their creativity affected in any way? Their ambition? Their capacity for love? Their self-reliance? Their happiness? Their ability to resist tyranny? What is their later impact on society? And if we cannot answer these questions—as in fact we cannot—what arrogance coupled with what blindness is causing us to inflict this Swiftian edifice of testing upon our own children?[30]

Quantification applied to group behaviour (such as that of the inmates of a prison) necessitates the same drastic simplification of a complex system[31], and promotes the same lack of will to confront the larger picture, in this case to locate a prison riot within the context of human life as a whole, with all its concerns, values, goals, and ideals. Thus, we encoun-

---

[28] Ehrenfeld, *The Arrogance of Humanism*, p. 63.

[29] Ehrenfeld, *The Arrogance of Humanism*, p. 63.

[30] Ehrenfeld, *The Arrogance of Humanism*, p. 74.

[31] The model applied—catastrophe theory—"can handle only two control variables and one behaviour variable. So a social system of quite remarkable complexity must be simplified almost out of existence" (Jonathan Rosenhead, "Prison Control and Catastrophe Theory," *New Scientist* 72 [1976]: p. 120).

ter "a veneer of unusually sophisticated mathematics applied over the all-too-common base of ignorance and contempt of fellow human beings in trouble"[32] Of these simplified models, Ehrenfeld observes:

> We cannot know and gather in advance all the information that will be relevant, we cannot know what questions to ask of it, and if we did we could not make errorless deductions from what we know. . . . [Therefore, even] if it could work, which it cannot, what is the point of this "model"? Is it so difficult to tell when conditions at a prison are bad enough to warrant a riot, and if we know this, isn't it more important to change conditions than to waste scarce resources trying to find the exact moment when the riot will occur?[33]

In the application of quantified science to the body, "the claims of predicting the unpredictable and of knowing the unknowable, the absolute faith in procedures whose end-results can never be comprehended"[34]reappear. Yet, if we once again apply "end-product analysis" to the technology we use to overcome sickness, we find that this technology necessitates all sorts of "trade-offs." Our machines and inventions are attempts to augment our capacities. However, they usually satisfy only one or two requirements, while creating unforeseen consequences. Apart from the fact that they escape the precise fit with their environment that organisms demonstrate—often leading them to fail—their fundamental flaw lies in their tendency to create residual problems, relating once again to the qualities of life. Wherever technology is used to assist biology (by providing, for example, contact lenses, bionic canes, or artificial limbs and organs) we find the human being is "locked into" an artificial system. Through a new reliance on that technology, a person loses independence and connection with more natural and qualitative ways of living. Therefore, in Ehrenfeld's words, "it would be very difficult in practice to make fundamental changes in our bodies that would better equip us *for what we consider life as a human to be.*"[35]

---

[32] Ehrenfeld, *The Arrogance of Humanism*, pp. 75-6.

[33] Ehrenfeld, *The Arrogance of Humanism*, pp. 76-77.

[34] Ehrenfeld, *The Arrogance of Humanism*, p. 77.

[35] Ehrenfeld, *The Arrogance of Humanism*, p. 85, emphasis added.

The machine is itself a manifestation of the application of quantity to the world. Initially conceived as a mathematically precise object, and rendered in this way as image, its creation relies on the exacting control of the dimensions of the materials of which it is composed. The emphasis on quantity inherent here seems to entail—while the machine lives in our imagination—a corresponding failure to see that its defect lies precisely in its denial of quality. "Because," says Ehrenfeld, "we cannot comprehend the entire value and variety of the human experience, we simplify it, proclaiming certain isolated features, 'engineered' features, to be the best."[36] Rather than see the machine as flawed, we switch this round to claim that "anything that a machine cannot do is superfluous."[37] Hence the curious and unjustified faith in the machine results in a tendency "to portray humans as machine-like in their better qualities, rather than the other way around."[38] A machine analogy applied to ourselves could only ever be valid if we ignored the genuine qualities in ourselves that are absent in them, which is precisely what we do when we insist on taking account of only quantifiable aspects.

The attempt to escape the limitations of our biology by chemical means has led to resistant strains of bacteria, necessitating the production of ever more powerful antibiotics. Drugs designed to alleviate problems such as psychological stress often mask the symptoms of an unhealthy social system, or help to create it:

> Our acts of diagnosis and treatment themselves cause enough (harmful) reverberations within the system that the original purpose for doing them is thwarted. . . . The society clever enough to perform sophisticated research on cancer is the society clever enough to invent the sugar substitutes, children's sleepwear ingredients, food coloring agents, and swimming pool test kits that may cause it.[39]

[36] Ehrenfeld, *The Arrogance of Humanism*, p. 118.

[37] Ehrenfeld, *The Arrogance of Humanism*, p. 102.

[38] Ehrenfeld, *The Arrogance of Humanism*, p. 100.

[39] Ehrenfeld, *The Arrogance of Humanism*, pp. 90-91.

Faced with such ironies, "the conclusion we must inescapably reach," says Ehrenfeld, "is that our arrogant assumptions about our present and future control over our bodies have kept us from evaluating the quality and total consequences of that control—[because] we perform no end-product analyses . . . we never calculate the real price."[40]

When the sense of quality is uppermost in our minds, we very easily see the folly of our faith in technology. In referring to the tragic attempt to preserve the windows of Chartres cathedral,[41] Ehrenfeld observes: "our ability to ruin the optical quality of stained glass with such efficiency and despatch has come about in an age in which stained glass of this transcendent beauty and quality can no longer be created."[42] But our environment—the natural world—is full of "transcendent" and equally fragile beauty. In engineering an Aswan dam and thereby ruining Nile agriculture and marine fertility or creating salinity and the spread of disease; in manufacturing solar powered pumps that cause falling water tables; in attempting to "design" a maximum sustainable yield for one species and so depleting many others; and in planning orbiting space colonies, we are forever implementing "quasi solutions" to problems which then leave "residual problems" in their wake.[43] If there is a certain readiness to admit in hindsight to the inappropriate or wrong use of science, there is often nothing to indicate that such use will be stemmed, or to persuade the scientifically minded against yet another application of technology to overcome the damage that has been wrought. In this way age-old beauties of human life, of society, and

---

[40] Ehrenfeld, *The Arrogance of Humanism*, p. 87.

[41] In 1974, some of the thirteenth century stained glass of Chartres, endangered by air pollution, was coated with a synthetic protective film. Subsequently it was found that "the light that fell from the three restored windows had turned as flat and insensitive as that dispensed by ordinary tinted glass" (Pierre Schneider, "Optics at Chartres Reported Ruined," *New York Times*, January 1, 1977).

[42] Ehrenfeld, *The Arrogance of Humanism*, pp. 105-6.

[43] For René Dubos, "Developing *countertechnologies* to correct the new kinds of damage constantly being created by technological innovations is a policy of despair. If we follow this course we shall increasingly behave like hunted creatures, fleeing from one protective device to another, each more costly, more complex, and more undependable than the one before; we shall be concerned chiefly with sheltering ourselves from environmental dangers while sacrificing the values that make life worth living" (Dubos quoted in Ehrenfeld, *The Arrogance of Humanism*, p. 108).

162

of nature are swept away. The epithet of "desert maker" Ehrenfeld uses for humanity is both literally and metaphorically true; a retreat to the desert that human existence becomes in space could only be contemplated by those who no longer have a clear vision of the Eden before them.[44]

This dulling of vision shows that, rather than an appreciation of ethics and beauty acting to direct the course of science, the advancement of science seems to modify the perception of both, so that what is positively ruled out today becomes admissible tomorrow. The incremental "progress" of genetic research, where ethical disputes seem to be viewed as so many hurdles to be negotiated; architecture which displays more and more contempt for the timeless qualities of natural materials and proportions; and the on-going replacement of nature with artificial landscapes, supports this dictum. Modern science's built-in momentum of discovery, manipulation, and control, combined with its ability to "pattern" human consciousness, explains why it has looked—to the perceptive—like a downhill trend. For Blake the scientistic mentality wreaks slow havoc upon the human soul, and unethical practices and blindness to beauty are the evidence of this havoc. "Newton's deadly sleep" expresses the effect on consciousness of the spell of science. In Blake's vision of Albion—his native land asleep— we have an apt metaphor for a state at the lowest extreme of the vertical dimension: through modern science, we have become *un*conscious.

GUÉNON

Visionary though he was, it is doubtful Blake anticipated the true depths to which the scientistic mentality could take human consciousness. Guénon, on the other hand, by clearly identifying the essential nature of the scientific enterprise, provided an adequate explanation for all that the twentieth century was to manifest.[45] In *The Reign of Quantity and the Signs of the*

---

[44] Ehrenfeld observes: "People in space are diminished people, out of their ancient, inherited, and supremely beautiful context. And like anything ripped from context, there is no point to them" (Ehrenfeld, *The Arrogance of Humanism*, p. 124).

[45] Guénon (1886-1951) and Blake share the same metaphysical influence, both being exposed to Indian thought. They also share the desire to propagate an "antidote." But while Blake's poetic sensibility appeals to those of like inclination, the writings of Guénon, who stands alongside Ananda Coomaraswamy as a clear progenitor of a re-emergent metaphysical tradition, may be thought more apposite to the highly "intellectual" climate prevalent today.

Times, he predicts the eventual outcome of the allegiance to quantification or measurement ("the tendency to bring everything down to an exclusively quantitative point of view"[46]) that has been a fundamental part of science since the days of Galileo. The tendency, he writes,

> is most marked in the "scientific" conceptions of recent centuries; but it is almost as conspicuous in other domains, notably in that of social organization: so much so that . . . our period could almost be defined as being essentially and primarily the "reign of quantity".[47]

However, for Guénon, "quantity itself, to which [modern science strives] to reduce everything is . . . no more than the 'residue' of an existence emptied of everything that constituted its essence."[48] Indeed, modern science represents the relinquishment of a once clearly understood difference between quality and quantity, or essence and substance. In all traditional metaphysics the two exist as universal principles, and the manifested universe and all entities are a "resultant of the action exercised by the active principle, Essence, on the passive principle, Substance."[49] These terms correspond in Aristotelian metaphysics to "act" and "potency," and in Scholastic philosophy to *forma* and *materia*.[50] Substance or "matter," conceived of as a thing capable of standing alone is, by this understanding, an impossibility, since that which makes a being what it is, is essence or quality:

> To say that every manifested being is a composite of "form" and "matter" amounts to saying that its existence necessarily proceeds

---

[46] Guénon, *The Reign of Quantity and the Signs of the Times*, p. 9.

[47] Guénon, *The Reign of Quantity*, pp. 9-10.

[48] Guénon, *The Reign of Quantity*, p. 13.

[49] Guénon, *The Reign of Quantity*, p. 20.

[50] Guénon makes it clear that *materia* is not the same as the modern term "matter," since it includes both *materia prima* and *materia secunda*. *Materia prima* is Universal substance, which itself acts to inform *materia secunda* or relative substance. A clear comparison can be made here with the Sanskrit *Prakṛti* which is the qualified *Puruṣha*, but itself acts to inform manifestation. "Substance," from *sub* and *stare*, "that which stands beneath," thus becomes a more accurate translation of the Scholastic *materia*. See Guénon, *The Reign of Quantity*, chapter II.

simultaneously from both Essence and Substance, and consequently that there is in each being something corresponding both to the one and to the other of these two principles.[51]

Hence:

> the explanation of things must not be sought on the substantial side, but on the contrary it must be sought on the essential side; translated into terms of spatial symbolism, this is equivalent to saying that every explanation must proceed from above downwards and not from below upwards.[52]

Since modern science can be defined by the latter approach, for Guénon,

> modern science actually lacks all explanatory value. . . . Anything that is quality must necessarily be referred to essence. . . . Modern physicists, in their efforts to reduce quality to quantity, have arrived by a sort of "logic of error" to the point of confusing the two, and thence to the attribution of quality itself to their "matter" as such; and they end up by assigning all reality to "matter", or at least all that they are capable of recognizing as reality: and it is this that constitutes "materialism" properly so called.[53]

Now, it has been shown in both the previous section and in this one that quantification—measurement—is the common basis of all scientific procedure, in any field of science. But, notwithstanding everything that has been said so far, it might still be thought that the worst effect of quantification—a thorough-going materialism—had reached its limit around the turn of the twentieth century when the new physics arose to dispel the myth of discrete entities; that the indeterminacy Heisenberg demonstrated, because it implied a complex interaction between our perceptions and the world, heralded a more sophisticated interpretation of reality. If, as Bohm thought, consciousness could no longer be considered distinct

---

[51] Guénon, *The Reign of Quantity*, p. 20.

[52] Guénon, *The Reign of Quantity*, pp. 26-27.

[53] Guénon, *The Reign of Quantity*, pp. 27 and 28.

from the world then perhaps the "elements of consciousness"—the qualities that were supposed to be only subjective, such as beauty—might be re-introduced as a component of the world.

However, despite the potential for a revolution in thought, the process of quantification which science started has continued to exert its influence. As Guénon observed, the momentum of Newtonian-Cartesian science has been remarkably strong, and the evidence around us today shows that it is still largely the viewpoint of this science that prevails.[54] Science continues to objectify both the realm of nature and, most significantly, the realm of human consciousness itself; and the observed, at least during observation, is still defined by its measurable boundaries. The non-measurable qualities of nature and the qualities of the human being have continued to be stripped from any identity with an essence of the sort Guénon refers to, and instead assigned a new status as the nebulous product of matter. And since qualities are the attributes of entities that make them different one from another, to "downgrade" them in favour of quantity is, knowingly or otherwise, to attempt to make entities more alike. Thus, for Guénon,

> A mere glance at things as they are is enough to make it clear that the aim is everywhere to reduce everything to uniformity, whether it be human beings themselves or the things among which they live, and it is obvious that such a result can only be obtained by suppressing as far as possible every qualitative distinction.[55]

To what extent can this statement be supported? In physics itself, the undisguised aim is to reduce the world *conceptually* to a structure entirely

---

[54] For Kathleen Raine, it is the "cosmology . . . which, imaginatively, modern Western man continues to inhabit" (Raine, "The Vertical Dimension," *Temenos* 13 [1992]: p. 203). Normally one might point to the "lag time" between the introduction of a new "paradigm" and its eventual assimilation. However, it seems the sophisticated nature of quantum science, combined with the way that the old has acted to *modify* consciousness, means that it will probably remain outside the orbit of general understanding or acceptance.

[55] Guénon, *The Reign of Quantity*, p. 61. The fatalistic tenor of this paragraph stems from the fact that Guénon, steeped in Indian metaphysics and its conception of cyclic time, recognized in the advent of scientific quantification a trend inherent within the movement of cycles. In this view, modern science is part of an inevitable historical process and does not so much create the mentality of the times as reflect it. See chapter V, "The Qualitative Determinations of Time" in Guénon, *The Reign of Quantity*.

mathematical in form—pure quantity.[56] If this involved only the wish to design an abstract "Theory of Everything," a final neat equation to describe everything of an empirical nature, we would have little to fear. However, the discovery of this "glittering central mechanism"[57] relies on far more than abstract reasoning could provide. The seemingly innocuous, even "heroic," ongoing attempt at discovering the basis of matter is inextricably bound up with a practical method that is more certainly "dissolving" in character. The long absorption in quantification has driven a machine technology of increasing sophistication, power, and manipulative capacity. Each level of invention, based now on subtler understandings of chemistry and physics has allowed a "ratcheting-up" of these characteristics. Today, computing ability (again, pure number) combined with the application of materials technology has given a level of control and manipulation of the world that may be just a step away from an actual *dissolution* of nature. Nuclear technology, nano technology, and gene technology, because they may instigate processes that become uncontrollable, are the "cutting edge" in the application of science that threatens to cleave the world asunder.[58]

[56] Chaos theory, because it sought to deal with complexity, flux, and disorder in such areas as meteorology, ecology, and economics, was initially interpreted as a challenge to determinism and reductionism. However, its non-linear mathematical equations were in fact able to describe regularity beneath apparent disorder.

[57] This phrase of John Wheeler's (qualified by his own doubt as to the capacity of science to uncover such a mechanism), captures the popular romanticized view of the scientific enterprise. We are meant to imagine science being responsible for finding extraordinary inner beauty in the world. In fact, what is found is uncovered by tearing away that very mantle which is, by common consent, the beauty that clothes the world.

[58] In a startling interview in 2000, Bill Joy, the founder of Sun Microsystems, conceded: "It is far easier to create destructive uses for nanotechnology than constructive ones . . . [and so] we are on the cusp of extreme evil, an evil whose possibility spreads well beyond that which weapons of mass destruction bequeathed to the nation states, on to a surprising and terrible empowerment of extreme individuals" (Bill Joy quoted in Zac Goldsmith, "Discomfort and Joy," *The Ecologist* Vol. 30, No.7 [2000]: pp. 36 and 39). In a scenario reminiscent of the almost cheerfully complacent days of the development of the atomic bomb, it has been conceded that the CERN Large Hadron Collider (LHC), capable of accelerating protons to close to c, could create a black hole that would grow by swallowing the matter around it. While even CERN acknowledges the possibility of black hole creation (in J.P. Blaizot, J. Iliopoulos, J. Madsen, G.G. Ross, P. Sonderegger, and H.J. Specht, "Study of Potentially Dangerous Events During Heavy-Ion Collisions at the LHC: Report of the LHC Safety Study Group," 2003, CERN), it presumes they would decay by thermal

In the human sphere, faith in scientific demonstration has succeeded in reducing our own nature to a parody of what it was. Recourse to measurement has relegated humanity to the status of beings that can be defined completely in terms of matter and psyche. Moreover, an assumed equivalence between mind and brain has meant that the psyche itself has born the brunt of measurement and is now studied from a biological perspective. The discovery of the DNA molecule, and then the sequencing of the human and other genomes in recent years, has provided an enduring contemporary view of what represents the essential in humans, and the growing belief that most human proclivities have their origin in a particular genetic make-up. Various exceptional qualities are set to one side in the attempt to find the basis of behaviour, motivation, emotions, reasoning, and even religious and spiritual "experience" in the structure of molecules and in the chemical and electrical activity of the brain.

A willingness to assume a reductionist viewpoint has meant that, in comparing ourselves with other species, we have concentrated on what is common, not on what is different,[59] despite this type of comparison being all but meaningless.[60] Since most of the qualitative difference of humans is

processes ("Hawking Radiation"). However, several physicists question the existence or the applicability of this hypothetical radiation. See, for example, A.D. Helfer, "Do black holes radiate?" *Reports on Progress in Physics* Vol. 66, No.6 [2003]: pp. 943-1008; W.G. Unruh and R. Schützhold, "On the Universality of the Hawking Effect" *Physics Review* D 71 [2005]; and V.A. Belinski, "On the existence of quantum evaporation of a black hole," *Physics Letters* A 209(1) [1995]: pp. 13-20.

[59] Ecophilosophy, we have seen, has inherited this approach and sees the essential commonality of species as supporting ecocentrism. But, interestingly, the word for "species" in Greek is the same as that used for "form"—*eidos*; and so, as Guénon points out, "species is properly speaking a nature or an essence common to an indefinite multitude of individuals. *Specific nature is of a purely qualitative order*, for it is truly 'innumerable' in the strict sense of the word, that is to say it is independent of quantity, being indivisible and entire in every individual belonging to the species" (Guénon, *The Reign of Quantity*, p. 22, emphasis added). Thus, attempting comparisons of species by appealing only to traits that are measurable is to betray the qualitative meaning of "species," and reduce it to quantity. Furthermore, a "species [can] in no way be conceived as a 'collectivity', the latter being nothing but an arithmetical total of individuals; a 'collectivity' is, unlike species, entirely quantitative" (Guénon, *The Reign of Quantity*, pp. 60-61).

[60] The comical discovery in molecular biology of the close genetic similarity of humans and potatoes, or the finding that humans and chickens may be paired as the closest relatives (*New Scientist* Vol. 103 [August 16, 1984]: p. 19) only serves to underscore the point made in a lecture by Bronowski when B.F. Skinner's experiments first inspired the behaviourist

found in consciousness,[61] the attempt to make a quantifiable equivalent of these qualities is to reduce the significance or importance of such qualities. It is to conceal or suppress these qualitative distinctions. Ultimately, it is to *consciously ignore aspects of consciousness.* Clearly, this is a recipe for their eventual disappearance over time.[62] This is so because here, as in most forms of reductionism, we are not being permitted a neutral survey of an alternative; we are, instead, directed along a particular path of thought by being continuously asked to adopt a particular and limited view of ourselves. Once we cease to see ourselves as qualitative beings, we are ready to imbibe a whole range of ideas that have as their basis the concentration on measurable aspects:

> The modern tendency to simplification . . . naturally always operates by the reduction of things to their most inferior elements, and so asserts itself chiefly by the suppression of the entire supra-individual domain, in anticipation of being able later on to bring everything that is left, that is to say, everything in the individual order, down to the sensible or corporeal modality alone, and finally that modality itself to a mere aggregation of quantitative determinations. It is easy to see how rigorously these steps are linked together, so as to constitute as it were so many necessary stages in a continuous "degradation" of the conceptions which man forms of himself and of the world.[63]

school of psychology: "If everything that we have to know about ourselves is stuff that we can get from the rats, why aren't the rats in here and why aren't we scurrying in the wainscoting?" (Jacob Bronowski, *The Origins of Knowledge and Imagination* [New Haven: Yale University Press, 1978], p. 8).

[61] The importance of this fact is not lost on the scientific mentality. The attempt to explain what the universe is must take account of the role of the very consciousness that attempts such explanation. In this connection see, for example, Paul Davies, *The Mind of God* (London: Penguin, 1992), chapter 9.

[62] In the social sphere, a tendency to obliterate the qualitative distinction between individuals is seen in the workings of modern political systems. Although Marxism is an obvious example here, Guénon rightly points out the way in which democracy, by also emphasizing equality amongst individuals, must downplay evidence of the inequality of human traits. In this context, universal education is "well fitted to suppress in everyone all possibilities above the common level" (Guénon, *The Reign of Quantity*, p. 66).

[63] Guénon, *The Reign of Quantity*, p. 111.

We can interpret this passage of Guénon's by bringing to mind the operation of the various disciplines that represent the application of scientific consciousness (quantification) to humanity: physics, chemistry, biology, anthropology, sociology, psychology, and economics—areas of thought which, taken together, largely define an anti-traditional "modernism." Crucially, this engagement with quantification affects consciousness over time. Changing ethical standards may now be seen as the outcome of a movement away from the affirmation of timeless qualities (that cannot be measured) towards the acceptance as real of only measurable things. They are an outward indicator of what is taking place "within." The human mind, persuaded as it is by modern science to adopt a pattern of thought that is rational and quantitative, becomes prey to that very mode of consciousness, so that the tendency becomes deeply entrenched. One of the outcomes is that the *process* of greater and greater alignment with quantification goes unrecognized. Each successive stage seems a reasonable step to take. Any controversy surrounding previous steps is largely forgotten, so there is no possibility of ever assessing the whole process, in the sense of adopting the outlook of the past and studying the future (now the present) with the sort of vision that was previously the norm. The example of medical intervention, not to say genetic engineering, is pertinent here. It does indeed take an effort of will to appreciate our current position from the perspective of the past. We know that earlier generations were often implacably opposed to organ transplants or *in vitro* fertilization, or the first genetic manipulations, or the patenting of genes, but find it nearly impossible not to dismiss their outlook as unnecessarily cautious. We can even be persuaded that ethics somehow advances and that the ethics of the past is no longer relevant. Yet to suggest that ethics is so malleable as to eventually allow practices that almost no one alive today would countenance, lends support to Guénon's view that we are dealing with a catastrophic change in consciousness itself.[64]

The prolonged attempt at creating equivalence between the world and the measurement of the world, has eventually led to a modern economic

---

[64] Pre-modern history records many examples of unethical behaviour amongst people, but usually against a background of general respect for human diversity, which prevented the extremes of intolerance we see today. Empirical evidence for this can be found in the existence, side by side for centuries, of church, mosque, synagogue and temple. There existed, too, examples of the accidental mistreatment of the Earth, but no examples equivalent to "deliberately blasting its guts out," to borrow Sherrard's phrase.

theory that reflects the belief that the world and human life can ultimately be represented by a monetary value.[65] Where common sense, or concern for ethics, or the wish to retain qualities in nature like beauty, might be thought to override this viewpoint, the reality is that it often does not. Hence, individuals, organizations, corporations, and governments are prepared to sacrifice various qualities in the environment and in the human sphere in exchange for this "important" quantity. This tendency is perhaps the most telling example of scientific quantification having influenced human consciousness. Neither ethics nor aesthetics have entirely disappeared; rather the influence of quantification is so pervasive that it works to override these factors.

In the light of the above, the temptation to imagine that, although the scientific tradition exists there is nothing to prevent us re-assessing it and, if we wish, rejecting it, is seen to be erroneous, because it presumes an ability to see it objectively in the first place. But of course, if our consciousness has been changed through long-term conformity to scientific principles, could we see an alternative if it was presented, or would we dismiss it? Guénon expresses well what happens when the quantification of consciousness becomes a self-perpetuating state:

There are some things that can never be grasped by men of learning who are materialists or positivists, and this naturally further confirms their belief in the validity of their conceptions by seeming to

---

[65] The word "value" here must be considered a misnomer, since to represent things in terms of money is to substitute values or qualities with abstract quantity. For Edward Goldsmith, the present economic paradigm creates the illusion that "all benefits, and therefore our welfare and our real wealth, are derived from the man-made world; this means, in effect, that they are the product of science, technology and industry, and of the economic development that these make possible" (Edward Goldsmith, *The Way: An Ecological Worldview* [London: Random Century, 1992], p. xiii). Alternatively, if the benefits provided by the planet's functioning *are* recognized, the attempt to represent them in economic terms leads only to parody: "In 1997 a team of biologists and economists tried to put a value on the 'business services' provided by nature—the free pollination of crops, the air conditioning provided by wild plants, the recycling of nutrients by the oceans. They came up with an estimate of $33 trillion dollars" (Tim Radford, "Most of world's resources 'used up,'" *Guardian Weekly*, April 8-14, 2005, p. 8). Making such a comparison only serves to reinforce a sense of the validity of quantification, and confound what is just an abstract concept with the very real phenomenon that is the Earth system, which could never be replicated by us anyway.

afford a sort of negative proof of them, whereas it is really neither more nor less than a direct effect of the conceptions themselves.[66]

Concentration on the modality of quantification and materialism engenders a "conditioning" process, whereby a self-fulfilling prophecy of the "real" occurs. Consciousness is turned back upon itself and confined, by its own self-imposed mode of operation, to a limited sphere that defines both its own world and necessarily the world around it.

[66] Guénon, *The Reign of Quantity*, p. 146.

CHAPTER EIGHT
Ascent

In the castle of human intellectual endeavour, modernist thought has tended to retreat to one room, shutting many doors behind it. In this room of empirical method based on quantification there are "windows" to the outside world, and from within we may view nature and point out its attributes. We are persuaded that we know it as well as is possible. Its ultimate reality cannot be experienced; its "essence" must remain unknown, since the "glass" of our own subjectivism separates us from that world. There are, it is maintained, two realities: the world, and our experience of the world.

The voices of those who testify to the existence of other rooms (other ways of knowing), or suggest there might still be a way "outside," by referring to Truth, Goodness or Beauty as not merely human ideas but essential aspects of reality which might reconcile the apparent duality, are marginalized. In academia—the "Schools and Universities" Blake lamented—it has long been unfashionable to subscribe to "outdated" metaphysics, or appeal to past authority. A belief in intellectual progress has meant an avoidance of all that seems a hindrance to the forward momentum of human thought.[1]

Confinement within this one "room" might remain a *fait accompli*. But a retreat to such a room in the first place requires the existence of a doorway that will lead out again. And in the context of the current metaphor the doorway cannot lead other than back into the corridor of consciousness, for it is consciousness itself that remains the *sine qua non* of any intel-

---

[1] This belief seemed justified by the unfolding of scientific discovery, something without precedent. In the nineteenth century, Darwinism became an obvious support for this "progressism." An organism with a history of profound development implied a corresponding development in consciousness. And the argument for development from the primitive intellectual capacity of our distant ancestors (the contemporary "equivalent" of which displayed "simple," "irrational," "superstitious," or "uncivilized" behaviour) suggested an ongoing linear development. If it could not be doubted that a certain brilliance of "intellect" must attach to many past thinkers, scientific progress provided more knowledge and a bigger picture into which would fit the "mistaken" beliefs of these thinkers. Hence, earlier metaphysical views could be superseded.

173

lectual position whatsoever, and certainly of modern science. As the previous chapter revealed, a recent version of the scientific paradigm—quantum physics—has been obliged to accept the ineluctable role of consciousness in the responses that nature gives to our empirical investigations. And while this has often been interpreted, by those who do science, to demonstrate the limitations of consciousness to an understanding of the reality that science endeavours to reveal, this is not the only possible deduction from the facts. It is just as sensible to reverse what is really a particular mental ordering that science *qua* science takes. Such an inversion means we are no longer attempting to look at consciousness as though it could be made an objective element of the paradigm. Consequently, we are no longer looking at the limitation of consciousness to know reality, but rather at the *limitations of the scientific paradigm*, the "reality" of which is being limited by a particular form of consciousness. In this alternative view, consciousness cannot be the objective or passive witness to a particular worldview; rather, consciousness is composed of—or, more accurately, is commensurate with—a particular worldview, in this case the world that science takes to be real (the quantified world). Far from the scientific paradigm being able to define consciousness, the scientific paradigm is a reflection of a particular form of consciousness.

An escape from the position we find ourselves in, then—a return through the "doorway"—cannot be made through an appeal to the same type of consciousness already operating (the scientific, quantifying one which, in seeking to apply measurement to things, is structured by this very process, and becomes as it were "quantified"), but only through a non-quantifying dimension of consciousness. Now, it may be surmised that if we shift our focus from those aspects of things that can be quantified or measured, to those which cannot be quantified or measured, we will be disengaging from the aspect of consciousness that deals with quantification—analytical or discursive thought, or rationality (the quintessence of the scientific consciousness)—and engaging with the usually dormant elements that lie outside the boundaries of quantifying consciousness. A focus on qualities that resist adequate description through quantification, then, will be expressive of a non-quantifying—or qualifying—consciousness. Consciousness that is structured by the perception of these qualities may be termed "qualified consciousness" and it is this mode of consciousness that is the key to a restoration of the vertical dimension.

RAINE

As the Blake scholar Kathleen Raine observed, "Of Plato's three verities, the Good, the True and the Beautiful, none can be understood in terms of the materialist values of modern Western civilization, and beauty least of all."[2] Precisely because beauty defies measurement,[3] while, at the same time, it is granted almost universal assent, beauty is the quality perhaps most suited to act as a catalyst for "qualifying" consciousness. In turning to the contemplation of beauty, we are now turning to face the upward movement of consciousness.

The perception of beauty can be understood in the light of a statement once made by Aldous Huxley:

> Knowledge is a function of being. When there is a change in the being of the knower, there is a corresponding change in the nature and amount of knowing. . . . The being of a child is transformed by growth and education. . . . Among the results of this transformation is a revolutionary change in the way of knowing and the amount and character of the things known.[4]

However, the transformation of being must itself be dependent on the form of knowing to which we are initially subject. When a particular form of knowing—scientific, or quantifying consciousness—sets limits on what can be perceived and what can be known, it must act as a restriction on conscious development. In relation to beauty, it would lead to a form of blindness. We may recall Blake's famous chiding of his employer who accused him of an inaccurate depiction of the world:

> I see Every thing I paint In This World, but Every body does not see alike. To the Eyes of a Miser a Guinea is more beautiful than

---

[2] Raine adds: "Truth can be confused with fact, with the measurable and quantifiable aspects of what is currently called 'the real world'. The Good may be seen as actions or events leading to desirable results; but Beauty cannot be quantified or measured in material terms" (Preface to Lane, *Timeless Beauty*, p. 8).

[3] As we saw in part three, the attempt to draw an equivalence between our perception of beauty and particular mathematical relationships in nature, is a facile one.

[4] Aldous Huxley, *The Perennial Philosophy* (London: Chatto & Windus, 1969), p. 1.

the Sun, & a bag worn with the use of Money has more beautiful proportions than a Vine filled with Grapes. The tree which moves some to tears of joy is in the Eyes of others only a Green thing which stands in the way. . . . As a man is, So he sees. As the Eye is formed, such are its Powers. You certainly Mistake, when you say that the Visions of Fancy are not to be found in This World. To Me This World is all One continued Vision of Fancy or Imagination.[5]

Blake claims a vision that is neither subjective nor unique, but indicative of a state of consciousness the participation in which allows an increased perception of beauty.[6] The following lines bear testimony both to the hierarchical nature of this vision and to the stultifying effect of remaining under the sway of quantified consciousness:

Now I a fourfold vision see,
And a fourfold vision is given to me,
'Tis fourfold in my supreme delight
And threefold in soft Beulah's night
And twofold Always. May God us keep
From Single vision & Newton's sleep.[7]

Aware of how that latter vision has predominated, and that we now "live in a world to which the very notion of a hierarchy of states of consciousness, is alien,"[8] Raine can still find, in the honour accorded to the poet,

a certain remote echo of that age-old belief that the poet is 'inspired'. An honour due to poetry only when, and insofar as, it does, in a measure, aspire to participation in a sacred vision of the

---

[5] William Blake quoted in Kathleen Raine, "The Vertical Dimension," *Temenos* 13 (1992): pp. 198-199.

[6] In chapter 4, we saw that the poets of the Romantic era were influenced by the influx of the esoteric from the East. Nevertheless, the poetic sensibility, which may well be inspired by the intellectual appreciation of a particular metaphysic, exists quite independently of it.

[7] Blake quoted in Raine, "The Vertical Dimension," p. 203.

[8] Raine, "The Vertical Dimension," p. 195.

Word that is 'with God', on that vertical ladder which has in our time for the most part been lost.[9]

To speak thus of Divinity is to be reminded of the epiphanic vision of nature to which the Romantic poets gave assent. To experience nature as supremely beautiful is to see nature unveiled through the unveiling of consciousness. Such a vision is not uncommon: "there are surely few . . . who have not at some time seen the simplest things 'apparel'd in celestial light'—in the phrase of . . . Thomas Traherne, for whom also the simplest pebbles on the path were radiant with that light."[10] Raine confirms that, in speaking of "a 'vertical dimension' . . . what is at issue is not any question of 'another world' but the manner in which we experience this one."[11] When nature appears without lustre, "it is not the pebbles or the trees that have changed: it is we who no longer participate in that light of vision."[12]

For Raine, the increasing absence of that vision of nature today parallels the increasing expression of scientific consciousness. Quantified consciousness (as it has been termed) demonstrates momentum and direction, and this is because, in continually reinforcing its own quantitative content and continually lessening any qualitative content, it is continually reinforcing itself. While the clearest evidence for this may be the ongoing change in the ethical stance adopted by those who do science or who are exposed to the scientific worldview, there is also the matter of the simplification of conscious experience and conscious expression. The lines by Coleridge that refer to the things of nature as

The lovely shapes and sounds intelligible
Of that eternal language, which thy God
Utters, who from eternity doth teach
Himself in all, and all things in himself.[13]

[9] Raine, "The Vertical Dimension," p. 197.

[10] Raine, "The Vertical Dimension," p. 199.

[11] Raine, "The Vertical Dimension," p. 198.

[12] Raine, "The Vertical Dimension," p. 199.

[13] Samuel Taylor Coleridge, "Frost at Midnight" (1798).

and which testify that the Divine presence is revealed through the "language" of nature, are opaque to science. Having little allegiance to qualities, quantified consciousness reduces the ontological status of the experiences or perceptions that cannot be quantified (such as those of beauty and its prolongation, the sacred). Just as significantly, because these qualities—to which the language of poetry and scripture refer—are divested of ontological reality, that language is no longer tied to anything substantial and so is itself remodelled by the language of quantification.[14] Support for this interpretation may be found in Raine's account of the effect of "materialist scientism" on the time-honoured field of poetry:

> Throughout the nineteenth century descriptive verse, and painting which reproduced natural appearances with minute and photographic accuracy abounded. Much of this continued to present the natural world as pleasing to behold, continuing unquestioned earlier schools which had held beauty to be a supreme value. Now beauty is a word scarcely used, for what meaning has the word in the context of the neutrality of nature, unrelated to the vital form-creating power of Imagination? We have seen the emergence first of 'social realism' and then of a grimmer realism of poets and painters who have ceased to discover beauty in nature or in human nature. There has emerged a school of writers and painters who describe appearances not to enhance, but to dislimn, not a discovery but a denial of form, beauty and meaning. . . . The song of birds has been a source of delight to poets from the troubadours to Chaucer, from the nightingales of Persia to Keats. . . . Now children's schoolbooks contain poems informing them that the voices of birds are not a song but a scream; it is deemed more 'honest' to note nature's warts and blemishes than to observe its daily panorama of sun and moon, clouds and stars, birds and trees as the epiphanic language of a living mystery.[15]

---

[14] This is ironical because the quantifiable aspects of things do not exist as realities independent of consciousness. It was established in part three that the quantitative aspects of things amount to nothing more than comparisons made between the outward forms of those things. Quantum physics shows that the measurements made through such comparisons are conceptual realities belonging to the consciousness that applies them. As such, they are less obviously real than the perceptible aspect of things that have not undergone comparison. Beauty is such an aspect since it is an immediate or direct perception.

[15] Raine, "The Vertical Dimension," pp. 201-202.

The belief in a more "honest" treatment of nature is the belief of a consciousness in sympathy with the ontology of a science that first instils a propensity towards the perception of nature as outward (quantified) form, and then treats this particular perception as if it were independent of human interpretation.[16] But the straightforward language of much modern poetry, for which nature is simply "an object to be described," is itself a language reflecting a mode of consciousness. Hence, while the figurative language common to Romantic poetry (which seems to replace an "unadulterated" form with symbol and metaphor) may appear at first a dishonest representation of what nature is, it actually reflects a greater awareness of the role of consciousness in perception. Thus,

> When Wordsworth wrote "'Tis my belief that every flower enjoys the air it breathes" he was not indulging in poetic make-believe, but affirming that nature is a *living* presence, as other cultures have held as a self-evident truth. As indeed it is, if not matter but spirit, not the object perceived but the perceiving consciousness, be taken as the ground of reality as we behold and experience it.[17]

To acknowledge the role played by consciousness, is to see that the knower *cannot be separated* from what the known *is;* and the special language of poetry expresses this truth. But more: poetic language is imbued with its own metamorphic quality. For Dante, there were four possible meanings of a work of art: the literal, allegorical, moral and anagogical.[18] Viewed as an ascending hierarchy, the presence in a poem of the anagogical, mystical, or esoteric meaning is a function of the poet's own participation in the corresponding level of conscious perception. In other words, "it is via the faculty of the Intellect that the poet receives inspiration." Equally significant is the converse of this: it is the anagogical aspect of a poem "that appeals to the supra-rational faculties in the person reading or hearing the

---

[16] This might be termed the "heresy" that environmental thought has inherited from scientism—the belief that nature's reality could be somehow unaffected by us. An ecocentric outlook seems to require that nature be somehow free of the constraints imposed by any particular outlook we might have, and this is not possible.

[17] Raine, "The Vertical Dimension," p. 202.

[18] Dante makes mention of these in a 1318 letter to his Veronese patron, Cangrande della Scala, concerning the subject of the *Divina Comedia.*

poem."[19] Since it is always nature that is the substance out of which poetry is made, nature itself is shown to be the true instrument of transformation for the consciousness that perceives it. Poetic language transforms nature in order that nature may transform consciousness. These are but two aspects of a process, each element of which does not exist without the other. Dwelling on beauty—nature's essence—leads to increased consciousness of its reality, which in turn leads to a greater perception of beauty. If we were to look for a supreme example of the way this works, we would find it in these lines from Shelley:

> Hail to thee, blithe Spirit!
> Bird thou never wert,
> That from Heaven, or near it,
> Pourest thy full heart
> In profuse strains of unpremeditated art.
>
> Higher still and higher
> From the earth thou springest
> Like a cloud of fire;
> The blue deep thou wingest,
> And singing still dost soar, and soaring ever singest.[20]

For Raine, Shelley's skylark "is the poet's spirit in flight, like Plato's rhapsodist, to the 'Garden of the Muses', the 'skies' of Blake's 'supreme delight', a region of spaciousness, freedom and light above common consciousness of which the 'skies' have always been the natural symbol."[21] Here, the vertical dimension of consciousness finds its exact correspondence in the dimension in which the skylark moves. And the way the lark ascends—"singing still dost soar, and soaring ever singest"—suggests the very manner in which poetical language works: nature may act to unfold consciousness, which in turn acts to unfold the vision of nature as "not a material world but a living, epiphanic cosmos."[22] The natural world is used, says Raine,

---

[19] Justin Majzub, "Martin Lings: Collected Poems," in *Sophia* Vol. 5, No. 2 (1999): p. 79.

[20] Percy Bysshe Shelley, "To A Skylark" (1820).

[21] Raine, "The Vertical Dimension," pp. 204-205.

[22] Raine, "The Vertical Dimension," p. 206.

as the poet's language, the keyboard, as it were, upon which he strikes resonances of inner experience, by the skilful use of correspondences. Mountain and river, tree and garden, bird and cloud, are words in the language of Eden in which Adam 'named' the creatures. . . . Poetry and the other arts are . . . the world we inwardly inhabit, the human kingdom built over a millennia in the full range of the height and depth of human experience by means of *symbolic correspondences on a vertical axis of consciousness.*[23]

The poet's presentation of the complex interaction possible between nature and consciousness stands in contradistinction to the language of quantified consciousness, where measurable nature corresponds only to itself. The power of nature to transform consciousness into something capable of seeing nature for what it is, suggests a beautiful synthesis of nature and ourselves. Admittedly, a vertical dimension to human consciousness does not lend itself to a "democratization" of nature of the sort ecophilosophy might wish for. Instead, Raine's "human kingdom" invokes a sense of the profound distinction this dimension confers on humanity. However, nature cannot be denied, at least not without consequences, and the turning away from what, until recently, has been considered our fundamental inner nature has had devastating consequences for the natural world. It would be ironic indeed, if, for the sake of this democratization, we were to suppress those very qualitative elements of our nature that allow us to unveil the deeper reality in nature, and prompt us to treat it with reverence.

To believe that the perception corresponding to any particular consciousness is still "only subjective" would be to remain entrapped in the net that quantified consciousness has woven. The supposition that the poetic consciousness is rooted in physiology is to confound the wholly different orders of reality to which Raine refers. If this confusion has come about, it is precisely because a conviction in, and concentration on, the material, has led to a study of the brain as if it were coterminous with consciousness and could explain what consciousness is. It is entirely to be expected that this would lead to the disappearance of the very mode of consciousness that challenges this outlook—to the disappearance of the "vertical dimension."

This has not yet happened,[24] but the poetical tradition that affirms a

---

[23] Raine, "The Vertical Dimension," pp. 204 and 207, emphasis added.

[24] Towards the end of the twentieth century Raine could still offer T.S. Eliot, Rainer Rilke,

vertical dimension to consciousness exists only precariously while it remains in the shadow of modernist thought, with the dismal shape of "psychologism"—which seeks to reduce everything of a higher order to the human level of the subconscious and unconscious—looming over it. This is why the attempt to draw, from the poetic experience of beauty and the sacred, an adequate understanding of it, requires us to seek a metaphysical basis for such experience that is rooted in a pre-modern world. It requires us to return in imagination to an earlier time, against the momentum and inertia that the scientific paradigm continually imparts to the very consciousness that attempts such a movement.

The Sophia

This imaginative venture is what the exponents of a traditional metaphysics are continually recommending. However, in confronting the current mode of consciousness through reference to an alternative mode of consciousness—now largely lost—they open themselves to charges of obscurantism, abstruseness, and woolly thinking.[25] Though modernism is in fact an aberration against the broad stretch of human civilization, its vision of progress, combined with a certain arrogance, has meant a corresponding myopia towards the past.[26] This seems to explain the near-

---

W.B. Yeats, Edwin Muir, Vernon Watkins, Dylan Thomas, and David Gascoyne as poets who have "continually explored the human kingdom in all its heights and depths, seeking to extend the frontiers of that kingdom and record its fine subtleties of wisdom and beauty and moral perception" (Raine, "The Vertical Dimension," p. 205).

[25] Raine herself often enough encountered the attitude of the "impervious rationalists who demand so aggressively that . . . [she] should 'explain what you mean by' (God, love, beauty, the good, the soul. . .)" (Kathleen Raine, *Autobiographies* [London: Skoob Books, 1991], p. 347).

[26] The bias of the modern West towards other cultures has been long-standing and stems largely from a belief in its possessing superior tools for providing knowledge. Current technological superiority causes it to conveniently overlook the earlier advantage the East had, as well as the East's huge contribution to the technical culture of the West. For numerous examples of this, see Joseph Needham, *Within the Four Seas* (London: George Allen & Unwin, 1979); and John M. Hobson, *The Eastern Origins of Western Civilisation* (Cambridge: Cambridge University Press, 2004). Meanwhile the vast metaphysical accomplishments of the East looked at through the lens of science, have been seen as misdirected or unnecessary steps along the path of "true" understanding. Any attempt to redress this bias, that is now clearly provincial and no longer excusable, can be protracted. For instance, it is now

invisibility of an alternative "school" of thought, whose soaring towers seem, to modernist thought, ethereal and without substance, precisely because they are founded on the great metaphysical systems of the past. To recognize a *perennial* tradition of knowledge of unchanging applicability is to defy the modernist conception of progress, and since this tradition is based on principles that are denied by modernist thought, it is also to defy much of modernist thought as such. Unsurprisingly, then, the present day exponents of the *sophia perennis*—perennial, or timeless, wisdom—remain largely unacknowledged by mainstream philosophy or theology.[27] To assert, as Martin Lings does, that the Renaissance represents not so much the rebirth of knowledge but rather "one of the great milestones of decline in Western Europe";[28] to dismiss, as Guénon does, most modern philosophy;[29] to claim, as Schuon does, that "it is impossible to prove

more than eighty years since the literature of traditionalism made its first appearance in the West, yet its reasonable outlook is still not understood. As Nasr says, "One of the remarkable aspects of the intellectual life of this [twentieth] century . . . is precisely the neglect of . . . [the traditional] point of view in circles whose official function it is to be concerned with questions of an intellectual order" (S.H. Nasr, *Knowledge and the Sacred* [Edinburgh: Edinburgh University Press, 1981], p. 67).

[27] In 1946 Aldous Huxley, in *The Perennial Philosophy*, gave an account of what he took to be "the metaphysic that recognizes a divine Reality substantial to the world of things and lives and minds; the psychology that finds in the soul something similar to, or even identical with, divine Reality; the ethic that places man's final end in the knowledge of the immanent and transcendent Ground of all being" (Huxley, *The Perennial Philosophy*, p. 1). Yet, a man of his own age—and steeped in scientific humanism—Huxley is consequently quite selective in his approach to perennialism. He favours the esoteric doctrine while dismissing the significance of many of the ritual practices of religion; he is also wont to appeal to scientific conceptions and explanations of reality, all of which make his "perennialism" very much a personal and modernist account, at odds with the universalist and unchanging character of the *sophia* that the traditionalists accept. For more on Huxley's perennial philosophy see the account by Kenneth (Harry) Oldmeadow in *Traditionalism: Religion in the Light of the Perennial Philosophy* (Colombo: Sri Lanka Institute of Traditional Studies, 2000), pp. 158-160.

[28] Martin Lings, *The Eleventh Hour* (Cambridge: Quinta Essentia, 1987), p. 50.

[29] Guénon writes: "modern philosophy . . . for the greater part represents no more than a series of wholly artificial problems, which only exist because they are badly propounded, owing their origin and survival to nothing but carefully kept up verbal confusions; they are problems which, considering how they are formulated, are truly insoluble, but on the other hand, no one is in the least anxious to solve them, and their sole purpose is to go on indefi-

the reality of the Intellect to every understanding," but that this "proves nothing at all against [its] reality";[30] to try to dislodge one of the cornerstones of modernist thought (evolution) as Titus Burckhardt does;[31] to see the progenitors of modern science as "instrumental in producing a body of thought representative of about the lowest level of intelligence to which the human mind has ever sunk," or insist that "we can obtain no genuine knowledge of the physical world unless we first attain a knowledge of spiritual or metaphysical realities"[32] as Sherrard does, is to invite dismissal and ridicule.

Yet these pronouncements are not made lightly, but in the context of a careful, rigorous, and scholarly defence of a metaphysics, the rupture of which has led first to a spiritual crisis, and consequently to an environmental crisis of unprecedented proportions.[33] The attempt to bring back into the light what has been overshadowed by modernism is to reveal just this spiritual antecedent to the crisis. And to speak of the "spiritual" is to be reminded of religion, and so the principal dwelling place of this metaphysics.[34]

nitely feeding controversies and discussions which lead nowhere, and which are not meant to lead anywhere" (Guénon quoted in Whitall Perry, A *Treasury of Traditional Wisdom* [Cambridge: Quinta Essentia, 1971], p. 732).

[30] Frithjof Schuon, *Logic and Transcendence* (London: Perennial Books, 1984), pp. 31-2.

[31] See Titus Burckhardt, "The Theory of Evolution," in *The Betrayal of Tradition*, ed. Harry Oldmeadow (Bloomington: World Wisdom, 2005), pp. 287-300.

[32] Sherrard, *Human Image: World Image*, p. 35 and p. 6.

[33] The underlying spiritual dimension to the environmental crisis was suggested as early as 1968 by Nasr in the seminal book *Man and Nature: The Spiritual Crisis in Modern Man* (Chicago: Kazi), which identifies the importance for humanity of the metaphysical knowledge contained within the great religious traditions. His later paper, "The Spiritual and Religious Dimensions of the Environmental Crisis" (which first appeared as *Temenos Academy Paper* No. 12 [1999]) serves to reinforce the urgency of seeing and applying this understanding. Sherrard, in *Human Image: World Image*, develops the theme from a mainly Christian perspective. And Angela Malyon-Bein's Ph.D. thesis, *In Search of the Timeless Wisdom: An Inquiry into the Ecological Implications of the Loss of Tradition in Western Civilization* (University of Tasmania, 2001), offers a comprehensive overview of this theme of "spiritual crisis" from the standpoint of environmental philosophy.

[34] Nasr states: "the term spirituality as it is used today began to be employed by French Catholic theologians in the mid-nineteenth century and then crept into English. . . . Today it denotes for many people precisely those elements of religion which have been forgotten in

Central to the religions of all cultures, up until that of the modern West, is a view of human potential that far transcends any account given by the anthropology, sociology, psychology, or biology of today. It is not inappropriate that religion is so often placed in opposition to the modernist worldview, since the word "religion" itself expresses precisely what modernism excludes. As we saw in chapter 4, the Latin word *religio* suggests the "ligament" or element that allows human consciousness to "reconnect" to a transcendent reality, where the duality of subject and object, knower and known, is overcome. An exposition of this core principle may be found at the heart of each of the world's religious traditions. It is the particular virtue of the traditionalist writers to bring fully to light the differing expressions of this common principle.[35]

The fullest and most recent expression of the *sophia* in Christianity—the foremost religion of the West—may be found in medieval Scholasticism.[36] Known for its rational discourse, Scholasticism yet retained, as part of its metaphysical doctrine, a perspective on reasoning that betrays the diminished character of the humanist and scientific revolutions that would follow. One of the great conceptions of medieval thought was the hierarchy (attributed to Boethius, 480-525 CE) of *sensus, imaginatio, ratio,* and *Intellectus*—the last, the Intellect, referring to the "faculty" by which direct or unmediated knowledge of a transcendent reality is gained. As James Cutsinger explains,

> While reason operates one step at a time, proceeding by stages from premises to conclusions, the Intellect goes straight to the

the West. . . . Traditionally the term religion would suffice since in its full sense it includes all that is understood by spirituality today" (*The Spiritual and Religious Dimensions of the Environmental Crisis*, pp. 6-7).

[35] To affirm and, more importantly, to be inspired by this basic principle, more clearly than anything else may be said to be what distinguishes traditionalist writers. For this reason, it would be only superficially pertinent to claim that these writers had adopted a Guénonian stance. Rather Guénon's role was to expose a long disused path to a forgotten goal. The writers who espouse similar ideas to Guénon may be likened to those who have subsequently, and independently, chosen to set out on this path.

[36] The Renaissance, which represents a turning away from Christian theology and a welcoming of Classical humanism, is like a cut-off point after which the full compass of the metaphysics belonging to the medieval world is no longer clearly seen.

conclusion. . . . Reason conceives—that is, it holds things together. But the Intellect perceives.[37]

And for Huston Smith,

Reason proceeds discursively, through language, and like a bridge, joins two banks, knower and known, without removing the river between. The Intellect knows intuitively and . . . identifies the knower with what he knows, causing one to become the other.[38]

As a form of perception, the Intellect is analogous to the sightedness of the eye. Its "locus" is the centre of the being, and therefore it is the "heart" or the "soul" which sees; it is the "soul's central faculty which, in virtue of its centrality, must be considered as being above and beyond the psychic domain."[39] Thus it is that for Augustine, "Our whole business . . . in this life is to restore to health the eye of the heart whereby God may be seen," for "God is light, not such as these eyes see, but as the heart seeth."[40] And for Eckhart (c. 1260-c. 1327), "The soul has two eyes—one looking inwards and the other outwards. It is the inner eye of the soul that looks into the essence and takes being directly from God."[41] Aquinas (1225-1274) could spend much of his life immersed in the rational systematizing of Christian theology but, upon experiencing the vision granted by the Intellect, would count his writings as of little importance compared to this immediate knowledge.

An understanding of this type of vision can be traced back through a number of Christian writers to Christ's own teachings.[42] In the Gospel of

---

[37] James Cutsinger, *Advice to the Serious Seeker* (New York: SUNY, 1997), p. 28.

[38] Huston Smith, introduction to *The Transcendent Unity of Religions*, pp. xiv-xv.

[39] Martin Lings, *Symbol and Archetype* (Cambridge: Quinta Essentia, 1991), p. 3.

[40] Augustine quoted in Perry, *A Treasury of Traditional Wisdom*, pp. 819 and 817.

[41] Eckhart quoted in Perry, *A Treasury of Traditional Wisdom*, p. 816.

[42] It can also be traced forward, but after the Renaissance and especially as the scientific revolution took hold, increasingly there was a failure to distinguish between *ratio* and *Intellectus*. Among the notable exceptions to this trend were Boehme; the Cambridge Platonists John Smith (1618-1652) and Peter Sterry (1613-1672); the contemplative poet Thomas Traherne (1637-1674); and, following them, the English Divine William Law (1686-1761).

Matthew we are told: "The light of the body is the eye: if therefore thine eye be single, thy whole body shall be full of light."[43] And, in the first centuries of Christianity, it is the ready adaptability of Plotinus to Christian intellectualism that demonstrates a correspondence with the earlier Platonic thought.

In the Socratic dialogues, especially the mature ones such as the *Republic* and the *Symposium*, this highest "faculty"—the *nous*—is, from the human point of view, the agent of noesis (Intellective intuition), the capacity for knowledge or apprehension of the transcendent, or inner reality of things. Thus, "there is an eye of the soul which . . . is more precious far than ten thousand bodily eyes, for by it alone is truth seen."[44] For Plato the agency of noesis reveals the ultimate form of Beauty, or the Good, or God. Accordingly, the philosopher kings of his imagined ideal State "must raise the eye of the soul to the universal light which lightens all things, and behold the absolute good."[45] And in the *Symposium*, Plato's great work on love and beauty, we are told that absolute beauty is known "with the faculty capable of seeing it."[46]

Clearly, Plato's writings have had a profound influence on Western thought; so much so that it might almost be concluded that we were witnessing a continuing reformulation of one man's thought.[47] Two things negate this appraisal. Firstly, we are dealing with a form of knowledge that by its nature escapes the merely conceptual. Evidence for this knowledge does not come through reason, and those who accept its reality, like Plotinus, Augustine, or Aquinas, experience it as an undeniable revelation completely unrelated to logical or rational proof or discursive thought. Crucial to the understanding of the *sophia* is that rather than being the expression of ideas formulated by any particular individual human consciousness, it is rather the expression, through language (and so through the *medium* of the rational mind), of what is experienced when individuated conscious-

---

[43] Matthew VI: 22

[44] Plato, *Republic*, 527e.

[45] Plato, *Republic*, 540b.

[46] Plato, *Symposium*, 212e.

[47] The famous observation, attributed to A.N. Whitehead, that "the history of Western philosophy is, after all, no more than a series of footnotes to Plato's philosophy"captures this feeling.

ness is transcended in the union of knower and known. Seen in this way it becomes understandable that the founders of the great religions, along with the mystics and sages, were led to adopt, or make use of, similar particularly clear, elegant, or apt expressions.[48] Secondly, the rise of comparative religion, after the West was exposed to the diversity of religions in the nineteenth and twentieth centuries, has given us a much greater perspective. Parallel expressions of the *sophia,* pre-dating Plato, are found in diverse metaphysical traditions, from India and China to that of the American Indians. Indeed, "belief in the transcendent intellect, a faculty capable, and alone capable, of direct contact with the real, is common to all traditional doctrines, of all ages and countries."[49]

Such a faculty cannot be shown or demonstrated to the rational mind, anymore than vision could to one without eyesight. As a *perception,* it is known through its own operation—just as sight is. Nor can its "object"— the Good, or Divinity—be described using reason, because it is not a thing reason comes to know.[50] This is why Socrates must take the most important truths as axioms or existential propositions, and why, in addition, they are "proved," not by reasoning but with the poet's language of allegory, simile, and metaphor.[51] To engage imaginatively in the transference of terms that

---

[48] As Schuon observes: "the deep-rooted agreement of the traditional doctrines shows itself . . . even in forms and details" (Frithjof Schuon, *The Feathered Sun* (Bloomington: World Wisdom, 1990), p. 51.

[49] Marco Pallis, *Peaks and Lamas* (London: Cassell, 1939), p. 166.

[50] Accordingly, Socrates declines to do so. See *Republic*, 506e.

[51] In an age when empiricism is the criterion of truth, it is common to favour the inductive and deductive elements of the arguments (after all, Socrates is famous for using logic to uncover confusion in belief), and treat the rest as unsupported. However, for Schuon, "what puts Plato in the clearest possible opposition to rationalism . . . is his doctrine of the eye of the soul" (Schuon, *Logic and Transcendence,* p. 46). The use of rational argument, says Guénon, "never represents more than a mode of external expression and in no way affects metaphysical knowledge itself, for the latter must always be kept essentially distinct from its formulation" (Guénon quoted in Oldmeadow, *Traditionalism,* p. 90). And Schuon writes: "that a reasoning might simply be the logical and provisional description of an intellectual evidence, and that its function might be the actualization of this evidence, in itself supralogical, apparently never crosses the minds of pure logicians" (Schuon, *Logic and Transcendence,* p. 37). Nevertheless, "In the intellectual order logical proof is only a quite provisional crystallization of intuition, the modes of which are incalculable" (Frithjof Schuon, *Spiritual Perspectives and Human Facts* [Middlesex: Perennial Books, 1987], pp. 9-10). And,

take place in figurative language is to escape the usual constraints of rationality, and thus find resonance with—even promote—the non-rational consciousness. In the *Phaedrus*, the winged charioteer (the *nous*) through the skilful control of two horses—the other elements of the soul—is able to ascend to the realms of true Beauty.[52] For Plato *noesis* is superior to *dianoia* (reasoning or discursive thinking) and the metaphor conveys both this superior position and the dominant role the faculty should have. Reason has the potential to control the body and mind but, without itself being informed by a knowledge of what truth, goodness, or beauty is, it is liable to go astray.[53] Thus, the progenitors of modern science, for whom reason became pre-eminent, could, while believing reason to be the discoverer of truth, actually be making reason subject to more arbitrary existential propositions that the imagination might suggest. From this standpoint the method of empiricism and inductive reasoning, to which we have become accustomed, is equivalent to the senses alone dictating to the mind what is real or true. When we include the fascination with the propositions of mathematics, we are looking at a reciprocal reinforcement taking place between the senses and reason that acts to obscure the noetic faculty. Reason persuades us to take as legitimate sensory experience only what can be quantified—to concentrate on the measurable—and to consider the rest as subjective. At the same time, whatever the senses supply of the reality inherent in nature is modified by reason. Reason cannot see an inherent nature, but it can conceal what is there by acting as a barrier to the faculty that *is* able to see.

It can be intuited from this that a consciousness that allows the propositions of the reason to influence what it apprehends through the senses is actively preventing the noetic faculty (which, when applied to nature, acts

---

"Metaphysical truths are by no means accepted because they are merely logically clear, but because they are ontologically clear and their logical clarity is only a trace of this imprinted on the mind" (Schuon quoted in Oldmeadow, *Traditionalism*, p. 89).

[52] Plato, *Phaedrus*, 246a-250c.

[53] This insight is made clearer in a remarkably similar metaphor found in the *Katha Upanishad*. Here, the higher Intellect, *Buddhi*—which "considered in relation to the human individuality . . . is . . . its immediate but transcendent principle" (Guénon, *Man and His Becoming According to the Vedanta*, pp. 65-66)—is the "charioteer" that holds the reins of the mind. Thus, "He . . . whose mind is never steady is not the ruler of his life, like a bad driver with wild horses" (Mascaró, *The Upanishads*, p. 60).

to uncover its qualitative aspects) to operate. It can also be intuited that, for it to operate fully, the reasoning mode must be suspended.

Since, for Plato the *immediate*, or unmediated, consciousness is like vision or sight (an analogy common in metaphysical literature[54]), in the allegory of the cave both the various levels of knowing, or perception, and the levels of knowledge attained by that perception, are rendered through the imagery of seeing and light.[55] In this allegory, our initial position is comparable to the darkness of a cave; our apprehension of things is limited by the feeble and distorting light of our faculties of sense and reason. It is only in and through the bright light of the Sun that we see clearly the nature of the world.

Now, *noesis* is usually portrayed as a perceptive faculty of the individuated consciousness that somehow extends the range of that conscious-

---

[54] Because the prominent instrument of sensible knowledge is sight, "this symbolism is carried even into the purely intellectual realm, where knowledge is likened to 'inward vision'" (Guénon, *Man and His Becoming According to the Vedanta*, p. 14).

[55] Plato, *Republic*, 514a – 521b. The allegory is set forth by Socrates thus: "Imagine the condition of men living in a sort of cavernous chamber underground, with an entrance open to the light and a long passage all down the cave. Here they have been from childhood, chained by the leg and also by the neck, so that they cannot move and can see only what is in front of them, because the chains will not let them turn their heads. At some distance higher up is the light of a fire burning behind them; and between the prisoners and the fire is a track with a parapet built along it, like the screen at a puppet-show, which hides the performers while they show their puppets over the top. . . . Now behind this parapet imagine persons carrying along various artificial objects, including figures of men and animals in wood or stone or other materials, which project above the parapet. Naturally, some of these persons will be talking, others silent. . . . Prisoners so confined would have seen nothing of themselves or of one another, except the shadows thrown by the fire-light on the wall of the Cave facing them. . . . Such prisoners would recognize as reality nothing but the shadows of those artificial objects. . . . Consider what would happen if their release from the chains and the healing of their unwisdom should come about in this way. Suppose one of them set free and forced suddenly to stand up, turn his head, and walk with eyes lifted to the light. . . . And suppose someone were to drag him forcibly up the steep and rugged ascent and not let him go until he had hauled him out into the sunlight. . . . At first it would be easiest to make out shadows, and then the images of men and things reflected in water, and later on the things themselves. After that, it would be easier to watch the heavenly bodies and the sky itself by night, looking at the light of the moon and stars rather than the Sun and the Sun's light in the day-time. . . . Last of all, he would be able to look at the Sun and contemplate its nature, not as it appears when reflected in water or any alien medium, but as it is in itself in its own domain" (Frances MacDonald Cornford, trans., *The Republic of Plato* [London: Oxford University Press, 1955], pp. 222-225).

ness and provides it with this enhanced knowledge.[56] This perspective—to see *noesis* as somehow belonging to the self—is inherent within the nature of the mind;[57] it *necessarily* experiences itself as *subject*, and objectifies. However, Plato's allegory subtly captures a very different relationship between *nous* and self. Upon leaving the cave of limited perception, things are seen by the light of the "Sun." But the "Sun" symbolizes the ultimate reality (or Form) of the Good. So the Sun is at once the *means of sight*, and *what is seen*. It is both perception and what is perceived. Symbolically, then, it represents both the knowing and what is known, and hence, at the highest level, the *identity* of *noesis* and *nous* (which might now be capitalized as "*Nous*"). Thus, what at first is taken by the mind to be its own latent potentiality becomes the knowing of an entity distinct from the mind. And the One, the Good or Divinity, which appeared to be object, is actually a subject whose object is the self. The "Sun" illumining all things becomes the Supreme subjectivity, the ultimate witness of the individuated consciousness. From the perspective of individuated consciousness, noesis is less a faculty than a "ray of light" that connects with and illumines individuated consciousness with the light of the Self.[58] Plotinus asserts this truth when he says: "Never did eye see the sun unless it had first become sunlike, and never can the soul have vision of the First Beauty unless itself be beautiful."[59]

This reversal of the usual ordering that the mind imposes on metaphysical truths is crucial to an appreciation of them, because it identifies

---

[56] For example, Cornford, in his classic translation, defines it thus: "*noesis* is . . . compared to the immediate act of vision and suggests . . . *the direct intuition or apprehension of its object*" (Cornford, *The Republic of Plato*, p. 218, emphasis added); the Pan *Dictionary of Philosophy* is content with: "mind" or the "rational part of the soul"; while the Citadel *Dictionary of Philosophy* defines it as "the highest part of the mind, viz. reason; the faculty of intellectual (as distinct from sensible) apprehension and of intuitive thought."

[57] The individuated consciousness—the *ahamtattva*—is, as Guénon says, defined precisely by "the notion that 'I am' concerned with external and internal objects, which are respectively the objects of perception and contemplation" (Guénon, *Man and His Becoming According to the Vedanta*, p. 68).

[58] From the Vedantic perspective: "if we view the 'Self' (*Atma*) . . . as the Spiritual Sun which shines at the centre of the entire being, *Buddhi* [the higher Intellect] will be the ray directly emanating from this Sun and illuminating in its entirety the particular individual state" (Guénon, *Man and His Becoming According to the Vedanta*, pp. 65-66).

[59] Plotinus quoted in Perry, *A Treasury of Traditional Wisdom*, p. 750.

the true ground of consciousness or subjectivity to be not in the individual, but in the Divinity. For Smith,

> the Intellect *is* the Absolute as manifest in the human soul. . . . What appears from mundane perspective as the Intellect coming to know the Absolute is in actuality the Intellect as Absolute-in-man becoming perceptible to phenomenal awareness.[60]

Concurrence with this interpretation may be found in diverse metaphysical traditions. In the *Taittiriya Upanishad*, we are told first of the limitations of the mind to approach *Brahman*, or the Absolute: "Words and mind go to him, but reach him not and return."[61] Then, in another *Upanishad*, it is revealed that the reason for this is because of a failure to appreciate the true ordering: "When all has become Spirit, one's own Self . . . how and whom could one know? How can one know him who knows all? How can the Knower be known?"[62] *Brahman* cannot be *known*, not because the *knowing* is impossible, but because *Brahman* is the knower; and this—in the *Bhagavad Gita*—is Arjuna's great revelation: "O Supreme Being, O Source of beings, O Lord of beings, O God of gods, O ruler of the universe, *Thou Thyself alone knowest Thyself by Thyself.*"[63]

The mysterious connection between the innermost "self" and the Divinity erases what seems paradox. The Jewish philosopher Philo wrote: "God is His own brightness and is discerned through Himself alone. . . . The seekers for truth are those who envisage God through God, light through light."[64] And Ali, the fourth *Khalifa*, declared: "I know God by God, and I know that which is not God by the light of God."[65] Throughout Christian history, the greatest thinkers have never failed to express this mystery. For

---

[60] Huston Smith, introduction to Schuon, *The Transcendent Unity of Religions*, pp. xiv-xv.

[61] Mascaró, *The Upanishads*, p. 110.

[62] Mascaró, *The Upanishads*, p. 132.

[63] *Bhagavad Gita* X: 15, quoted in Perry, *A Treasury of Traditional Wisdom*, p. 752, emphasis added.

[64] Philo quoted in Perry, *A Treasury of Traditional Wisdom*, p. 751.

[65] Ali quoted in Perry, *A Treasury of Traditional Wisdom,* p. 751.

Saint Paul, "The things of God knoweth no man, but the Spirit of God."[66] And for Augustine, "His divinity can in no wise be seen by human sight, but is seen by that sight with which those who see are no longer men, but beyond men."[67] In the thirteenth century, Aquinas could write: "the intellect sees . . . [God's essence] through the divine essence itself; so that in that vision the divine essence is both the object and the medium of vision."[68] At the end of that century, Dante would voice the same understanding in poetry:

> O light Eternal fixed in Self alone
> known only to Yourself, and Knowing Self,
> You love and glow, knowing and being known![69]

It can be surmised that these descriptions reflect experience.[70] Therefore, the significant and continuing decline in the occurrence of references to such vision or states of consciousness after the Scientific Revolution, suggests that the manifestation of this Intellective knowledge was in decline.[71] This would explain the increasing confusion over its reality, and, as

---

[66] 1 Corinthians, 2: 11.

[67] Augustine quoted in Perry, *A Treasury of Traditional Wisdom*, p. 754.

[68] Aquinas, *Summa Contra Gentiles*, III, li.

[69] Dante, *The Divine Comedy: Paradise*, trans. Mark Musa (Harmondsworth: Penguin, 1986), Canto XXXIII, 124-6. A different translation renders the same verse: "O Light eternal who only in thyself abidest, only thyself dost understand, and self-understood, self-understanding, turnest love on and smilest at thyself" (Dante quoted in Perry, *A Treasury of Traditional Wisdom*, p. 750).

[70] To consider that they reflect only "what people have believed" is perhaps more common. "There will be those," writes Schuon, "who will question how the existence and effectiveness of this knowledge can be proved: the only possible reply is that such proof is given by the expressions of Intellection themselves; just as it is impossible to prove to every soul the validity of a given religion . . . so also it is impossible to prove the reality of the Intellect to every understanding, which again proves nothing at all against the said reality" (Schuon, *Logic and Transcendence*, pp. 31-32).

[71] The symbolism of "light" or "fire," when present in poetry, can be taken to reflect a poet's mystical vision. In *The Fire and the Stones*, Nicholas Hagger traces the decline in the use of such visionary symbolism in European poetry. He concludes that, in England, "The Fire or Light virtually disappeared . . . after Hopkins"—T.S. Eliot, Auden, Vernon Watkins,

we have seen, the redefining of consciousness without that element in it. Considering the decline took place at the same time as the rise of science, we might blame modern science with its emphasis on the experience of quantity, rather than quality, as the culprit. Alternatively, we might say that the convictions of men like Descartes, and the fact that they were listened to, were but an outward *reflection* of this decline.[72] Whatever the case, once the revolution took hold it operated to keep consciousness directed along a particular course, that of reason-modified empiricism, and towards a quantified state, or—as Blake would have it—"sleep."

To re-invoke Blake is to be reminded of the impact of the initial influx of the Vedantic tradition into the West in the nineteenth century. Blake's "mental fight" against passivity in the face of scientism was unsuccessful to the extent that the unique vision of science continued to grow rather than wane in influence, as though it must run the course it had set itself before finally running up against its own limitations. By the time the limit was reached, the West had become used to an extreme rationalism or intellectualism wherein an appeal to "heart knowledge" would look like no more than emotion and sentiment. Precisely because the rational mind has become so overextended, it now requires an intellectual account of the *sophia* equal to the demands of its own world. As Schuon explains:

> The usual religious arguments, through not probing sufficiently to the depths of things and not having had previously any need to do so, are psychologically somewhat outworn and fail to satisfy certain needs of causality. If human societies degenerate on the one hand with the passage of time, they accumulate on the other hand experiences in virtue of old age, however intermingled with errors their experience may be; this paradox is something that any

David Gascoyne, and Dylan Thomas being the last to refer to it. In Germany, Holderlin (1770-1843) "knew the Light," but Rilke (1875-1926), who wrote imaginatively of others' vision, "never experienced it." Mallarme and Paul Valery represent the last glimmers in French poetry. See Nicholas Hagger, *The Fire and the Stones* (Shaftesbury, Dorset: Element, 1991), especially pp. 313-331.

[72] "One of the great unresolved psychological enigmas of the modern western world," says Sherrard, "is the question of what or who has persuaded us to accept as virtually axiomatic a self-view and a world-view that demand that we reject out of hand the wisdom and vision of our major philosophers and poets in order to imprison our thought and our very selves in the materialist, mechanical and dogmatic torture-chamber devised by purely quantitative and third-rate scientific minds" (Sherrard, *Human Image: World Image*, p. 6).

pastoral teaching bent on efficacy should take into account, not by drawing new directives from the general error, but on the contrary by using arguments of a higher order, intellectual rather than sentimental.[73]

Thus, in modern times it was Guénon who would once again turn to the Vedanta for inspiration:[74] As an expression of pure, unveiled, metaphysics the Vedanta[75] escapes the usual distinction that must be made between "esoteric" and "exoteric" content. For Guénon, the Vedanta, being "accessible in its entirety to all those who are intellectually 'qualified,'" fulfils, as far as is possible, the requirements of the Western mentality, which, even so, must still accept the limits of language, "since words and symbols, all told, serve no purpose beyond acting as aids to conceiving [the inexpressible]."[76] In *Man and His Becoming According to the Vedanta*, Guénon writes:

> The "Self" is the transcendent and permanent principle of which the manifested being, the human being, for example, is only a transient and contingent modification, a modification which . . . can in no way affect the principle. . . . The "Self", as such, is never individualized and cannot become so, for since it must always be considered under the aspect of the eternity and immutability which are the necessary attributes of pure Being, it is obviously not susceptible of any particularization, which would cause it to be "other than itself".[77]

---

[73] Frithjof Schuon, *Islam and the Perennial Philosophy* (World of Islam Festival Publishing Company, 1976), pp. 53-54.

[74] Ananda Coomaraswamy said of Guénon: "If [he] wants the West to turn to Eastern metaphysics, it is not because they are Eastern but because this is metaphysics. If 'Eastern' metaphysics differed from a 'Western' metaphysics—as true philosophy differs from what is often so called in our modern universities—one or the other would not be metaphysics. It is from metaphysics that the West has turned away" (Coomaraswamy quoted in Rama Coomaraswamy, *The Essential Ananda K. Coomaraswamy* [Bloomington: World Wisdom, 2004], p. 90).

[75] The "end of the Vedas," composed chiefly of the *Upanishads* and the *Brahma Sutras*.

[76] Guénon, *Man and His Becoming According to the Vedanta*, p. 22.

[77] Guénon, *Man and His Becoming According to the Vedanta*, p. 29.

Further:

> The "Self" is not . . . distinct from *Atma*, except when one considers it particularly and "distinctively" in relation to a being, or, more accurately, in relation to a certain definite state of that being, such as the human state, and in so far as one considers it from this special and limited point of view alone. In this case, moreover, the "Self" does not really become distinct from *Atma* in any way, since . . . it cannot be "other than itself," and obviously cannot be affected by the point of view from which we regard it, any more than by any other contingency. What should be noted is that, to the extent that we make this distinction, we are departing from the direct consideration of the "Self" in order to consider its reflection in human individuality. . . . The reflection in question determines what may be called the centre of this individuality; but if isolated from its principle, that is, from the "Self," it can only enjoy a purely illusory existence, for it is from that principle that it derives all its reality, and it effectually possesses this reality only through participation in the nature of the "Self".[78]

At the limit of the vertical dimension, then, we encounter a strange inversion of reality. The familiar dualism of knower and known has become a mirror image of itself: the known becoming the knower, and the knower the known. The witnessing counterpart to what is, is not the "self," but the "Self." Moreover, since the Self—the Divinity—encapsulates all that is, the original human knower is not a separate entity, but a "fragment" of this Unity.

To apply this new understanding to the question of immanence spoken of by the Romantic poets requires that immanence itself undergo this subtle change, so that rather than God being in, or interpenetrating, the world, the world that we know is fully and entirely immersed or—as Schuon has it—"mysteriously plunged" in God. This means that the *qualities* of the Divine do not so much belong to the world, rather these qualities are what the world is. The highest Platonic Forms of the Good and the Beautiful – which in *The Symposium* coincide as the object of love—do not exist in an abstract elsewhere, but are potentially ever-present, veiled only by a

---

[78] Guénon, *Man and His Becoming According to the Vedanta*, pp. 31 and 32.

failure of perception, such failure being the "illusion" of *Maya,* which refers not to the illusory nature of the world but to the illusion of perception generated by the existence of the individuated self.

We can now see that the symbolic language of poetry confronts the deepest implications of this truth. When poetry makes nature a symbol for states of being, it is not just offering analogies. It is identifying an actual relationship between ourselves and nature—a relationship of consciousness. Since our highest or innermost consciousness or being is divinity, and since nature is divine, then nature is not other than our own highest being. Because there is an exact correspondence between nature's qualities and the qualities to which we are potentially heir, the way nature appears is but a reflection of our own conscious state, of our position on the vertical ladder of our being. Our own failings concerning nature stem from the false view we inevitably have of it when we fail to engage with the higher element of our being.

But, if this non-rational element—the Intellect—is a bridge that connects our own being with divinity, then it must also be the element that connects us with what nature is. Here, the first "steps" on the bridge suggest themselves to be the perception of qualities in nature—divine qualities—like beauty. Movement "across the bridge," between the states of duality and non-duality, would then be signalled by an increasing level of perception of beauty. This recalls and affirms the hierarchy of perceptions, and the corresponding hierarchy of conscious states related to those perceptions, found to be a component of Leopold's thought. More significantly, however, by virtue of its harbouring the qualities that are potentially ours, nature must possess a means of "producing" the qualities within ourselves that are our *own* true nature. A directing of consciousness towards beauty in nature and towards the uncovering of beauty could be considered the very same thing as the manifesting of the subtle element of consciousness. To uncover the depths of beauty in nature would be to unveil the reality of the Intellect. And to seek beauty in nature would be to seek, and move towards, the essence of nature, and the consciousness of the Divine.

Part Five

THE NATURE OF NATURE

CHAPTER NINE
The Primacy of the Spirit

At the heart of each religious tradition is the understanding that the fundamental reality is the *Oneness of Being*. When, in applying this understanding, we use the term "essence" to designate the world's underlying reality, it should be remembered that this essence is not an ontological reality distinct from the rest of reality; it is not a "spiritual substance" that interpenetrates and is found within *another* substance. Rather, the "two" are actually one, the apparent duality only arising because of the existence of the human state itself, this state being defined, precisely, by the relativity of individuated consciousness. The human being is by definition a localized knower facing an "external" known; it is the human mind that conceptualizes the idea of "essence" and "substance." Oneness must remain only *virtual* while conceptualizing persists; even the *contemplation* of Oneness entails and perpetuates the ontological and epistemological divide.

Clearly, the usual operations of individuated consciousness, such as reason and imagination, do not of themselves provide the means of closing this gap, but instead act to keep it open. Thus it is that traditional metaphysics approaches the quest for knowledge not, as in the manner of modern philosophy and science, from the starting point of individuated consciousness seeking or directing itself towards a goal, but rather through an awareness of the primacy of the Spirit, which need only be allowed to impinge upon or be mirrored in this consciousness. This possibility is alien to both modern science and modern philosophy, whose method relies on retaining the primacy of the individuated consciousness. The method of esoterism appears to make no sense, because it seems bent on undermining the very thing that is supposed to support knowledge in the first place. Yet, if the primacy of the Spirit is accepted, it is only reasonable to suppose that it alone is responsible for the structure of reality, and that any genuine knowledge resides wherever the distorting influence of duality has been overcome. As we have seen, the outcome of several centuries devoted to the methods of science seems only to have confirmed that individuated consciousness, in thrall to the reasoning faculty, becomes like a distorting lens applied to one part of the world at a time.

A traditional metaphysics could never be primarily an edifice built upon the foundation of rational thought in the way modern philosophy is, since it was never intended to be a speculative venture. As the analysis of Plato revealed, it is a structure of a different kind. An outer shell of non-speculative doctrine exists only to enclose and safeguard a kernel, the revelation of which is *methodic* in nature, a practical means whereby the Spirit becomes manifest. The relationship between the two elements might be thought akin to the manner in which a lighthouse signals the presence of a light within. The building does not bring the *light* into being, rather the light is the reason for the structure being established, and for the form it takes.[1] It is the cessation of discursive thought, the relinquishment of conceptualization, that allows the inner qualities of the Spirit to manifest in consciousness, and the degree to which they do this is what defines the level of consciousness.

Since the centrality of the divine in the human is mirrored by the same centrality in the world, a similar process must apply to the revelation of *nature's* essence. From a metaphysical standpoint, the world is sacred because it participates in the nature of God. The sacred qualities of nature are an ever-present reality; if they seem "inherent within" nature, and are not readily perceptible, it is only because the consciousness we are used to wielding when we approach nature inevitably masks them. The nature that we know as "wilderness" or "virgin nature"—the wild, untamed and free splendour of deserts, forests, lakes, rivers, and mountains, distinct from our artificial world, and for untold millennia the matrix in which we lived—cannot be other than a direct and pure manifestation of divinity, and, as such, always stands ready to provide an opening into that essence. However, a bridge between "outer" nature and its inner reality cannot take place through the usual operations of individuated consciousness. The

---

[1] To equate light—so often used to represent the *aim* of method—with method itself, is not misplaced because, from the esoteric point of view, the method corresponds closely to that which it is applied to—the Spirit. From the traditionalist point of view, there is very real identity between certain practices in which the human being engages, and the Spirit itself. This is the reason, in esoterism, for the invocation of the name of God, since, in sacred scripts such as Arabic and Sanskrit, there is identity between the name and what is being named. In Sufism, *al-ism huwa'l-musamma*—"the Name is the Named"—indicates that the Divine is present in its name and therefore invocation has an incalculable effect on the consciousness of the invoker. See the chapter "The Quintessential Esoterism of Islam" in Frithjof Schuon, *Sufism: Veil and Quintessence* (Bloomington: World Wisdom, 1981).

duality can only be overcome by the *Being* of nature interpenetrating and reforming consciousness.

PRIMAL HUMANITY

Nature as *theophany* stands at variance with the vision of modernism. It is considered today that we are part of an all-embracing "ecosphere," living not just *upon* a world, but immersed *in* it. The breath of plants surrounds us; we ingest, and are formed from the cascading waters, the minerals of the earth, and the bodies of the once living. The sun's warmth and light which animates our waking hours, and the stars under which we sleep and dream, have shaped what we are. Our nature is defined—and inevitably *confined*—by material boundaries. If ecology has shown us a picture of interconnectedness, it is one appropriate to an age and an eye already used to seeing things in a certain way. The elements of this picture are empirical facts, applied with the brush of reason. While it displays originality and an intricate and complex pointillism, the picture appears curiously flat and lifeless. Understandably so, since this reassembled image of nature is the product of the same hand that first broke nature apart by wielding the knife of analysis. Historically, the ongoing process of dividing nature has presented us with changing images of an inner world, images which in turn have come to live in, and so shape, our imagination (our inner vision) and hence, our thought and perceptions.

The rise of urban civilizations such as those in Mesopotamia, Egypt, China and South America, from the modern standpoint signify progress, but they also represent the beginning of a slow divorce of humanity from nature—both a physical and a psychic separation. A sedentary lifestyle produces agriculture, towns, the stratification of society, and the development of arts and sciences. This artificial world is shaped by dismantling and re-fashioning the environment. To do this it is no longer possible for the mind simply to respond to nature as it presents itself; it must create an alternative picture of nature as *outer form hiding an underlying structure*. And the process by which the underlying structure is revealed is one where hand and imagination interact. Stone will shape stone or cut wood. Fire will harden wood and split stone; more importantly, as a "knife that cuts below the visible structure"[2], fire will "create" and transform metals. Copper, bronze, and iron tools enabled the creation of an increasingly sophisticated

---

[2] The phrase is Bronowski's. See *The Ascent of Man*, p. 125.

artificial world. Moreover, slicing into nature, we fashion for ourselves an inner imagery, one that is based on our own creations. The more we extend the artificial world, the greater the sense of the reality and importance of our particular view of the world, and so, too, the greater the sense of autonomous power. Long before the Greek world began to make formal propositions regarding the underlying structure of nature, humanity was already well advanced on the road of practical analysis, the unmediated images from nature being replaced with ones of our own. An acceleration of human inventiveness, the insight into how nature is put together, the harnessing of the energies in nature, and the destruction of nature, all began at this time and represent the birth of a wholly new form of civilization. Modern science represents the most recent outcome of an *imaginational* history; the inner world has *become* the "real" one and is what defines the nature we now behold—a thing detailed in the extreme, but now lacking the elements found in earlier times.[3] In seeking an image of nature that conveys the same sense of interconnectedness, but rendered richly and in depth and relatively free of the distorting images brought about through the analysis of nature, it would be necessary to reach back into a world that pre-dates the unfolding of urban civilization.

For primal peoples the natural world is ever-present before the senses. Since the action of cutting nature open is as yet rudimentary, there is no "beneath-the-surface" image, no "world within a world" of the sort we have grown used to, to conflict with what is directly experienced.[4] Be-

---

[3] Nasr writes: "Nothing is more dangerous in the current ecological debate than that scientistic view of man and nature which cuts man from his spiritual roots and takes a desacralized nature for granted while expanding its physical boundaries by billions of light years. This view destroys the reality of the spiritual world while speaking of awe before the grandeur of the cosmos. It destroys man's centrality in the cosmic order and his access to the spiritual world" (S. H. Nasr, *Man and Nature* [London: Unwin Hyman, 1990], p. 7).

[4] The following account adequately sums up the modern secular view of nature: "For contemporary Western consciousness landscape is barren, empty, unalive. Far from being animated by ancient spirits of place, landscape is seen as a dead objective background to our busy, ego-centred and self-propelling human lives. . . . Western intellectual tradition has a host of terms and concepts to explain away any attempt to animate the land in life or art: projection, personification, anthropomorphism, pathetic fallacy. Any life 'out there' was *put* there by an overactive or 'creative' mind. Indeed, the contemporary postmodern view is not even sure that there is a real landscape at all, or whether our experience of the land is entirely created by our own subjectivity. All we know, according to this bleak intellectualist position, are our own internal images, which we project vainly upon the world"

cause sensory experience is unencumbered by images *about* nature—which for us continually seek to project themselves upon the world—it can be conjectured that whatever qualities nature possesses are more readily experienced.

There are still enough wild or natural places where, removed from the trappings of modern civilization, we can begin to test this simpler vision. In the solitude of nature, we encounter the fundamentals of existence. We find ourselves at the central point of a world, which encircles us. Turning around on the summit of hill or mountain or on a plain, the curving horizon clearly defines this spatial relationship. Standing still, four cardinal directions suggest themselves: we face one, another lies behind us, the third and fourth are to either side. What we see in the world orients us and fixes these directions. The sun's place of rising and setting defines the first two—east and west—while the north-south axis crosses this. We are aware, too, of another circularity—the arching dome above—and our central position between earth and sky. If we were to express symbolically this relationship between nature and ourselves, we might choose the circle divided with a cross, the cross's intersection marking the centre where we are. Our bodily stance also represents a cross, the central point of which is our centre of being, our heart.

Two peoples in whose art this symbol manifests are the Aborigines of Tasmania, and the Plains Indians of America. The first have left a record in stone. Huge slabs on the north-west coast of their island home have been carved with such glyphs—plain and concentric circles, and crosses.[5] The "old people" who carved these stones are long gone, and much of their culture is now a dim memory. Yet to account these stones as only silent testaments to an unfathomable culture is to overlook the universality of certain human experience and the desire to express that experience. When these same symbols can be correlated with a living tradition, that of the American Indians, we are at once permitted to hear and see more. Schuon, who, in the latter half of the twentieth century made a point of studying the American Indian tradition firsthand, and who drew upon the pioneer-

(David J. Tacey, *Edge of the Sacred: Transformation in Australia* [Melbourne: Harper Collins, 1995], pp. 148-9).

[5] The most elaborate non-figurative designs are found at Sundown Point. An example of the circle with internal cross occurs at Greens Creek. See Josephine Flood, *Rock Art of the Dreamtime* (Sydney: Harper Collins, 1997), chapter 8.

ing work of Joseph Epes Brown who set down the narrative of Black Elk (the Oglala Sioux), could write:

> The whole tradition of the Indians of North America . . . is contained in the cross inscribed in the circle. . . . The cross marks the Four Directions of space and all the other quaternaries of the Universe; it also marks the vertical ternary Earth Man-Sky, which puts the horizontal quaternary on three levels.[6]

Thus, the same image of circle with its centre—which adorns the Indians' dress, their *tipis*, and their sacred objects of ritual, and which is often a disc of rawhide painted red or blue—can be made to express three different realities. Within the domain that the first circle describes, the great movements of nature take place: the heat of day and the cool of night, wind, rain, storms of fire and snow, the cycle of the seasons, and the moon's waxing and waning. New life is ceaselessly generated, grows, then dies. Earth, air, fire, and water are the four elements or fundamental principles of nature that communicate to our senses its basic make-up. All within this sphere is in flux. Only the clear night sky reveals unchanging perfection, and an awareness of this quality brings us closer to an appreciation of the full meaning of the other two "circles," and to what is fundamental to all primal peoples. For the stars signify another world altogether; they delineate a *heaven* above our head, the obvious "dwelling-place" or symbol of a Spirit that animates everything. As Titus Burckhardt reminds us, "A fact that must never be lost sight of is that, to the ancients . . . physical space, envisaged in its totality, is always the objectivation of 'spiritual space.'"[7] Moreover (as noted earlier), primal "man" is rarely, if ever, a pantheist, but has often seemed so to ethnologists used to the concept of creation *ex nihilo* which makes God distinct from His creation. For the Sioux, the things of nature *are* created, but in the sense of being actual expressions of *Wakan-Tanka* (the Divinity or "Great Spirit"); the quality of sacredness comes about through the fact that all beings are manifestations of this Spirit.

---

[6] Frithjof Schuon, *The Feathered Sun* (Bloomington: World Wisdom, 1990), p. 14.

[7] Titus Burckhardt, *The Universality of Sacred Art* (Colombo: Sri Lanka Institute of Traditional Studies, 2001), p. 23.

The second level represents the domain of the human being, who, subjectively, is always at the centre of the world and whose own centre is the Divinity or Spirit, "the center of all things," as Black Elk says.[8]

At a still higher level, the circle of the sky represents the Divine in its cosmic or transcendent aspect—*Wakan-Tanka*, "who dwells at the depths of the heavens."[9] The sun—the "centre" of the sky—also represents the Divinity, but in its immanent aspect. Conceived as Spirit, this "central" light is the light that shines in the "heart" of "man";[10] the centre of the Great Spirit is the centre of the human being.

The mystery of the Divine as simultaneously both transcendent and immanent, both outward and inward, both centre and periphery, and of "man" as being both great and small, the centre of a world but having a world at "his" centre, is thus beautifully represented by the use of one symbol which must be viewed in different ways, and in fact shifts under our gaze even as it is contemplated. The use of this symbol to convey a profound and subtle metaphysics with simple beauty demonstrates that symbols of this kind are not expressive of a crude conception, but rather great subtlety of thought—a cognizance of the highest ontological realities, together with an awareness of the insufficiency of accurately representing the formless in other than abstract terms.[11] As Schuon warns, there are

[8] Joseph Epes Brown, *The Sacred Pipe* (Norman: University of Oklahoma Press, 1989), p. 71.

[9] Brown, *The Sacred Pipe*, p. 71.

[10] Brown explains: "*Wakan-Tanka* as Grandfather is the Great Spirit independent of manifestation, unqualified, unlimited, identical to the Christian Godhead, or to the Hindu *Brahma-Nirguna*. *Wakan-Tanka* as Father is the Great Spirit considered in relation to His manifestation, either as Creator, Preserver, or Destroyer, identical to the Christian God, or to the Hindu *Brahma-Saguna*" (Brown, *The Sacred Pipe*, p. 5).

[11] In *The Feathered Sun*, Schuon cites a fatal misrepresentation by a modern author that begins with an eighteenth century account of a meeting with Delaware Indians: "In the course of the conversation (William) Penn asked one of the Lenape (Delaware) interpreters to explain to him the notion which the Natives had of God. The Indian . . . sought in vain for words. Finally he drew a series of concentric circles on the ground, and, indicating their centre, said that this was the place where the Great Man was symbolically situated" (Werner Muller, *Die Relgionen der Waldindianer Nordamerikas* [Berlin: D. Reimer, 1956]). Schuon explains that the "argument based on this incident [was] that for the Delawares God was a drawing, thus something 'concrete' and not an 'abstraction'!" (Schuon, *The Feathered Sun*, p. 5).

grave problems associated with attempting to assess the beliefs of primal peoples without an adequate understanding of spiritual or metaphysical truths: "scientific 'specialization' alone . . . does not amount to the intellectual qualification enabling one to penetrate ideas and symbols."[12] Anthropology and ethnology as scientific disciplines proceed with the handicap of the rational viewpoint:

> According to a very prevalent error . . . all traditional symbols were originally understood in a strictly literal sense, and symbolism properly so called only developed as a result of an "intellectual awakening" which took place later. This is an opinion that completely reverses the normal relationship of things. . . . In reality, what later appears as a superadded meaning was already implicitly present, and the "intellectualization" of the symbols is the result, not of an intellectual progress, but on the contrary of a loss . . . of primordial intelligence.[13]

With the American Indian example before us, the danger of reading simple images as indicative of simple conceptions or a primitive consciousness is clear.[14] A scientific mentality that could conceive the great symbols

---

[12] Schuon, *The Feathered Sun*, p. 4. Schuon adds: "While the Indians of North America are one of the races which have been most studied by ethnographers, it cannot be said that everything about them is fully known, for the simple reason that ethnography does not embrace all possible forms of knowledge—any more than do other ordinary sciences—and therefore cannot possibly be regarded as a general key. There is in fact a sphere which by definition is beyond the reach of ordinary science ('outward' or 'profane' science, that is to say), but which is the very basis of every civilization: this is spirituality—the knowledge of Divine Reality and of the means of realizing It, in some degree or other, in oneself. Clearly no one can understand any one form of spirituality without knowing spirituality in itself; to be able to know the wisdom of a people we must first of all possess the keys to such wisdom, and these indispensable keys are to be found, not in any subsidiary branch of learning, but in intellectuality at its purest and most universal level" (Schuon, *The Feathered Sun*, pp. 45-6).

[13] Schuon, *The Feathered Sun*, p. 3. In regard to Jung's psychological interpretation, Burckhardt writes: "What is absolutely false is the view that the origin of the symbol is to be found in the so-called 'collective unconscious' . . . in a chaotic substratum of the human soul. The content of a symbol is not irrational, but supra-rational, that is to say, purely spiritual" (Titus Burckhardt, *Mirror of the Intellect* [Cambridge: Quinta Essentia, 1987], p. 117).

[14] A determination to apply scientific reductionism to the universal imagery in the art of

of the Tasmanian Aborigines to be akin to the first faltering artworks of children, is the same one that could overlook the powerful significance of their belief that the Spirit dwells in the "left breast," and departs at death.[15]

The indications of a complete metaphysical tradition in human society existing outside the usual matrix of formalized religion may suggest a continuity of tradition stretching into the remote past, and require us to re-assess the principle of progress so dear to modernists. In *Ancient Beliefs and Modern Superstitions,* Lings argues the case for a re-interpretation of early humanity, based on a view inclusive of metaphysical tradition.[16] Scepticism regarding the *scientific* appraisal of human history as a retreat into a more and more primitive past is made easier when it is considered that the

---

primal peoples, inevitably leads to the positing of a behavioural or biological cause. Thus, first Desmond Morris finds a similarity between the images produced by primates and those of young children (see D. Morris, *The Biology of Art: A Study of the Picture-making Behaviour of the Great Apes and its Relationship to Human Art* [New York: Knopf, and London: Methuen, 1962]). Next, the pictures of pre-school children, analyzed by Rhoda Kellogg in the 1950s, are equated with phosphenes—the images that the eye and brain produce on their own (see R.M. Kellog, M. Knoll and J. Kugler, "Form-similarity between phosphenes of adults and preschool children's scribblings," *Nature* Vol. 208 [1965]: pp. 1,129-30). Finally, a comparison is made between phosphenes and aboriginal rock art (see R.G. Bednarik, "On the Nature of Psychograms," *The Artefact* Vol. 8, 3-4 [1984]: pp. 27-32), leading to the hypothesis that "some of the earliest art is . . . thought to be an externalisation of these images" (P.G. Bahn, and J. Vertut, *Images of the Ice Age, Facts on File* [New York: Oxford, 1988], p. 20); and the "possibility that the capacity to reduce three-dimensional sensory information to a two-dimensional image was not present to the people who produced the most archaic rock art in Australia" (Bednarik quoted in Flood, *Rock Art of the Dreamtime,* p. 243). Such speculations not only overlook any metaphysical explanation, but even ignore the incisive testimonies of early ethnographers and Aborigines themselves. George Augustus Robinson, for example, states that the Tasmanian Aborigines' body adornment of circular cicatrices is "in imitation of the sun and moon," which "having the power of those luminaries they imagine it will have the same influence" (N.J.B. Plomley, ed., *Friendly Mission: The Tasmanian Journals and Papers of George Augustus Robinson, 1829-1834* [Hobart: Tasmanian Historical Research Association, 1966], p. 582).

[15] Lyndall Ryan, *The Aboriginal Tasmanians* (Crows Nest, NSW: Allen & Unwin, 1996), p. 11. Indeed, as Oldmeadow points out, "It is in the primal cultures (so often dismissed or patronized as 'primitive' and 'preliterate'), such as those of the Australian Aborigines, the African Bushmen, or the American Indians, that we find the most highly developed sense of the transparency of natural phenomena and the most profound understanding of the 'eternal language'" (Oldmeadow, "The Firmament Sheweth His Handiwork," p. 43).

[16] Martin Lings, *Ancient Beliefs and Modern Superstitions* (London: Unwin, 1980).

significant contacts with primal people—in, for example, the Americas, the Pacific islands and Australia—came about only after the Renaissance and Scientific Revolution, when metaphysical understanding was in decline and there was increasing emphasis on material culture:[17]

> If science . . . knows much about [humanity's] prehistoric past . . . [this] knowledge would have taught our ancestors little or nothing that they did not already know, except as regards chronology, nor would it have caused any general change in attitude. For in looking back to the past, they did not look back to a complex civilization but to small village settlements with a minimum of social organization; and beyond these they looked back to men who lived without houses, in entirely natural surroundings, without books, without agriculture, and in the beginning even without clothes. It would be true then to say that the ancient conception of early man, based on sacred scriptures and on age-old tradtional lore handed down by word of mouth from the remote past, was scarcely different, as regards the bare facts of material existence, from the modern scientific conception, which differs from the traditional one chiefly because it weighs up the same set of facts differently.[18]

Today, the belief in material evolution, from the simple to the complex, almost demands a corresponding historical development in expres-

---

[17] Thomas Hobbes' seventeenth century assessment is well known: "No arts; no letters; no society; and which is worst of all, continual fear and danger of violent death; and the life of man, solitary, poor, nasty, brutish, and short" (Hobbes, *Leviathan*, i.13). Rousseau, in the eighteenth century, favoured the state between "primitive" and "civilized" ("*la société naissante*") to be ideal, because he assumed that before that man was "a solitary, moving, stupid but unmoral beast" (Rousseau quoted in *The Aboriginal Tasmanians*, p. 49). Even as short a time ago as 1971, David Davies could write of the Tasmanian Aborigines: "If wanting little for the body, they required even less for the soul. With no gods, no form of worship, their vague fears were due only to the wild, dread voices of the constant storms, the darkness, and the eyes of the Tasmanian Wolf . . . peering at them out of the blackness beyond the fire. With these fears life must have been all the more terrible because they did not have the slightest understanding of the laws of the universe" (David Davies, *The Last of the Tasmanians* [Sydney: Shakespeare Head Press, 1973], p. 10).

[18] Lings, *Ancient Beliefs and Modern Superstitions*, pp. 6-7.

sions of human intelligence or thought. Yet, for Lings, this inclination can easily be challenged by the facts of language alone:

> [The] conception of man's primordial speech as having been the most perfectly expressive or onomatopaeic of all languages is . . . beyond the reach of any philological verification. None the less philology can give us a clear idea of the general linguistic tendencies of mankind, and in doing so it teaches us nothing which in any sense weighs against the traditional report. On the contrary, every language known to us is a debased form of some more ancient language, and the further we go back in time the more powerfully impressive language becomes. It also becomes more complex, so that the oldest known languages, those which are far older than history itself, are the most subtle and elaborate in their structure. . . . The passage of time always tends to diminish the individual words both in form and sonority, while grammar and syntax become more and more simplified.[19]

If language corresponds to perception, in the sense that it exists to communicate inner and outer experience, then subtlety in language certainly reflects subtlety of perception. We need only bring to mind the terminology of ancient Sanskrit or even classical Arabic to be reminded that there were once "more things in heaven and earth" than modern philosophy now dreams of. When perception extends beyond outer form, and language, like art, is asked to describe that perception, language must extend beyond *its* "outer" or literal form; it must be symbolic. Then, words, like images, are no longer always meant to be taken at face value, but represent subtler truths. The assumption of our own time, which is, more or less, that everything modern science can measure is real, and everything else is merely the expression of a subjective consciousness, obliges us to disregard this interpretation of language as an indication of subtle perception, because science peremptorily denies the existence of what the sym-

---

[19] Lings, *Ancient Beliefs and Modern Superstitions*, pp. 11-12. Relevant in this context is Davies' telling comment concerning the language of the Tasmanian Aborigines: "A language, albeit with no ordinary grammatical niceties, proved their kind: though, as with all primitive people, it was complicated and difficult to understand" (Davies, *The Last of the Tasmanians*, p. 10).

bol applies to. Similarly, we will also overlook the use of everyday language to express symbolically—in the same manner as images—a deeper truth.[20]

NATURE AS SYMBOL

The subtlest perception derives from unitive knowledge, the heart knowledge to which Black Elk refers:

> When the light comes from Above, it enlightens my Heart and I can see, for the Eye of my Heart (*Chante Ishta*) sees everything. . . . The heart is a sanctuary at the Center of which there is a little space, wherein the Great Spirit (*Wakantanka*) dwells, and this is the Eye. This is the Eye of *Wakantanka* by which He sees all things, and through which we see Him.[21]

Unmediated awareness reveals that the phenomenal nature known to individuated consciousness conceals an inner essence.[22] The innermost of the known is the same as the innermost knower—that is, Divinity. In this state, knower and known are indistinguishable. Nature is sacred now, not because it *reflects* Divinity but because its divinity is realized.

When the essence of things is experienced, there is no need for their symbolic representation through word or image.[23] When the true "art" of nature is known, there is little need for another art that refers back to this one. For Ananda Coomaraswamy,

---

[20] This may remind us of Kant's dismissal of the ontological argument for God. Imaginary dollars are possible, he says, but this does not mean they exist in reality. However, this overlooks the subtlety of the argument. The image of dollars arises because of the existence of the real money, which hints at the truth that the perception of Divinity comes before the symbolic images of Divinity.

[21] Black Elk quoted in Perry, *A Treasury of Traditional Wisdom*, pp. 819-20.

[22] The inner quality of things brought by such perception is only "inner" because the subtlety of perception is not the norm. The heart knowledge given to Black Elk is exceptional today.

[23] The *Bhagavad Gita* expresses this idea thus: "As is the use of a well of water where water everywhere overflows, such is the use of all the Vedas to the seer of the Supreme" (*Bhagavad Gita*, II: 46).

It is evident that symbols . . . can serve no purpose for those who have not yet, in the Platonic sense, 'forgotten'. . . . The need of symbols, and of symbolic rites, arises only when man is expelled from the Garden of Eden; as means, by which a man can be reminded at later stages of his descent from the intellectual and contemplative to the physical and practical levels of reference.[24]

By this reasoning, the paucity of external images in a culture may indicate not underdeveloped consciousness, but the existence of a less individuated awareness.[25] Although this is not easy to prove, what is more certain is that the initial *prolongation* of Intellectual perception—what is carried away from this experience and acts to permeate a people's culture—is the felt experience of the sacredness of nature. The phenomena of phenomenal awareness then stand as symbols for the essential nature of nature. And the symbolism in question is of the nature of a direct correspondence; there is nothing arbitrary about it, as the following passage from Schuon makes clear:

It would be quite erroneous to believe that the symbolist mentality consists in selecting from the exterior world images on which to superimpose more or less farfetched meanings; this would be a pastime incompatible with wisdom. On the contrary, the symbolist vision of the cosmos is a priori a spontaneous perspective that

---

[24] Ananda Coomaraswamy, "Symbols," in *What is Civilisation?* (Ipswich: Golgonooza Press, 1989), pp. 126-127. "We assuredly have 'forgotten,'" continues Coomaraswamy, "far more than those who first had need of symbols, and far more than they need to infer the immortal by its mortal analogies; and nothing could be greater proof of this than our own claims to be superior to all ritual operations, and to be able to approach the truth directly. It was as signposts of the Way . . . that the motifs of traditional art, which have become *our* 'ornaments', were originally employed. In these abstract forms, the farther one traces them backward . . . the more one recognises in them a polar balance of perceptible shape and imperceptible information" (Coomaraswamy, *What is Civilisation?* p. 127).

[25] Josephine Flood observes that despite the well documented "complexity and richness of the religious and ceremonial life of the 'nomads' of central Australia" they were labelled "primitive," "because of the simplicity of their few tools and lack of metal, pottery or agriculture." Yet, "such concepts are derived from the undue value placed on material culture . . . in our Western possession-dominated way of thinking. . . . This is a totally alien concept to traditional Aboriginal societies, whose preoccupations are much more with the intangible world of religion and law" (Flood, *Rock Art of the Dreamtime*, p. 2).

213

bases itself on the essential nature—or the metaphysical transparency—of the phenomena, rather than cutting these off from their prototypes.[26]

The symbolist outlook is in accord with the structure of reality:

> The science of symbols—not simply a knowledge of traditional symbols—proceeds from the qualitative significance of substances, forms, spatial directions, numbers, natural phenomena, positions, relationships, movements, colors, and other properties or states of things; we are not dealing here with subjective appreciations, for the cosmic qualities are ordered in relation to Being and according to a hierarchy which is more real than the individual; they are therefore independent of our tastes, or rather they determine them to the extent that we are ourselves conformable to Being; we assent to the qualities to the extent that we ourselves are "qualitative."[27]

While all of nature is of the Spirit, the Spirit vastly transcends its immanent aspect. The symbolist vision is to see evidence of this transcendence as it is "reflected" disproportionately in the differing aspects of nature:

> The symbolism of a thing is its power to recall its higher reality, in the same way that a reflection or shadow can give us a fleeting glimpse of the object that casts it; and the best symbols . . . are those things that are most perfect of their kind, for they are the clearest reflections, the sharpest shadows, of the higher reality which is their archetype.[28]

Thus it is that, when the *Bhagavad Gita* wants to list those phenomena that most clearly indicate the presence of the Divinity in nature, it includes "only the greatest":

---

[26] Schuon, *The Feathered Sun*, p. 6.

[27] Schuon, "Seeing God Everywhere," in *Seeing God Everywhere*, pp. 4-5.

[28] Martin Lings, *The Sacred Art of Shakespeare* (Rochester: Inner Traditions, 1998), p. 135.

Of luminaries [I am] the radiant sun. I am the lord of the winds and storms, and of the lights in the night I am the moon. . . . Of radiant spirits I am fire; and among high mountains the mountain of the gods. . . . Of lakes I am the vast ocean. . . . Of trees I am the tree of life. . . . Of beasts I am the king of the beasts. . . . Among things of purification I am the wind. . . . Of fishes in the sea I am Makara the wonderful, and among all rivers the holy Ganges . . . and of the seasons the season of flowers. . . . I am the beauty of all things beautiful.[29]

From a traditional perspective, nature could never be a "democracy" where everything is considered equivalent in value because of a basic material similarity.[30] Instead, because of the primacy of the Spirit, non-material *qualities* must be re-introduced as ontological aspects of the world. And since there are some things that more perfectly express, for instance, the qualities of beauty or majesty—which are the reflections of *divine* beauty and majesty—nature must be structured hierarchically.

Since the essence or esoteric core of religion is the knowledge of the inner reality of both the world and of ourselves, "pre-civilized" peoples who have the same understanding as that of the American Indians could rightly be said to possess all that is essential as regards metaphysical knowledge.[31] For primal humanity immersed in nature it is the natural world, not scripture, which reveals the truth of things, and in a manner that is direct. Indeed, constantly in the presence of the artistry of the Divine, art which seeks to remind of metaphysical truths is largely unnecessary, the "shadows or reflections of spiritual realities"[32] being too apparent.

For the American Indians, as for most primal people, the sun is one of the clearest manifestations of the spiritual qualities inherent in nature. It

---

[29] *Bhagavad Gita* X: 21-36.

[30] And, from the same perspective, to force it to be so in order to support once again, a particular conception of things and a particular exigency, would amount to an irrational denial of what nature is.

[31] Brown remarks that for the Lakota, "each form in the world around them bears such a host of precise values and meanings that taken all together they constitute what one would call their 'doctrine'" (J.E. Brown quoted in Oldmeadow, "The Firmament Sheweth His Handiwork," p. 43).

[32] Lings, *The Sacred Art of Shakespeare*, p. 135.

would be impossible to over-emphasize the significance of the source of all light and life:

> The sun is the Heart of the Macrocosm, the human heart is the sun of the microcosm that we are. The visible sun is only the trace of the Divine sun, but this trace, being real, is efficacious and allows the operation of "analogical magic".[33]

In his account of the sacred rite of the Sun Dance, recorded by Brown, Black Elk specifies that

> A round rawhide circle . . . be made to represent the sun, and this should be painted red; but at the center there should be a round circle of blue, for this innermost center represents *Wakan-Tanka* as our Grandfather. The light of this sun enlightens the entire universe; and as the flames of the sun come to us in the morning, so comes the grace of *Wakan-Tanka*, by which all creatures are enlightened. It is because of this that the four-leggeds and the wingeds always rejoice at the coming of the light. We can all see in the day, and this seeing is sacred for it represents the sight of that real world which we may have through the eye of the heart.[34]

The moon is a lesser light, illuminated by the sun, and enlightens the world in the hours of darkness. "When the moon is full it is as if the eternal light of the Great Spirit were upon the whole world," says Black Elk.[35] The moon's nature is to wax and wane as "everything created waxes and wanes, lives and dies."[36] Its "living" nature allows it to represent all living things. Significantly, though, "the growing and the dying of the moon reminds us of our ignorance which comes and goes."[37] A night without moonlight is the soul without knowledge, while the full moon's reflected light aptly

---

[33] Schuon, *The Feathered Sun* pp. 94 and 97.

[34] Brown, *The Sacred Pipe*, pp. 71-2.

[35] Brown, *The Sacred Pipe*, p. 67.

[36] Brown, *The Sacred Pipe*, p. 71.

[37] Brown, *The Sacred Pipe*, p. 67.

suggests the full light of the Spirit in the heart, and therefore the moon is the symbol of the enlightened human soul. For Lings:

> The sun and the moon . . . symbolize respectively the Spirit and the Heart: just as the moon looks towards the sun and transmits something of its reflected radiance to the darkness of the night, so the Heart transmits the light of the Spirit to the night of the soul.[38]

If light is so obviously the symbol of connectivity between what is above and what is below, it may be asked what in the terrestrial world acts to reciprocate such a movement and define the vertical dimension in terms of the soul's aspiration. Between Earth and Sky, what great symbols are there?

The birds that rise from the earth, ascending skyward free of our physical limitations, are the most powerful of symbols. Most sacred to the American Indian is the eagle, whose soaring flight, so clearly visible in the blue expanse above our head, seems to bring it to the realm of the sun:

> O You, Spotted Eagle of the heavens! we know that You have sharp eyes with which you see even the smallest object that moves on Grandmother Earth. O You, who are in the depths of the heavens, and who know everything.[39]

As part of the Sun Dance rite Black Elk advises:

> You should prepare a necklace of otter skin. . . . At the center of the circle you should tie a plume taken from the breast of the eagle, for this is the place which is nearest to the heart and center of the sacred bird. This plume will be for *Wakan-Tanka*, who dwells at the depths of the heavens, and who is the center of all things.[40]

---

[38] Lings, *Symbol and Archetype*, p. 3.

[39] Brown, *The Sacred Pipe*, p. 77. The spotted eagle's significance lies in its being the highest flier.

[40] Brown, *The Sacred Pipe*, p. 71.

The visible relationship between eagle and sun, that takes place over-head, is a symbol from the hand of nature herself. However, the same symbolism is reflected in Indian art as the "feathered sun"

> found on buffalo hides used as cloaks and occasionally as a back-ground for ceremonies. The Sun is composed of concentric cir-cles formed of stylized eagle feathers; the resulting impression is particularly evocative in that the symbol simultaneously suggests center, radiation, power and majesty. This symbiosis between the sun and the eagle . . . [is] found again in the celebrated headdress of feathers formerly worn by chiefs and great warriors.[41]

The symbolism of the sacred rite of the Sun Dance, one of the "seven ways of praying to *Wakan-Tanka*,"[42] is that "man is spiritually transformed into an eagle soaring towards Heaven and becoming identified with the rays of the Divine Sun."[43]

The second great symbol in nature of hierarchy in both the spheres of being and knowing is the tree. Although firmly fixed upon "Grandmoth-er Earth," it too rises heavenwards with outstretched limbs and lives and moves in the "sky." In the rite of the Sun Dance,

> one of the standing peoples has been chosen to be at our center; he is the *wagachun* (the rustling tree, or cottonwood); he will be our center and also the people, for the tree represents the way of the people. Does it not stretch from the earth here to heaven there? [44]

---

[41] Schuon, *The Feathered Sun*, p. 100.

[42] Brown, *The Sacred Pipe*, p. 68.

[43] Schuon, *The Feathered Sun*, p. 100.

[44] Brown, *The Sacred Pipe*, pp. 69-70. Black Elk adds: "I think it would be good to explain to you here why we consider the cottonwood tree to be so very sacred. I might mention first, that long ago it was the cottonwood who taught us how to make our tipis, for the leaf of the tree is an exact pattern of the tipi. . . . Another reason why we choose the cottonwood tree to be at the center of our lodge is that the Great Spirit has shown to us that, if you cut an upper limb of this tree crosswise, there you will see in the grain a perfect five pointed star, which, to us, represents the presence of the Great Spirit. Also perhaps you have no-ticed that even in the very lightest breeze you can hear the voice of the cotton wood tree; this we understand is its prayer to the Great Spirit, for not only men, but all beings pray to

Schuon comments:

> The central element of the rite is the tree, image of the cosmic axis which joins earth to Heaven; the tree is the presence—necessarily vertical—of the Celestial Height over the terrestrial plane; it is what allows the contact, both sacrificial and contemplative, with the Solar Power.[45]

The third great symbol is "man," who in his vertical stance, motivity, and upward gaze, stands for that which re-links earth and heaven, and most clearly embodies a receptivity to the "light" from above.[46] From the traditionalist perspective, "man himself as he was created . . . is the greatest of earthly symbols."[47] The initial qualification is significant, for "man" *as he has become*—man of the modern world—no longer assents to or even understands such a status. By contrast, for Black Elk, representative of a pre-modernist tradition, "This which is over your head is like *Wakan-Tanka*, for when you stand you reach from Earth to Heaven; thus, anything above your head is like the Great Spirit. You are the tree of life."[48]

A simple recognition of a human being's innate capacities, and not an arrogant assumption of superiority or licence to do as we wish, is what lies behind the understanding of humanity's unique position.[49] Black Elk, like other representatives of tradition, finds in this position cause for profound humility. Indeed, this "favoured" position implies a responsibility with which no other creature is similarly burdened. As mediator between earth and heaven, humanity is responsible for how the earth fares. It is this sense of duty to earth and heaven which infuses both the everyday lives and

---

Him continually in differing ways" (Brown, *The Sacred Pipe*, pp. 74-5).

[45] Schuon, *The Feathered Sun*, p. 97.

[46] In the words of the *Chandogya Upanishad*, "There is a Light that shines beyond all things on earth, beyond us all, beyond the heavens, beyond the highest, the very highest heavens. This is the Light that shines in our heart" (Mascaró, *The Upanishads*, p. 113).

[47] Lings, *Symbol and Archetype*, p. 2.

[48] Brown, *The Sacred Pipe*, p. 123.

[49] This is why for the traditionalists a sense of humanity's difference should remain. To efface this uniqueness in the interests of promoting an equality amongst species is to risk the effacement of this position of mediator.

the sacred rites of primal man. The rites re-establish and re-confirm man's connection to heaven, but more than anything establish the understanding of how the world as sacred presence is to be treated, and the means by which this is to be done. Such rites have little meaning to post-Renaissance rational man because the link between heaven and earth, which primal man takes to be an essential characteristic of man *qua* man, is not there. The breaking of the link—effected for the most part by its denial—and the rejection of sacred rites is, for primal peoples, the loss of ability to effect harmony in the universe.[50] When the environmental philosopher Edward Goldsmith says, "the overriding goal of the behaviour pattern of an eco- logical society must be to preserve the critical order of the natural world or of the cosmos,"[51] he is fully aware that for traditional peoples this critical order or sacred balance is not thought to be preserved just by taking only what is necessary or being mindful of the needs of other creatures. More than anything it is the rites, of which Black Elk speaks, that are directed towards restoring the balance and harmony between people and between humanity and nature. In recalling that these are religious rites that have their parallel in all religions, we can see why Goldsmith refers to "the role that religion can and must play in saving what remains of the natural world."[52] We can see, also, the reason Nasr, after more than thirty years speaking in defence of the environment, can say, "In the deepest mystical sense, nature is hungry for our prayers."[53]

The disparity between the outlook of pre-urban civilization and our own may bring to mind the occasions when the beauty of primal people— whether it be their physical grace, manner of expression, or moral behav- iour—was first documented. For the Christian explorers of the Renaissance and Enlightenment, convinced though they were of the merits of their own civilization, the discovery of the "children of nature" could still evoke a sympathetic response. Their own religion spoke of simplicity, purity and innocence, and this is what they found. Columbus, "going ashore in the

---

[50] This is why the American Indian culture, like many other traditional cultures, expects unavoidable calamity if the balance is not redressed.

[51] Edward Goldsmith, *The Way: An Ecological World-View* (London: Random Century, 1992), p. xvii.

[52] Edward Goldsmith, *The Ecologist* Vol. 30, No.1 (2000): p. 3.

[53] S. H. Nasr, *The Spiritual and Religious Dimensions of the Environmental Crisis*, p. 13.

Antilles, was struck by the profound well-being of the island of Arawak. ('There is not in the world, a better nation. They love their neighbours as themselves, and their discourse is ever sweet and gentle.')"[54] Bougainville took from his experience of the natives of Tahiti a vision to confirm Rousseau's doctrine of the "noble savage." Cook counted the Aboriginal people of Australia among the most fortunate in the world.[55] In Tasmania, d'Entrecasteaux, Labillardière, and Péron—who, significantly, represented peaceful research expeditions—received only "friendliness, kindness, and generosity [from] the inhabitants."[56] However, the vision of a Pacific "paradise" and a "noble savage" soon disappeared once the same "savages" made to defend their paradise against those bent on possession.[57]

The parallel found between those living in close harmony with nature and nobility of spirit can be explained most easily, not through Rousseau's sentimental view of childlike innocence, but by an *integrity of being* wherein the full range of human faculties is either expressed or affirmed. Through an immediacy of vision, or its prolongation in the language, images, and ritual of a culture, nature itself becomes the "book of revelation." The need for a secondary expression of religion as we know it, is circumvented. For Schuon,

[54] Peter Matthiessen, *Indian Country* (London: Fontana, 1986), p. 15. "It has been suggested," says Peter Matthiessen, "that he named them Indios not because he imagined them to be inhabitants of India . . . but because he recognized that the friendly, generous Taino people lived in blessed harmony with their surroundings—*una gente in Dios*, a people in God." Matthiessen adds: "The Indians strove to live honourably and responsibly as well as generously, and perhaps it was the very goodness of a 'heathen' people, so civilized in all meaningful ways, that was so disturbing to religious men who had to wrestle with the bestiality in their own natures" (Matthiessen, *Indian Country*, pp. 15 and 16).

[55] Cook wrote: "the Natives of New-Holland . . . are far more happier than we Europeans; being wholly unacquainted not only with the superfluous but the necessary Conveniences so much sought after in Europe, they are happy in not knowing the use of them. They live in a Tranquility which is not disturb'd by the Inequality of Condition" (Philip Edwards, ed., *The Journals of Captain Cook* [Harmondsworth: Penguin, 1999], p. 174).

[56] Ryan, *The Aboriginal Tasmanians*, p. 61.

[57] See Ryan, *The Aboriginal Tasmanians*, chapter 2. The subsequent conflict which obliterates initial goodwill does nothing to disprove innate tendencies, but demonstrates only what should be obvious: in the struggle for survival, the more subtle elements of a culture are the first to disappear.

[Virgin nature] . . . plays the role of Temple, as well as of Divine Book. In this there is an element of esoterism—obviously so, since it is a question of a survival from the primordial religion—which monotheistic and Semitic exoterism had to exclude because it was obliged to oppose the naturalism of religions that had become pagan, but which, on the plane of the *religio perennis* or simply of truth as such, retains all its rights . . . for nothing can prevent Nature in general and its noble contents in particular . . . from manifesting God and being the vehicle of graces, which they can communicate in certain conditions both objective and subjective.[58]

Integrity of being necessarily implies humility towards the earth, which is absent when the awareness of humanity's position in the scheme of things disappears. The conquering spirit of the Enlightenment, arrogant through having lost the inner, or esoteric, awareness, was blind to the more subtle aspects of those cultures it encountered. The exoteric outlook of a civilization explains its missionary zeal and its inability to understand the heedlessness of the conquered people to the form of religion they are subjected to, which appears meaningless precisely because it lacks any connection with the obvious manifestation of the Spirit in the natural world. The root of the tragedy of the European encounter with primal peoples was not merely the assumption that a worthwhile civilization should contain just those elements familiar to a *post*-Renaissance age, but the incapacity to register the inner dimension of their culture. The Renaissance lived in the imagination as an era during which unquestioned belief was augmented by knowledge drawn from the Ancient world, so producing a greater clarity of vision. Yet, as we have seen, the knowledge gathered was highly selective, and instead impressed itself upon European history and the European mind like a screen, blocking a clear view of the past that would make coherent both our own long-standing theocentric civilization and the religion of nature to which the primal peoples adhered. The diverting of attention towards the rational faculty and away from the intuitive meant that the world, which through Intellective vision is perceived as a translucent reality both hiding and revealing its theophanic character, came to look opaque under the scrutiny of a gaze more myopic. The new consciousness was such as to prevent awareness of the unity lying "behind" phenomena, and,

---

[58] Schuon, *The Feathered Sun*, pp. 92-3.

instead, it became convinced of the solidity of the sensory world. The following claim by Leo Schaya—which would have made perfect sense and been assented to by the pre-Renaissance mind—is more likely now to be categorized as conjecture:

> The whole of existence . . . is the expression of the one reality, that is to say the totality of its aspects, manifestable and manifested, in the midst of its very infinity. Things are no more than symbolic "veils" of their divine essence or, in a more immediate sense, of its ontological aspects; these aspects are the eternal archetypes of all that is created.[59]

Nature interpreted as symbol may draw the accusation that it is not being appreciated for itself. However, such a view fails to appreciate the deeper meaning of symbolism first mooted in chapter 1. From a traditionalist perspective, symbolism does not substitute the reality of nature with something more abstract, but instead claims for natural phenomena a participation in a greater reality. The symbolist mentality denies the validity of the ordinary human perspective on nature, since it is through this perspective that the nature we know "suffers" from the veil which our consciousness draws over it. The ineluctable—and fatal—connection between what nature "is" and what our consciousness is, is nowhere more clearly seen, and merely to entertain the doctrine of symbolism is at once to confront the question of our own epistemological shortcomings. In Schuon's words:

> The man of rationalist formation, whose mind is anchored in the material as such, starts from experience and sees things in their existential isolation. Water is for him—when he considers it aside from poetry—a substance composed of oxygen and hydrogen, to which an allegorical significance can be attributed if one wishes, but without there being a necessary ontological connection between the material thing and the idea associated with it. The symbolist mind, on the contrary, is intuitive in a superior sense, reasoning and experience having for it the function of an occasional cause only and not of a foundation. The symbolist mind sees appearances in their connection with essences: in its manner of vi-

---

[59] Leo Schaya, "Creation, the Image of God," in *Seeing God Everywhere*, p. 241.

sion, water is primarily the sensible appearance of a principle-reality, a *kami* (Japanese) or a *manitu* (Algonquin) or a *wakan* (Sioux); this means that it sees things, not "superficially" only, but above all "in depth," or that it perceives them in their "participative" or "unitive" dimension as well as in their "separative" dimension.[60]

The question, "what is the nature of nature?" cannot be meaningfully asked—and certainly not answered—without being aware that our own nature, or our own consciousness, is drawn into the very framework of the question. The particular vision we now have of nature is one slowly formed during the five hundred years or so in which our allegiance to Intellective perception became increasingly diminished. A withdrawal of consciousness into the shell of rationality meant that we believed the world and our knowledge of it were distinct, one from the other. Our science fostered a belief that only some of the qualities we experienced should remain in the world, while the rest must be brought within the domain of our own consciousness. This view has worked to undermine the qualitative experience of nature, so that attributes like beauty seem now like projections onto nature of exclusively human values, feelings, and sentiments. Both a belief in our own separateness and a conviction that our minds are the origin of many of the qualities, mark the "absolutizing" of the human being. Inevitably, the attempt to quantify all characteristics has led to a reduction of the value of even the qualities we have been left with, and they have come to appear more and more abstract.

This process of reduction has been through measurement of the world—the imaginative association of aspects of sensory experience with measuring tools, ultimately with mathematical symbols. Mathematics is the basic language of science, and through this language the Western consciousness has been "quantified"—it has succumbed to a faith in the legitimacy of quantified reality.

In contrast, from a traditional perspective ("traditional" precisely because it represents the perennial outlook of humanity) all of nature, being of the Spirit, cannot but express the qualities or attributes of Divinity. Although the world is immersed in God[61] and there is nothing that exists

---

[60] Schuon, *The Feathered Sun*, pp. 6 and 9.

[61] The *Bhagavad Gita* expresses it thus: "All beings are in Me and I am not Myself in them. . . . My Being upholds beings and, without being Itself in them, it is through It that they

independently, diversity is not compromised by this ultimate unity since, as Lings says, existence is projected forth from the essence of Absolute, Infinite Perfection in the manner of a ray of light which grows increasingly dim as it recedes from its source.[62] Distance from the Unity, if treated hierarchically, becomes a measure of how the Absolute is divided again and again. Such divisions are numerous but, for Lings, the main divisions are those between the Absolute and the relative Absolute or Creator (*Nirguna* and *Saguna Brahma* in Sanskrit); then the division of Spirit and soul; and below this, the division into soul and body. In the cosmogony of the Vedanta, after *Purusha* manifests *Prakrti*, the elements of manifestation (*tattvas*) are *Mahatattva* (*Buddhi* or Intellect), *Ahamtattva* (the sense of "I"), *Manas* (mind), then the five *koshas* (or "envelopes"), the last of which is corporeality. This view almost exactly reverses modern cosmogony, which imagines simple matter giving rise to an increasing complexity, and eventually human consciousness emerging. Yet, if manifestation is a prolongation of the nature of Divinity—"the true principle to which everything must ultimately be referred"[63]—it is to be expected that all of existence will be a manifestation in varying degrees of the attributes of the Divinity. When ontological hierarchy is viewed from the top down as it were, it can be seen that the qualities (which, when the human state is "absolutized," are taken to be qualities of human consciousness) arise not from the human state, but are projected "into" this and all the states of existence from above; the *ahamtattva* is responsible for the delusion of originality. Since the qualities are *non-material*, it is impossible that they could be discovered within the material realm by utilizing that very realm as a means of measurement.

Considering the nature of their origin, the qualities must be considered innumerable. Nevertheless, Islam's "ninety nine" Names of God give some indication of these qualities. Here, Beauty, Majesty, Grandeur, Nobility, Wisdom, Truth, Glory, Sublimity, Bounty, Compassion, Peace, Love, and Life, are divine archetypes whose ultimate nature vastly transcends the limited reality we normally ascribe to them. Since there is a continuity

---

exist" (*Bhagavad Gita*, IX: 4-5, trans. René Guénon, in *Man and His Becoming According to the Vedanta* [New Delhi: Oriental Books Reprint Corporation, 1981], p. 81).

[62] Lings, *Symbol and Archetype*, p. 13.

[63] Guénon, *Man and His Becoming According to the Vedanta*, p. 58.

to existence—a consequence of the fundamental ontological identity—nature inevitably reflects (or, more accurately, is a manifestation of) all these divine attributes to some degree. Moreover, nature reflects the very structure of this reality. The infinite blue of the sky, or oceanic limitlessness which is ever one but is shaped into multiple forms, are reflections of this sort; while the spider and her web are more than metaphor for this structure—their very existence is made possible because they are a symbol in the true sense, that is, a reflection of ontology. According to Lings,

> The concentric circles represent the hierarchy of the different worlds, that is, the different planes of existence; the more outward the circle, the lower its hierarchic degree, each circumference being in itself a disconnected outward (therefore 'downward') projection of the centre. The radii of the web on the other hand are images of the radiance of the Divine Mercy, and they portray the relationship of connection between the centre and all that exists.[64]

Through modernism's long concentration on the *psychic* and *material*, we are inclined to split the holism that Lings wants us to see into two separate categories: the symbol and what is symbolized. The first we consider real, and the other only an idea or metaphor. Furthermore, we want to reverse the ordering, so that what is actually the more real of the "two"— Divinity—becomes imaginary, while the less real is thought more substantial. Insisting upon this interpretation, though, actually demonstrates the extent to which human consciousness has been subverted by scientific thought. The quantifying process, by which all non-quantifiable things become psychic things, means that the qualities of nature are not recognized as qualities of nature, but as elements of consciousness. But, according to the traditionalists, the human state is itself a reflection of the qualities of the Spirit, and, therefore, its nature and mode of seeing is dependent upon what "light" from the Unity is reflected in it.[65] Furthermore, due to the

---

[64] Lings, *Symbol and Archetype*, pp. 6-7. The spider, Lings adds, "would be incapable of weaving its web from its own substance if creation were not woven out of the substance of the Creator" (Lings, *The Eleventh Hour*, p. 37). It is possible to take from the *Mundaka Upanishad* the same meaning: "Even as a spider sends forth and draws in its thread . . . even so the whole creation arises from the Eternal" (Mascaró, *The Upanishads*, p. 75).

[65] From the traditionalist perspective, being made "in the image of God" (Genesis 1: 27)

inseparability at the deepest level of knower and known, there is an exact correspondence between the qualities reflected in the human state and those within nature. Therefore, the sense we have of the beauty of nature is not something we create; it does not rely on manufactured conceptions. Nor does it come simply from the world and impinge on consciousness. It is rather the other way around: our subjective awareness of beauty is the relative existence within consciousness of the quality *Beauty* itself, which allows us to "see" it "outwardly" because it resonates with the quality *Beauty* in our environment; "*we assent to the qualities to the extent that we ourselves are 'qualitative'*."[66] When the rays from the divine Beauty strike and illumine individuated consciousness, they *qualify* consciousness; that is, they allow the quality of beauty to be perceived. This qualification is the lessening of the divide between ontology and epistemology, since the nature of the Spirit, which is both knower and known, begins to replace egoic or individuated consciousness.

The identity—at the deepest level—of knower and known, and the fact that most of the divine qualities belong to both nature and human consciousness, means that there is a two-way relationship between nature and ourselves. *Immediate* awareness (in the sense of being unmediated by rational or discursive thought) of the natural world allows the actual nature of that world—its beauty, for instance—to impinge upon consciousness. The qualities of nature—which are the qualities of God—may then act to qualify consciousness, thus reversing the movement taking place under the impact of the quantification of science. Significantly, the process will be self-reinforcing: the presence of beauty in consciousness allows an increasing *perception* of beauty, while the world's beauty lends to consciousness a further capacity to experience it. Understood in this way, nature is revealed "as a multitude of more or less pure images of God or of his qualities, as a hierarchy of more or less pure truths leading towards the only truth."[67] Since "wilderness" or "virgin" nature is a perfect reflection of the Spirit's qualities, this type of nature provides the means whereby a *remembrance*, or recollection of the soul's true nature can most readily take place. By one interpretation of a famous *hadith qudsi*, the world exists to allow its own

means the potential to express all the divine qualities.

[66] Schuon, "Seeing God Everywhere," pp. 4-5, emphasis added.

[67] Schaya, "Creation, the Image of God," p. 241.

deepest nature to be understood: "*I was a Hidden Treasure and I loved to be known, so I created the world.*" And in the Qur'an, we are told: "*We shall show them our signs on the horizons and within themselves until they know that this is the Truth.*"[68] To be receptive to nature as symbol is to begin to withdraw a veil from consciousness.

---

[68] *Qur'an*, LXI: 53.

CHAPTER TEN
The Imprint of the Sacred

THE GENESIS OF SACRED ART

To see with a symbolist's eye is to see the world in the light of tradition, and to be aware, like Black Elk, of the language in which nature "speaks." It is also to uncover the hidden language that primal peoples use in their art, for "symbols are the language of sacred art."[1] When vision is no longer direct, sacred art offers a reminder of what the essence of nature is by referring directly back to the symbol already "hidden" in nature. As such, it is an art whose expressions must themselves be treated as symbolic; in this approach alone do we come to see how primal peoples experienced nature.

Now, if there were no continuity between the vision of primordial humanity and that of more recent civilizations, such an understanding would remain unlikely. However, the fundamental perception that defines for primal people their "religion of nature," is the same as that referred to in the esoterism of all religious traditions; hence, when we look to the sacred art of those later traditions we may expect to encounter a symbolism that captures some of the same basic perceptions regarding nature.

It is worth reminding ourselves, once more, that only in the brief span of ten or twelve thousand years have we created an alternative to an ancient and almost timeless pattern of human life. As the last ice age drew to a close, in certain areas of the warming world the life of the hunter-gatherer, the nomad and the pastoralist, gave way to settled communities. A record of this dramatic and relatively sudden change is preserved in the Torah. Cain, who represents the new sedentary existence, destroys his nomadic brother Abel. Since God favours the latter it may be assumed that a life immersed in nature is closer to an ideal, while the way of agriculture is associated with degeneration.[2] In the crucible of the Agrarian Revolution

---

[1] Lings, *The Sacred Art of Shakespeare*, p. 136.

[2] Even today, writes Lings, "there are some nomadic or semi-nomadic peoples . . . who have a spontaneous contempt for anything which, like agriculture, would fix them in one place

we find not just the dissolving of the old way of life, but the formation of formalized religion, as though the second was a prolongation of what had been, and necessary to shore against the danger inherent in moving away from the vision provided by nature.[3] This agrees with an accepted principle of the *sophia perennis* that, at the outset of a religion (which is also the start of a civilization as such), the esoteric dimension is uppermost and

and thus curtail their liberty" (Lings, *Ancient Beliefs and Modern Superstitions*, p. 8). Thus, the American Indian "has no intention of fixing himself on this earth where everything, according to the law of stabilization and also of condensation . . . is liable to crystallize; and this explains the Indian's aversion for houses, especially stone ones, and also the absence of a writing, which, from this perspective, would fix and kill the sacred flow of the Spirit" (Frithjof Schuon, *Language of the Self* [Bloomington: World Wisdom, 1999], pp. 196-7). An echo of this sentiment is found in Tasmania, where one of the earliest contacts carried the presentiment of what would eventually turn to conflict. At Recherché Bay, the naturalist, Jacques Labillardière, had an area of scrub cleared to make a vegetable garden. The Aborigines, although delighted to meet the French explorers, were unimpressed by this or the food the men brought, or other accoutrements of their civilization. Indeed, the conflict which arose and would later become the "black wars," stemmed as much from the European determination to alter the landscape by shooting the kangaroos and introducing sheep, as from an unwillingness on the part of the Aborigines to share the land. Even after nearly a hundred years, when the original population of 12,000 had diminished to a few dozen, the resistance to white civilization had persisted. The Aborigines, cooped up on the much smaller Flinders Island in the north, and pressed to live in small cabins, read and write, and attend church services, preferred to hunt the wild shearwater, collect shellfish, and paint their bodies and dance, than submit to such iniquities. See Bob Brown, *Tasmania's Recherché Bay* (Hobart, Australia: Green Institute, 2005); Lyndall Ryan, *The Aboriginal Tasmanians;* and Colin Dyer, *The French Explorers and the Aboriginal Australians 1772-1839* (St Lucia: University of Queensland Press, 2005).

[3] Because, for us, this knowledge has all but disappeared, we have learned to make of the road travelled an "ascent," and to believe what people of even the recent past did not, that primal peoples were less advanced. As inheritors of the post-Agrarian culture, our identification with it is almost complete. The lineage that "Cain" inspired has carried a wilful independence, self-satisfaction and even contempt for the world left behind. We have interpreted nearly all the elements that have arisen from this sedentary culture as being more sophisticated, even though, as Lings points out, "agriculture, after a certain degree of development had been reached, far from marking any 'progress', becomes in fact 'the thin end of the wedge' of . . . man's degeneration" (Lings, *Ancient Beliefs and Modern Superstitions*, p. 7). Thus, our own religious expressions are also thought to contain greater subtlety of thought and greater meaning, and, consequently, primal peoples were thought to be without true religion. This failure to remain sufficiently cognizant of esoterism and a perennial wisdom presents the single greatest difficulty in assessing the merits of a pre-Agrarian past. The idea of *devolution* would be far more prominent if it were otherwise.

fully expressed.[4] Consequently, while ethical precepts—which later come to dominate an *exoteric* side of religion—are important when people set themselves in a struggle to assert themselves against nature, it is the general outlook prevailing in the earliest days of a religion that is initially suggestive of "primordiality."

Certainly, both the religious founders and the sages who followed them often expressed a deep sympathy with the beauty and simplicity of the natural world, and with a life close to virgin nature. As the prototypal "king of the yogis," Shiva is said to live in the "abode of the snows" and the rivers that flow from the Himalaya are considered to be his shining locks. Accordingly, it became common when Hinduism was still an oral tradition, for guru and disciple to frequent wild, often mountainous places, eschewing the trappings of urban civilization. To this day, "among the Hindus . . . it is still an ideal—and a privilege—for a man to end his days amid the solitudes of virgin nature."[5]

Christ's whole life was a lesson in the virtues of the simple life, of relinquishing the attractions of the "marketplace," and being mindful that the flowers of the field are arrayed in a beauty that surpasses the raiment of a king. The early Christian ascetics of the Holy land and Egypt frequented the remote deserts in their search for wisdom. And in the Middle Ages, the hermits who chose to live in the seclusion of natural surroundings—and were often venerated because of this—"felt a certain benevolent pity for their brethren's servile dependence upon 'civilization'."[6]

Muhammad spent his early life among the desert Bedouin, whose nomadic ways and purer language were esteemed by town dwellers.[7] Later,

---

[4] See Lings, *The Eleventh Hour*, p. 57.

[5] Lings, *Ancient Beliefs and Modern Superstitions*, p. 7.

[6] Lings, *Ancient Beliefs and Modern Superstitions*, p. 7.

[7] Among the pre-Islamic Arabs, "it was the custom of the nobles of Mecca to send their sons to be brought up among the Bedouins of the desert because these entirely illiterate nomads were known to speak purer Arabic than their more 'civilized' brethren of the town" (Lings, *Ancient Beliefs and Modern Superstitions*, p. 10). Lings explains: "however accustomed we may be to thinking of linguistic prowess as inseparable from literacy, a moment's reflection is enough to show that there is no basic connection between the two, for linguistic culture is altogether independent of the written alphabet, which comes as a very late appendix to the history of language as a whole" (Lings, *Ancient Beliefs and Modern Superstitions*, pp. 8-9). See also in this connection Ananda K. Coomaraswamy, *The Bugbear*

the caves of the desert became his retreat, and it was in one of these that, at the age of forty, he began to recite the *Qur'an*. Afterwards, Islam's communal worship was performed in the open air, the first "mosques" being nothing more elaborate than walled enclosures. The *Qur'an* itself is a continuous reminder of the beauty and majesty of created nature, so much so that Burckhardt has called Islam "the renewal of the primordial religion of humanity."[8]

The origins of the symbolic art of the various religions are to be found in the origins of art itself. One of the very first arts—a prolongation of the circularity found in nature—is shelter. "Nomadic sanctuaries, made like tents or cabins of live branches, are generally round; their model is the dome of the sky. Similarly nomadic encampments are arranged in circular form."[9] The American Indian *tipis* of buffalo hide, and the Tasmanian Aborigines' bark huts conform to this pattern. As we have seen, circularity reflects centrality. Since the world of the Spirit and its immediate manifestation—nature—is pre-eminent for primordial people, the human figure in their art is usually insignificant when compared with the portrayal of other species.[10] Hence, the square structure, derived from the cross of the four directions, but ultimately defined by the human figure itself, makes its appearance later. The cross (representing humanity) together with the square of the earth (the cardinal axes) is found, for example, in the Hindu temples,[11] and the square combined with the circle (representing the sky or heaven) form the principle elements of later sacred architecture—the basilicas of Christianity and mosques of Islam.

---

of Literacy (Bedfont, UK: Perennial Books, 1979), p. 25.

[8] Titus Burckhardt, *The Universality of Sacred Art* (Colombo: Sri Lanka Institute of Traditional Studies, 2001), p. 14.

[9] Burckhardt, *The Universality of Sacred Art*, p. 9.

[10] And this is so apparently deliberately, since the "stick" figures familiar in such art often sit side by side with the beautifully modeled images of animals. The cave paintings of Lasaux and the rock paintings of Australian Aborigines are examples here.

[11] "According to the Hindu tradition the square obtained by the rite of orientation is the symbol of *Purusha* insofar as he is immanent in existence. *Purusha* is pictured in the shape of a man stretched out in the fundamental square" (Burckhardt, *The Universality of Sacred Art*, p. 10).

In contrast with other religions, Islam's avoidance of representational imagery reflects a deep appreciation for symbolism in the traditional sense, and hence a more acute understanding of the risk of confusing what is only symbol with what is important in its own right. Islamic art tends to be restricted to the abstract, which more adequately corresponds to the fundamental nature of divinity, which is not outer form but inner essence. Islamic architecture recapitulates in a relatively pure form the existential realities to which primal humanity, living in nature, was subjected. Since Islam regards itself as the "seal" of all previous religions, it affirms the right to "take to itself the heritage of more ancient traditions, while stripping that legacy of its mythological clothing, and reclothing it with "abstract" expressions more nearly in conformity with a pure doctrine of Unity."[12] Accordingly, although the original "mosque" was earth and sky, the square of the earth and the dome of the sky had already been transposed in Byzantine architecture into a rectangular base surmounted by a cupola, and this was eventually assimilated by Islam, which often added an octagonal drum between the two:

> The building as a whole expresses equilibrium, the reflection of the Divine Unity in the cosmic order. Nevertheless since Unity is always Itself, whatever the degree at which it is envisaged, the rectangular shape of the building can also be transposed *in divinis*, the polygonal part of the building will then correspond to the 'facets' of the Divine Qualities (*as-sifat*) while the dome recalls undifferentiated Unity.[13]

The mosque itself is essentially empty. It contains no image because Divinity is not localized in space and time but transcends both:[14]

> The absence of images in mosques has two purposes. One is negative, namely, that of eliminating a "presence" which might set itself up against the Presence—albeit invisible—of God, and which

---

[12] Burckhardt, *The Universality of Sacred Art*, p. 14.

[13] Burckhardt, *The Universality of Sacred Art*, p. 13.

[14] The "centre" to which Muslims pray—the Kaaba—is also empty and therefore must be thought pure symbol, standing for the Divine presence in the Heart to which Sufism attests.

might in addition become a source of error because of the imperfection of all symbols; the other and positive purpose is that of affirming the transcendence of God, since the Divine Essence cannot be compared with anything whatsoever.[15]

If the divine presence within the world finds its natural symbol in the infinite blue spaces of the sky above, and this realm is mirrored in the dome and in interior emptiness, then the natural symbol for the divine within humanity is the enclosed spaces of the earth. For primal people some of the most sacred rites took place in caves. The ancient cave art of the Aborigines, like that of the hunter-gatherers of Europe, celebrates both the life that sustains them, and the hand which represents the unique power they have within the world, and may even be found where no outside light penetrates, but where light must be brought in.[16]

The significance of the cave in early Islam has been acknowledged. But a similar connection between the cave as both retreat and protection from the world, and as an opening onto an inner world, may be found in all traditions. The stylistic representation of this natural form in architecture is the niche, which, in Hinduism and Christianity holds the sacred image, and in Islam has become the empty prayer niche or *mihrab*. The very interiority of the mosque—as any enclosed sacred space—suggests inwardness, while the *mihrab* suggests a further inwardness within this enclosure—a gateway to another world. All these symbolic elements are captured and given glorious expression in the Verse of Light (*Surah Al-Nur*), where the niche has become, unmistakably, the Heart:

> God is the Light of the heavens and the earth. The Parable of His Light is as if there were a Niche and within it a Lamp: the Lamp enclosed in Glass: the glass as it were a brilliant star: lit from a blessed Tree, an Olive, neither of the East nor of the West, whose oil is well-nigh luminous, though fire scarce touched it: Light upon Light! God doth guide whom He will to His Light.[17]

---

[15] Burckhardt, *The Universality of Sacred Art*, pp. 13-14.

[16] For example, "The art of *Ballawinne* (. . . 'ochre') Cave [in south-west Tasmania] . . . is in complete darkness. This is extremely rare among Australian art sites, but more nearly parallels decorated caves of the Upper Paleolithic in Europe" (Flood, *Rock Art of the Dreamtime*, p. 225).

[17] *Qur'an, Surah Al-Nur*, 24: 35 (Yusuf Ali translation).

While it would be legitimate to say that since everything partakes of divinity, therefore everything could be taken as a symbol for the Divine, it is nevertheless true, as we saw earlier, that

> "symbol" means "sign" or "token," which implies an opera-
> tive power to call something to mind, namely its Archetype. . . .
> Whether this or that can rightly be called symbolic depends on
> whether its "praise" is powerful or faint. The word symbol is
> normally reserved for that which is particularly impressive in its
> "glorification."[18]

If light has long been pre-eminent in this regard, then water is like liquid light, belonging to the earthly realm yet having the unique capacity to mirror the light of "heaven." The association of water with life is close, and uppermost in the minds of most primal people and those who live in an arid climate. After nearly 400 years of scientific analysis, it has remained impossible to explain what life is in terms of materialism. For Lings, "life is a presence of the Spirit, and therefore altogether transcendent. . . . The miracle of life which is always with us, both in us and about us . . . the powers of illusion persuade us to take entirely for granted."[19] Nor do all the attributes or qualities of water—life's essence—hope to be explained by the count of atoms.[20] From the point of view of symbolism, both water and life are prolongations or projections of Archetypes in the domain of the Spirit "into" the world of matter. In the *Qur'an*, it is through the divine quality of Mercy (*ar-Rahman*, the Infinitely Good, Compassionate or Merciful) that both revelation and water are "sent down" (*tanzil*). Thus, water here is not being used as an arbitrary symbol for the spiritual, but on the contrary it bears the imprint of the spiritual—put simply, "water is Mercy."[21] Ritual ablution, common to most religions, finds its rationale in

[18] Lings, *Symbol and Archetype*, p. 6.

[19] Lings, *Symbol and Archetype*, pp. 73 and 76.

[20] For instance, water's ability to imprint the character of that with which it is associated has long been testified to by homoeopathy. More recently, Masaru Emoto has made claims for its ability to imprint thought. See his *The Hidden Messages in Water* (New York: Atria Books, 2004).

[21] "And," writes Lings, "it would be true to say that even without any understanding of

this understanding. In Hinduism, the rivers of India are considered sacred, and bathing in them imparts this sacrament. In the ancient *medina* of Fez, as in many Islamic towns, a river's water is channeled below ground to emerge in clear fountains in the courtyards of a dozen mosques.

If water, like light, is a reflection of a higher reality, then part of its nature is to embody this very principle, since it is itself reflective. Water may express the apparent continuity that exists between the reflection and the original, but it also shows that the one is quite unlike the other: a mountain that appears in a still lake is both the same mountain and utterly different. In the *Qur'an*, it is the waters of two seas[22] which do not mix that represents the fundamental dissimilarity of what is "above" and what is "below," a duality originating, above all, with the human state. The two seas are the worlds of the Spirit and the soul,[23] and while there may be some reflection of the Spirit in the psychic domain, the psychic is ultimately as illusory as the mirage that shimmers on the desert air. When the psychic elements that ruffle the surface of the soul are stilled, the qualities of the Spirit are permitted to shine forth.

To speak of reflection in this way recalls the two greatest symbols of spiritual light, and how they pertain to the domain of the soul:

> The sun and the moon . . . symbolize respectively the Spirit and the Heart: just as the moon looks towards the sun and transmits something of its reflected radiance to the darkness of the night, so the Heart transmits the light of the Spirit to the night of the soul. The Spirit itself lies open to the Supreme Source of all light, thus making, for one whose Heart is awake, a continuity between the Divine Qualities and the soul, a ray which is passed from Them by the Spirit to the Heart, from which it is diffused in a multiple refraction throughout the various channels of the psychic substance.

symbolism and even without belief in the Transcendent, immersion in water has an inevitable effect upon the soul in addition to its purification of the body. In the absence of ritual intention, this effect may be altogether momentary and superficial; it is none the less visible on the face of almost any bather emerging from a lake or river or sea, however quickly it may be effaced by the resumption of 'ordinary life'" (Lings, *Symbol and Archetype*, p. 67).

[22] The seas are mentioned often, but see, for example, *Qur'an*, XXV: 53 and XVIII: 60-82.

[23] See the chapter "The Quranic Symbolism of Water," in Lings, *Symbol and Archetype*, pp. 67-82.

The virtues which are thereby imprinted on the soul are thus nothing other than projections of the Qualities, and inversely each of these projected images is blessed with intuition of its Divine Archetype. As to the mind, with its reason, imagination and memory, a measure of the 'moonlight' which it receives from the Heart is passed on to the senses and through them as far as the outward objects which they see and hear and feel; and at this furthest contact the ray is reversed, for the things of the macrocosm are recognised as symbols, that is, as kindred manifestations of the Hidden Treasure, each of which has its counterpart in the microcosm.[24]

Metaphysically there are many dualities, or occasions where "oneness" becomes two, but from the human perspective, the only duality of significance is the one comprised of knower and known, or subject and object, which confirms us in our separation from Reality. Hence, for the human being it is the expressions in nature that are indicative of both dividedness and its transcendence that are meaningful. Duality is seen replicated throughout the "earthly" sphere or nature, such as in night and day, the male-female duality, and, within individual forms, by the two-fold symmetry of the body and its features. Between night and day there exists the brief but symbolically significant twilight of opportunity; while the sexual union of what is otherwise two is symbolic of the union of, first, the masculine and feminine elements of the psyche or soul, and then the soul's marriage, at a higher level, to the Spirit, whence subject and object are fused. The Gods and their consorts in Indian mythology and art (*Shiva and Shakti*, for example), are the archetypes of this union.[25]

An initial division when prolonged becomes multiplicity. Then, the sun of Divine Unity has been "shattered" and becomes as the light of diamonds upon the waves. All the diversity in nature might be represented by its limitless colours, seen to be the mixture of just three primaries— red, blue and yellow, irreducible beyond this unless they undergo what amounts to an abrupt, discontinuous transformation into the unity of white or colorless light. Unity in multiplicity and the hidden essence is nowhere more strikingly revealed than in the beauty of flowers. A singular bud opens to reveal its multiple petals, while the flower has a centre that

---

[24] Lings, *Symbol and Archetype*, pp. 3-4.

[25] Lings, *Symbol and Archetype*, p. 21.

points back to its origin. Pre-eminent among flowers are the rose and the lotus, which for Islamic and Hindu mysticism have always been symbols of the hidden Treasure. The essence of the rose is its perfume, while for the lotus it is its purity.

The many fruits of nature contain a hidden kernel, once again indicating the hidden essence. In the *Chandogya Upanishad,* a guru instructs his son thus:

> "Bring me a fruit from this banyan tree."
> "Here it is, father."
> "Break it."
> "It is broken, Sir."
> "What do you see in it?"
> "Very small seeds, Sir."
> "Break one of them, my son."
> "It is broken, Sir."
> "What do you see in it?"
> "Nothing at all, Sir."
> ". . . My son, from the very essence in the seed which you cannot see comes in truth this vast banyan tree. Believe me, my son, an invisible and subtle essence is the Spirit of the whole universe. That is Reality. That is Atman."[26]

When the imagery is reversed and the kernel is taken to be not the Supreme Subject, but the more relative subjective consciousness, then the significance of fruit *without* a kernel becomes evident. In the four Qur'anic Paradises the higher of each pair are the ones that contain the fig and the pomegranate, fruit which, unlike the date and the olive of the lower pair, have no separate "kernel of individuality."[27]

A supreme symbol of the Essence is the night sky. "Hidden" in the brightness of day, it represents Reality within illusion. The Arabic word for night, *Layla,* is also the name of the heroine of romantic poetry; hence, the symbol of human love or devotion is transferred to the Sufic aspiration towards the hidden glory of the essence, the supreme Archetype to which the incomparable mystery and majesty of the night sky attests.

---

[26] Mascaró, *The Upanishads*, p. 117.

[27] See *Qur'an* LV: 46-68.

The symbols of the Essence or Unity, to which we have access through the sense of sight, have the power, by virtue of their being inextricably associated with the Archetype, to refer us back to it. There are some things in nature we hold to be supremely beautiful, and we believe we are attracted to them because of this beauty. Yet to say, instead, that they are beautiful because they are attractive, more closely captures the mystical approach to nature. The "clearest reflections"[28] attract by recalling to mind, or producing in consciousness, the world that they partially embody. That is, they have the capacity—if we allow it—to affect consciousness by drawing it closer to the Archetype. The felt sense of beauty, then, is the soul partaking, through the operation of the Intellect, in the Archetype whose essence is Beauty itself. Logically, the depth to which beauty is felt corresponds to the extent of movement in that direction.

The function of attraction to the Spirit and to Beauty that the visual world displays is just as evident in the world of sound and hearing. The melodious song of certain birds, for instance, could be likened to the beauty of flowers in their power to stir a longing for transcendence. Yet the function of attraction, which in the visual world depends upon a certain passive contemplation, becomes, in the world of sound, more dynamic, both in regard to Divine expressiveness and from the point of view of our own involvement.

The Spirit's immanence, and its movement through all of nature, is aptly symbolized by the wind, which "bloweth where it listeth." [29] The initial creative act of the Spirit is as a breath of wind "upon the face of the waters,"[30] and when Adam is created he has the life of the Spirit breathed into him. Our own breath is of the same substance, and so our own vocalized words have been considered to correspond mysteriously to the things they name. In Genesis II: 19 and in the *Qur'an*, II: 31, it is given to Adam to name the creatures, "these names ... [being] the phonations that exactly corresponded to what they expressed, echoes or symbols of the verbal archetypes."[31] The supreme words of a language are the names of God, and in conformity to this rule of correspondence, tend towards what is

---

[28] Lings, *The Sacred Art of Shakespeare*, p. 135.

[29] John 3: 8.

[30] Genesis 1: 2.

[31] Lings, *Symbol and Archetype*, p. 60.

essential. For instance, the forgotten sound of the long unspoken Hebrew name YHVH, has been considered to be the sound made by the inhaled and exhaled breath.[32] In Sufism, the supreme name *Hu* ("He")—the sound of the expelled breath—is *Allah's* essence. While, to sound the holy *Om* (AUM) of the *Vedas* is to echo the threefold nature of *Brahman*. The mysterious *identity* of the Supreme name and the Archetype to which it refers, is acknowledged in all metaphysical systems: "Hindu *japa-yoga* (union by invocation) and its equivalents in all other esoterisms[33] have, as their guarantee of efficacy, the truth which Sufism expresses with the words 'the Name is the Named'."[34]

The ability of human language to capture or reflect the divine qualities, confirms the traditional idea of *imago divinis*: "Man is, by his theomorphism, both work of art and artist: work of art because he is an 'image' and artist because this image is that of the Divine Artist."[35] Nature, viewed as creation, is divine artistry, and within nature, "man" is pre-eminent because he may re-express the creative act through the "art" of his very being. Thus, language may be considered one of the first sacred arts, since its original purity of form and expression, attested to by phonology, almost requires that for our earliest ancestors "speech was poetry." Similarly, their movements "had the beauty of dance."[36] For the reverberations of this ideal in recent times we have the example of primal peoples.

Insofar as the artist is aware of the divine imprint of the indwelling Spirit, so will his or her art depart from personal or egoic expression and reflect the reality of this inner essence.[37] And, "to the extent that [the artist's] objectivation reflects the secret depths of his being, it will take on

---

[32] David Abrams, *The Spell of the Sensuous* (New York: Vintage, 1997), p. 246.

[33] For instance, the Jesus prayer in Christianity and the *nembutsu* in Amidist Buddhism.

[34] Lings, *Symbol and Archetype*, p. 12. Cf. St John's *Et Verbum erat apud Deum, Et Deus erat Verbum* ("And the Word was with God, And the Word was God").

[35] Frithjof Schuon, *Castes and Races* (London: Perennial Books, 1982), p. 61.

[36] Lings, *Symbol and Archetype*, p. 58.

[37] This is why, whenever art aspires to be sacred, "it must not be the 'I', that root of illusion and of ignorance of oneself, which arbitrarily chooses [the means of expression]. . . . They must be borrowed from tradition, from the formal and 'objective' revelation of the supreme Being who is the 'Self' of all beings" (Burckhardt, *The Universality of Sacred Art*, p. 4).

a purely symbolic character."[38] This must be so because inner insight is what reveals nature itself to be symbolic, and sacred art, to be authentic, is obliged to conform to this truth. While nature's symbols are a prolongation of their supreme archetype, so the symbols of sacred art are also prolongations: "a sacred symbol is in a certain sense that to which it gives expression." Moreover, this is why a "traditional symbolism is never without beauty . . . [since] the beauty of an object is nothing but the transparency of its existential envelopes, and an art worthy of the name is beautiful because it is true."[39]

Traditionally, the archetypal human being is one in whom the divine qualities manifest strongly, permitting a vision concordant with "primordiality." The prophet, or religious founder, is an ideal who defines the outlook at the birth of a religion; an inner spiritual quality is pre-eminent, and its expression and propagation is mostly through spoken language. Mindful of expressing only the essential, the sacred art associated with such personages initially demonstrates an understandable reluctance to portray the human image, since outer form is inadequate as a means to express inner qualities. Instead, this art at first parallels the art of earlier times, in recognition that the human being in whom the divine is realized is one to whom the fundamentals of the circle and the centre are most apposite.

Burckhardt notes that the earliest Christian symbol, found in the catacombs beneath Rome, was the superimposed Greek letters *chi* (x) and *rho* (p), a six-pointed "star" that recalls the four cardinal directions and the

---

[38] Burckhardt, *The Universality of Sacred Art*, p. 4. Although sacred art inevitably looks to nature, "this in no way implies that the complete Divine creation, the world such as we see it, should be copied, for such would be pure pretension; a literal 'naturalism' is foreign to sacred art. What must be copied is the way in which the Divine Spirit works. Its laws must be transposed into the restricted domain in which man works as man, that is to say, into artisanship" (Burckhardt, p. 3).

[39] Burckhardt, *The Universality of Sacred Art*, p. 2. "It must be recognized," says Ananda Coomaraswamy, "that although in modern works of art there may be nothing, or nothing more than the artist's private person, behind the aesthetic surfaces, the theory in accordance with which works of traditional art were produced and enjoyed takes it for granted that the appeal to beauty is not merely to the senses, but through the senses to the intellect: here 'Beauty has to do with cognition'; and what is to be known and understood is 'an immaterial idea (Hermes), a 'picture that is not in the colours' (*Lankavatara Sutra*), 'the doctrine that conceals itself behind the veil of the strange verses' (Dante), 'the archetype of the image, and not the image itself' (St Basil)" (Coomaraswamy, "Symbols," in *What is Civilisation?* p. 126).

vertical axis, expressive of the centrality of both the human state and the Spirit. To this was often added the symbol of the cross, and the resulting eight-pointed star, when inscribed within a circle, forms an eight-spoked wheel. The symbol of the wheel (together with the tree of life) was utilized up until the Middle Ages, in the tympana above the doorway and in the rose windows of church and cathedral. In like manner the cosmic wheel and the sacred tree, traditional in Hinduism, were used in early Buddhist art to depict Gautama Buddha.[40]

The profound symbolism of the wheel begins with its depiction of unmoving centre and turning periphery, which, in Hinduism, is the ever-cycling world of *Samsara*—"this vast Wheel of creation wherein all things live and die."[41] The Spirit that moves this world remains as the core reality from which the world springs and to which it returns.[42] The wheel also echoes the circle of the horizon, which is contiguous with both earth and sky. Analogously, from a metaphysical point of view there is no discontinuity between heaven and "earth"—the essence at the centre of heaven (Divinity in its cosmic aspect) is the same as the essence at the centre of humanity. Therefore, our "position" on the wheel's circumference does not preclude access to the Spirit at the centre through one of the radial spokes, which in one sense are the various religions, and in another the esoteric teaching of the prophets themselves, who, by virtue of what they express, are a bridge between rim and hub. The wheel as *dharma* can be considered "Truth," but also the innate tendency or nature of things, or the order or structure of reality.[43]

THE FIGURATIVE IN SACRED ART

Sacred art is not, of course, restricted to such fundamental symbolism. For

---

[40] Burckhardt, *The Universality of Sacred Art*, p. 31.

[41] Mascaró, *The Upanishads*, p. 86.

[42] In early Taoist art "the disc represents the heavens or the cosmos, and the void in the centre the unique and transcendent Essence" (Burckhardt, *The Universality of Sacred Art*, p. 35).

[43] *Dharma* may be considered equivalent to *Tao, Sharia, and Nomos*. All these terms "demonstrate that there is an order that governs man as well as nature, from which comes our modern word *cosmos*. The Greek word *cosmos* means both order and beauty" (Nasr, *The Spiritual and Religious Dimensions of the Environmental Crisis*, p. 23).

Schuon, the human image is in one sense the *opposite* of the simplicity of the circle; it represents perfection in complexity, as the circle represents perfection in simplicity.[44] When a religion is based on the presence of a human "archetype," then, it seems to demand a figurative art.[45] In the case of Christianity, a model was found in the Greco-Roman tradition, modified in accordance with the dictum that sacred art seeks to express an inner spiritual quality that is archetypal and universal, while naturalism expresses an outer form that is individualistic and transient.[46] When Christ or the Virgin are first portrayed figuratively, the image is stylized. As Lings says, "The traditional painter . . . depicts the face of man with human features subtly but distinctly transfigured."[47] The intention is always to avoid elements of style or technique that would situate the figure within a merely material setting, or make it obviously a work of individualistic interpretation. For Burckhardt,

> The style is the direct result of the function of the symbol: the picture must not seek to replace the object depicted which surpasses it eminently; in the words of Dionysius the Aeropagite, it must "respect the distance that separates the intelligible from the sensible." For the same reason it must be truthful on its own plane, that is to say, it must not create optical illusions, such as arise from a perspective in depth or from modelling that suggests a body projecting a shadow.[48]

Instead, the figure should be "translucent," its outer form scarcely veiling its opening onto an inner world of timeless relevance. The holy personages, thus presented, stand

---

[44] Schuon, "Seeing God Everywhere," p. 10.

[45] Burckhardt, *The Universality of Sacred Art*, p. 18.

[46] Having such a model, meant Christianity was always open to reverting to a style that was anthropocentric, largely secular, and naturalistic. The art of the Renaissance betrays this movement; while religious themes are still depicted, they are less expressive of essential reality and more of contingent form. Michelangelo's and Raphael's brilliantly executed sensual forms are more a celebration of the sensory world, and show little mark of the more subtle inner qualities of traditional symbolism.

[47] Lings, *Symbol and Archetype*, p. 66.

[48] Burckhardt, *The Universality of Sacred Art*, p. 22.

ready to convert the beholder from his restricted and limited point of view to the full view of their spiritual vision. For the art of the icon is ultimately so to transform the person who moves towards it that he no longer opposes the worlds of eternity and time, of spirit and matter, of the Divine and the human, but sees them as united in one Reality, in that ageless image-bearing light in which all things live, move and have their being.[49]

The mystery of this possibility lies in the transformation that has already taken place in the artist. All art celebrates the consciousness of the artist as much as the subject of their work, and when a particular model or form of expression is imposed upon an artist from outside, as it is in sacred art, it can act to efface individualism or ordinary egoic consciousness. In the willingness to submit to the "strictures" of style and technique, lies the seed of an inner transformation. Seeking to portray the inner quality or beauty of the human image is no different from treading the path towards the discovery of one's own inner being. Hence, in the end, the beauty that flows from a work of art is a measure of the consciousness the artist had of beauty; in essence, it is a measure of the beauty of the soul of the artist.

An awareness of the essential nature of humanity would, in Hinduism, create an art which always captures the "quasi-spiritual quality of the human body."[50] In Shiva as *Nataraja* ("Lord of the Dance")—perhaps the pre-eminent example of this—the human form is a symbol of the Divine in its plenitude—transcendence and immanence. As both Creator and Destroyer, He is there before the world exists, and after it is gone. And it is His energy which keeps it from perishing: while the dance continues, the world persists.[51] The Divinity in human form is the clearest reminder, too, of the divine *within* the human form, and our role as *pontifex* or "bridge-maker." The divine dance becomes the archetype for a human ritual—"the first of the figurative arts"[52]—that seeks, through a participation in God's own moving dance of nature, not to destroy but to preserve the world.

---

[49] Philip Sherrard, *The Sacred in Life and Art* (Ipswich, UK: Golgonooza Press, 1990), p. 84.

[50] Burckhardt, *The Universality of Sacred Art*, p. 24. For Burckhardt, the temple sculptures depicting sexual union do not compromise this quality; here sensuality is transmuted "by saturating it with spiritual awareness" (Burckhardt, p. 23).

[51] Burckhardt, *The Universality of Sacred Art*, p. 23.

[52] Burckhardt, *The Universality of Sacred Art*, p. 24.

The energy within nature—the winds, falling waters, tides, lightning, fire, the fecundity of animals and plants—have for primal people been the clearest expressions of the Spirit in the world. Their own breath, the heart's "fire," or the energy in their bodies, is no less a divine presence that, when "brought forth" in song, prayer, dance, or sexuality, enables a participation in the ways of the Spirit. Hence, rites

> link the earth with the highest levels of reality. A rite always links us with the vertical axis of existence, and by virtue of that, links us with the principles of nature. This truth holds not only for the primal religions, where certain acts are carried out in nature itself—let us say the African religions or the Aboriginal religion of Australia, or the religions of the Native American Indians—but also in the Abrahamic world, in the Hindu world, and in the Iranian religions. . . . From a metaphysical point of view a ritual always re-establishes balance with the cosmic order.[53]

There could be few more potent reminders of humanity as "bridge-maker"—and even fewer that are as enduring—than the hand stencils of the Australian Aborigines. Within the secret recesses of the earth—her heart, as it were—the hand placed upon the rock shows both an understanding of the need and a willingness to form a bond with the earth. But how much more meaningful a gesture, when breath is used upon this union and, with liquid ochre, the hands own imprint is left upon the stone, defining and fixing the link between Spirit and earth.

---

[53] Nasr, *The Spiritual and Religious Dimensions of the Environmental Crisis*, p. 13. For traditionalists, the entire structure of the cosmos operates according to laws that require of us participation in order to preserve the integrity of the whole system. "The religious worldview points to a kind of mystery—because it is really a mystery from a purely human point of view—the mystery of the relationship between laws that should govern us morally and spiritually and the laws that govern the universe" (Nasr, p. 23). "We are like a window of the house of nature through which the light and air of the spiritual world penetrate into the natural world. Once that window becomes opaque, the house of nature becomes dark. That is exactly what we are experiencing today. Once we have shut our hearts to God, darkness spreads over the whole of the world" (Nasr, p. 13). The rites of primal peoples are often "laughed at by official science, but . . . such a science neglects the *sympathaeia* which exists between man and cosmic realities. . . . It is impossible for a human collectivity to live in harmony with nature without this ritualized relationship with the natural world and harmony with God and the higher levels of cosmic hierarchy" (Nasr, pp. 13 and 14).

Buddhism, centred on the historical personage of the Buddha, reverses the Hindu perspective, which is primarily theocentric. Gautama refused to discuss the "indeterminate question" of God; his focus was humanity and its transformation. And since the human quest for transcendence begins with individuated awareness, the human image in Buddhist art naturally crystallizes into a depiction of the Buddha himself, a man—motionless now—whose inner spiritual state, achieved not through action but contemplation, is portrayed in serenity of expression and symbolic placement of limbs.[54]

When Taoist art becomes figurative, it becomes so almost without conviction, as though the material world was only an idea. The landscapes of mountains, lakes and trees are ephemeral, emerging from and dissolving into a background of nothingness—the void, or Essence, or *Tao*—which can no more be painted than spoken of, although its light, which suffuses such works, testifies to its existence. For the contemplative painter, who "is never unconscious of the non-manifested, the less solidified physical conditions are, the nearer they would seem to be . . . to the Reality underlying all phenomena."[55] While the beauty of nature provides the ini-

---

[54] The question of whether Buddhism is to be considered a religion in the usual sense is answered by Burckhardt in the affirmative: "Instead of starting its exposition from a supreme principle, which could be likened to the apex of a pyramid made up of all states of existence—and this is what the universe looks like from a theocentric point of view—it proceeds only by way of negation, as if it were taking man and his nothingness as starting point, and building thereon an inverted pyramid which expands indefinitely upwards towards the void. But despite the inversion of perspective, the quintessence of the two traditions [Hinduism and Buddhism] is the same. The difference between their respective points of view is this: Hinduism envisages divine Realities in an 'objective' manner by virtue of their reflections in the mind, such a reflection being possible, outside and independently of their immediate spiritual realization, because of the universal nature of the Intellect. Buddhism on the other hand lays hold on the Essence of man—or the Essence of things—only by way of a 'subjective' path, that is to say, by the spiritual realization of that Essence and by that alone; it rejects as false or illusory every purely speculative affirmation of supraformal Reality. This attitude is justified by the fact that the mental objectivation of Divine Reality may often constitute an obstacle to its realization because reflection involves an inversion with respect to that which it reflects . . . and because thought limits consciousness and in a sense congeals it; at the same time thought directed to God appears to be situated outside its object, whereas God is infinite and nothing can really be situated outside Him; all thought about the Absolute is therefore vitiated by a false perspective" (Burckhardt, *The Universality of Sacred Art*, p. 27).

[55] Burckhardt, *The Universality of Sacred Art*, p. 36.

tial impulse in the direction of contemplative consciousness, and in turn permits the imbibing of the quality of beauty, the attempt to paint nature continues this process of discovering nature through discovering the inner Self. Taoist art, perhaps more than any, reveals itself as primarily "a method for actualizing contemplative intuition,"[56] the process by which the artist comes to know the essence of the natural world he or she paints.

Only in Islam do we find a consistent attempt to eschew the figurative in art. By avoiding the Greco-Roman artistic influence, Islamic art spans, as it were, the distance between the primal world and the modern, and provides a channel in which a genuinely Intellectual current is contained and is able to flow unimpeded by humanism. To equate Islam with the "primordial religion," as Burckhardt does, is to see in it a recapitulation of the particular outlook which values above all the essence of things and sees nature as the most translucent veil of this essence. Islam is not foremost a celebration of any one man, but of Divinity; Muhammad is one among many messengers of God (*Rasulu'Llah*), the revelation being the "book" he recited (*qur'an* means "recitation"). If there is paradox in Islam, it is that the reverence for the beauty of nature that saturates the pages of the *Qur'an* is not usually allowed to spill over into figurative works. Yet this seeming contradiction really preserves the integrity of nature by not making of this original revelation an idolatrous image.

The *leitmotif* of the *Qur'an* is the essential Unity of reality. This Oneness of Being finds a formula in the declaration, *la ilaha illa'Llah*—"there is no god but God," or "no truth but Truth," or "no reality but Reality."[57] The *Qur'an*, which, within the context of the Prophet's life and times, ranges over the great questions of human existence, continually emphasizes that all things have their origin and end in Divinity: *God originates creation, then brings it back again, then unto Him you shall be returned;*[58] and: *Everything perisheth but His Face.*[59] The glories of the world upon which we

---

[56] Burckhardt, *The Universality of Sacred Art*, p. 36.

[57] In Sufism, the formula—which condenses all of reality into unified essence like a prism focusing the colours of diversity into a singular light—is itself the mystical means by which the veil is penetrated and the "Hidden Treasure" revealed.

[58] *Qur'an*, XXX: 11. The same is expressed in the *Mundaka Upanishad*: "As from a fire aflame thousands of sparks come forth, even so from the Creator an infinity of beings have life and to him return again" (Mascaró, *The Upanishads*, p 77).

[59] *Qur'an*, XXVIII: 88.

gaze have their ultimate ground in the divine Being: *Whithersoever ye turn, there is the presence of God.*[60] However, the profound relevance of manifestation, creation, or nature, is not denied, since the world—immersed in God—is contiguous with the divine; if God's nature vastly transcends phenomena (*If all the trees in the earth were pens, and if the sea eked out by the seven seas more were ink, the Words of God could not be written out unto their end.*[61]), nevertheless making divinity distinct from the world is prohibited by the Oneness of Being (*Wahdat al-Wujud*). The expression, *I was a hidden Treasure, and I loved to be known so I created the World,*[62] testifies both to the divine qualities hidden in nature, and to the part played by nature—especially human consciousness—in unveiling those qualities by knowing them. Since nature and humanity are both part of the divine expression, the qualities are not ultimately known by any but God, which is to say that knowing the creation fully—discovering the "hidden treasure"—is to manifest within our being, the knowing of God; to manifest the ultimate knower.

To make relevant the announcement of a hidden treasure or a willingness to be known, requires the provision of signs that would lead to this knowledge or treasure. To this end, the already quoted *surah* LXI promises: *We will show them Our signs upon the horizons and within themselves, until they know that this is the Truth.*[63] The two-fold nature of the signs here might be conceived once again in terms of the epistemological and ontological divide. Thus, paramount among the *inner* "signs"—those relating to knowing—is that confidently identified by Lings when he says,

> Every human soul is imbued with what might be called the sense of the Absolute or of the Transcendent, the sense of a Supreme power that is both Origin and End of the created universe which It infinitely transcends. This sense belongs to the faculty of the Intellect.[64]

---

[60] *Qur'an*, II: 115 (Yusuf Ali translation)

[61] *Qur'an*, XXXI: 27 (Martin Lings' translation).

[62] "World" meaning all that exists, or "stands out" from God.

[63] *Qur'an*, XLI: 53.

[64] Martin Lings, *The Eleventh Hour*, p. 1.

As to the signs on the "horizons," we are asked—as we were in the *Bhagavad Gita*—to look to the natural world: *And among His Signs is the creation of the heavens and the earth. . . . He shows you the lightning . . . and He sends down rain from the sky and with it gives life to the earth after it is dead.*[65] At the time of the Prophet, as in all religious cultures prior to the Age of Reason, the forcefulness of this "argument" relied on more than just prior belief in God. Drawing attention to such things was equivalent to being asked in our day whether we are not profoundly moved by the reality of what exists, by ontology at the deepest level. The response that we are not, often demonstrates the learned preference for a particular imaginative vision of the world and ourselves. We are bent on *objectifying* the world rather than engaging with it fully.[66] And we are unable to engage with it fully because we are not complete ourselves, and so only take part of ourselves to the world. To imagine ourselves rational beings receiving sensory images, the interpretation of which is dependent upon our consciousness, is to immediately restrict ontology to what the reason and senses make of it. Imagination is here being used to negative effect, by perpetuating a view of ourselves and the world that is the opposite of the one testified to by tradition. If imagination were instead used to re-animate the traditional conception that both we and nature are much more, and that there is a correspondence between not the sensory world and the individuated consciousness, but between the essence of the world and the essence of consciousness, it would open the way to a different vision of reality.

ADAEQUATIO

The ways in which imaginative vision can be used to present this more complete ontology are the stuff not only of poetry and art, but also of metaphysics. A particularly enlightening metaphor is one Reza Shah-Kazemi uses to effect. The multiplicity of manifestation could be likened to innumerable mirrors each reflecting the qualities that are the divine Oneness:[67]

---

[65] *Qur'an*, XXX: 23-24 (Yusuf Ali translation).

[66] A profound response to the world is even still possible in modern philosophy: "It is not *how* things are in the world that is mystical, but *that* it exists," proclaimed Ludwig Wittgenstein (*Tractatus Logico-Philosophicus*, trans. D.F. Pears and B.F. McGuiness [London: Routledge and Kegan Paul, 1961], proposition 6.44).

[67] The aptness of the symbolism of the mirror, found in all mysticisms, lies in its being, as

God's most beautiful names and qualities display the "hidden treasure" in just the same way that an object displays itself in a mirror. It is the mirror that, in a sense, "produces" the reflection—the object remains inactive, it remains what it is, it does not have to exert any influence other than that which derives from its *presence*: it simply has to be present before the mirror, and the mirror "does" the rest. . . . It is by virtue of the different shapes and forms and colours of these mirrors that the one and only beauty of God assumes innumerable forms, apparitions, faces.[68]

Since the "mirror" is none other than God, nature is *the self-disclosure of God.* As such, it cannot be other than a wondrous and sacred presence, fully justifying Sherrard's claim that "everything that lives is holy."[69] Immanent aspects are truly signs *of* God; nature is not a "guidepost" that points elsewhere, but that which marks the very *presence* of the "treasure." And considering that all the Names, or attributes, or qualities of God, being infinite, necessarily "contain" every other Name, it is entirely justifiable to claim that the hidden treasure is Beauty itself. *Truly, God is beautiful and He loves beauty,* says a *hadith.* "[God's] beauty is cast into the mirrors of creation, which thereby display to Him the multiple expressions of this one and only beauty."[70]

Only when we consider our own "mirror-like" being do we find cause for the denial of this vision. A mirror may be clouded and the image it reflects dimmed. The "Heart" may be capable of reflecting all the attributes of Divinity, but if the over use of rationality has darkened the glass and prevented the "light" of the Intellect from penetrating, true Beauty cannot

Burckhardt says, "the symbol of the symbol." A symbol is a reflection of its Archetype, and the mirror—like still water—is a symbol for this very process of reflection.

[68] Reza Shah-Kazemi, "Verily God is Beautiful and He Loves Beauty: Aesthetics in Islamic Metaphysics," (unpublished paper, pp. 5 and 6).

[69] "For Every Thing That Lives Is Holy"—the concluding line of Blake's "The Marriage of Heaven and Hell"—is the title of an essay by Sherrard. See *A Sacred Trust: Ecology and Spiritual Vision,* eds. David Cadman and John Carey (London: Temenos Academy Papers 17 [2002]): pp. 1-32.

[70] Shah-Kazemi, "Verily God is Beautiful and He Loves Beauty," p. 6.

be known.[71] Moreover, when our imperfect "mirror" is turned on nature it too appears as veiled, although the very "absence" of Intellective intuition means this veiling is not apparent. Blindness to the true significance of natural phenomena is a recurrent theme in the *Qur'an*, which concedes: *It is not the sight that is blind but the hearts that are blind.*[72] The blindness or "hardness of heart"—the clouding of Intellective intuition—has, even today, its prolongation in the attitude of being heedless of, or unmoved by, the subtler qualities of the world.

Through the above metaphor, the intimate correspondence between nature and ourselves is revealed; the initially incomprehensible idea of nature manifesting the qualities which we believe belong to us, is resolved— if temporarily—when we imaginatively withdraw ourselves from the rationalistic framework we are used to:

> Multiplicity of meaning inheres in the very essence of a symbol; and this is its advantage over rational definition. For, whereas the latter organizes a concept in respect of its rational connections—at the same time fixing it on a given level—the symbol without losing an iota of its precision or clarity, remains 'open upwards'. *It is above all a "key" to supra-rational realities.*[73]

The traditional view of reality exactly reverses the modern scientific view. While for science this very exercise in imagination only serves to firm the conviction that the idea being entertained is less real than what is "out there," from the traditionalist perspective *imaginatio* has been used as a useful tool in the service of the Intellect, which *knows* that the qualities or the Archetypes—the Names of God—are the more real, and exist independently of us. In the words of the *Svetasvatara Upanishad*: "Even as a mirror of gold, covered by dust, when cleaned well shines again in full splendour, when a man has seen the Truth of the Spirit he is one with him."[74] *Adaequatio* (the medieval term to which the economist and

---

[71] For Burckhardt, "the Intellect itself is the mirror of the divine Being" (Burckhardt, *The Mirror of the Intellect*, p. 118).

[72] *Qur'an*, XXII: 46.

[73] Burckhardt, *The Mirror of the Intellect*, p. 117, emphasis added.

[74] Mascaró, *The Upanishads*, p. 88.

philosopher E.F. Schumacher refers[75]) means our being is adequate to the knowledge of reality, not because individuated consciousness is superhuman in capacity, but because at the deepest level everything takes part in a reality that transcends such consciousness.

The correspondence between symbol and Archetype, phenomena and *noumenon*, or nature and God, is what defines how primal people perceived the world. It explains their profound respect for it, the attempt to live in harmony with it, and an art which sought to express this principle of correspondence or reflection. To accept the primacy of the Spirit is to acknowledge that whatever is seen with ordinary vision is but a shadow of what is seen with the eye of the Heart. Hence, to lose this vision is to lose not merely knowledge of transcendent perfection, but the vision of nature as a supremely beautiful reflection of this state.

THE GARDEN

A fading vision would, logically, be indicated by an increasing tendency towards an outward expression—either visual or in writing—of what had previously been an inward knowing. This trend is all too apparent when we compare the "primordial" state with "civilization" in general, or study the evolution of any particular religious civilization. To the traditionalist, the glorious expressions in art, architecture and literature, which from one perspective signal the flowering of religious sentiment, are also, paradoxically, the testament to an inner failing:

> When the Spirit has need of such a degree of exteriorization, it is already well on the way to being lost; exteriorization as such bears within itself the poison of outwardness, and so of exhaustion, fragility and decrepitude; the masterpiece is as it were laden with regrets.[76]

When a fading vision is combined with a nostalgia associated with the loss of the natural state itself, it is unsurprising that the faint memories of a lost paradise should be crystallized in the form of the garden.

---

[75] See E.F. Schumacher, *A Guide for the Perplexed* (London: Abacus, 1995), chapters 4 and 5.

[76] Schuon, *Understanding Islam*, p. 162.

In Islamic culture, the re-creation of an Edenic garden[77] finds its immediate model in the Qur'anic description of the "Gardens of Paradise." For Emma Clark, the celestial Paradise is "symbolic of the serenity and peace of heart and mind that the soul yearns for."[78] For the desert Arabs—both nomad and city dweller—water, a tree's shade, and the green of foliage, took on a mystical significance: "water—particularly rain—and vegetation were direct symbols of God's mercy."[79] Clark identifies the oft-used Qur'anic phrase, "Gardens underneath which rivers flow," as that which most nearly suggests the nature of the Islamic garden. *Surat ar-Rahman* ("The All Merciful"[80]), the longest Qur'anic reference to Paradise, introduces the four fruits—dates, figs, pomegranates and olives—and the springs of flowing water, while a *hadith* which describes the Prophet's *miraj* or ascent to the heavenly realm, and *Surat Muhammad*,[81] present the four rivers flowing from a centre. This four-fold symmetry, which recalls the cardinal directions of the earth, is reproduced in the classic Islamic garden (the Persian *chahar-bagh* or "fourfold garden").[82] A pre-eminent example is the garden of the *Taj Mahal*, where water flows quietly in channels and below paved walkways into a central pool[83] from four directions, thus delineating the four squares of the garden which are filled with flowering plants

---

[77] A Chinese equivalent of the garden as reflection of Paradise is found in the Taoist garden of the Tang Dynasty, where great care is taken to make the garden imitate nature closely, and provide a means whereby all the yin-yang qualities and symbols are brought together. See J.C. Cooper, "The Yin and the Yang in Nature," in *Seeing God Everywhere*, pp. 227-238.

[78] Emma Clark, *Underneath Which Rivers Flow* (London: Prince of Wales' Institute of Architecture Research Department, 1996), p. 11.

[79] Clark, *Underneath Which Rivers Flow*, p. 9.

[80] *Qur'an*, LV.

[81] *Qur'an*, XLVII: 15.

[82] Clark, *Underneath Which Rivers Flow*, p. 16. Clark reminds us that this symmetry of the square is not unique to Islam but is found in the medieval monasteries and cathedral closes, and "the layout of the great Botanical Gardens of the sixteenth and seventeenth centuries, such as those at Padua and Oxford, was also based on the four-fold pattern; the gardens were intended to be representations of the original Garden of Eden containing, in theory, samples of every plant in the world" (Clark, pp. 23-24).

[83] This centerpiece is often octagonal, the octagon being a shape midway between the square of the Earth and the circle of "heaven."

and trees. However, the jewel of such gardens may be found within the fortress-like walls of the Alhambra in Spain, one of the glories of Islamic civilization. Here, a series of secluded courtyards are filled with the sound and sight of water:

> Rivers flowing, running water and fountains are the most powerful and memorable images one retains after reading the portrayals of Paradise in the *Qur'an*. The apparently endlessly flowing, splashing and trickling water in the gardens of the Generalife at the Alhambra must be one of the most evocative representations of the Gardens of Paradise anywhere in the Islamic world. [84]

An echo of these classic gardens is found in the traditional Islamic house where a square courtyard is enclosed by the four walls of the building. The word "paradise" is from the Persian *pairi* ("around") and *daeza* ("wall"), and "the courtyard is itself a kind of paradise garden in miniature since it represents the inward, contemplative aspect of man."[85] Such a "paradise" may contain, for practical reasons, only the element water (highly significant since water, like light, is "a symbol of spiritual knowledge"[86]); in this case, the trees and flowers live on within the colourful patterns of the carpets which adorn the interior of the house.

As sacred art, the Islamic garden is created to imitate its metaphysical counterpart in the Qur'anic revelation, which in turn draws *its* inspiration from the revelation that is nature. If all these "gardens" are actually symbolic (as Sufi poets like Rumi, Hafiz and Sadi remind us), then ultimately they are symbols for a consciousness in need of awakening. Significantly, the word *ayat* ("signs") is used by the *Qur'an* to describe both the signs in nature and its own verses. Furthermore, the signs are there for those with "understanding." This indicates not only that the two "books" cannot be read without sufficient knowledge, but that they are also wellsprings of this knowledge. When the book of nature is translated into the more human language of the garden, we have an art that is able to imitate the very function that nature has herself. If, as Rumi affirms, "the real gardens and

---

[84] Clark, *Underneath Which Rivers Flow*, p. 13.

[85] Clark, *Underneath Which Rivers Flow*, p. 22.

[86] Clark, *Underneath Which Rivers Flow*, p. 36.

flowers are within, they are in man's heart not outside,"[87] then the garden's truest purpose is to provide serenity and isolation, and so aid the contemplative and interiorizing mode of consciousness. The garden contains flowing and falling waters that make the sunlight sparkle, gentle airs which move foliage and waft scents, and green plants like the cypress and box to "cool the eyes." "At the sight of glittering waves or of leafage trembling in the breeze," says Burckhardt, "the soul detaches itself from its internal objects, from the 'idols' of passion and plunges, vibrant within itself, into a pure state of being."[88] Its response is to a "sign" or symbol that appeals not to "conceptual intelligence, but to aesthetic intuition and, more fundamentally, to the sense of the sacred."[89]

Whether it be patterned on Islamic ideals, or those of Christianity or any other religion, or whether it is something we are just moved to create for ourselves, the garden, with its water's gentle sounds, the sweet scented flowers, colourful blooms and fruit trees, cannot but be an attempt to capture or prolong, somewhere within our artificial environment, a portion of the glory of its prototype which lies without those walls. Its beauty is an echo of a once familiar beauty; the garden's creation is ultimately in praise of nature and the Supreme creator. As Schuon writes, "unless we are able to content ourselves with that shadow of Paradise that is virgin nature, we must create for ourselves surroundings which, by their truth and their beauty recall our heavenly origin."[90]

The garden as sacred art fulfils three functions. Firstly, it is a direct prolongation of wild nature itself, containing many pre-eminent symbolic forms where the beauty of the essence shines strongly. Secondly, like nature, it provides the environment in which the mind is liberated from the suffocating grip of discursive thought, and the serene and still light of Intellective intuition is free to manifest and allow Beauty to be known. Its third function rests on its ability to do what much of sacred art does: to *re-mind*

---

[87] *Mathnawi*, IV: 1357, quoted by Annemarie Schimmel, *The Celestial Garden* (Washington DC: Dumbarton Oaks, Trustees of Harvard University, 1976).

[88] Titus Burckhardt, *Sacred Art in East and West* (Bloomington: World Wisdom, 2001), p. 101.

[89] Frithjof Schuon, *From the Divine to the Human*, p. 103.

[90] Frithjof Schuon, *Esoterism as Principle and Way* (Bloomington: World Wisdom, 1990), p. 196.

us of the nature of nature. It is as though part of nature had been captured, like a bird from the wild, and placed in the confines of civilization. Its "song" is in praise of the world of its origin:

> Virgin Nature is at one with holy poverty and also with spiritu-al childlikeness; she is an open book containing an inexhaustible teaching of truth and beauty. It is in the midst of his own artifices that man most easily becomes corrupted, it is they that make him covetous and impious; close to virgin nature, who knows neither agitation nor falsehood, he has the hope of remaining contempla-tive like Nature herself.[91]

In the clamour of civilization, we have grown used to valuing our own works as more glorious, and believing nature to be silent. Yet, nature has always been the foundation upon which our artificial world is built, and it has always provided the foremost means of disclosing its own, and our, nature. Indeed, in the light of what nature embodies, "the marvels of tra-ditional culture are like swan songs of the celestial messages; [they] exte-riorize gloriously all that men are no longer capable of perceiving within themselves."[92] For this reason,

> had we to make a choice between the most magnificent of tem-ples and inviolate nature, it is the latter we would choose; the destruction of all human works would be nothing compared to the destruction of nature.[93]

To set up civilization in *opposition* to nature is to see it inevitably fail. If the earth's serene inner voice continues to go unheeded, still she will have the last word, although it will then be harsh. There can be few things more important now than to hear a message that speaks for nature. The esoteric, or inner, dimension of our religious traditions, which sacred art represents, is the most valuable aspect of civilization, since it alone has the capacity to re-orient us so that we look, once more, back into the heart of

---

[91] Schuon, *The Feathered Sun*, p. 41.

[92] Frithjof Schuon, *To Have a Center* (Bloomington: World Wisdom, 1990), pp. 34-35.

[93] Schuon, *Understanding Islam*, p. 163.

nature. If we were to seek a supreme metaphor for this function, we would find it, again, in the Alhambra, where sacred art dovetails beautifully into the "art" of nature, and where the art we create serves as key to open, as it were, the beauty contained in creation. In one of the rooms of the palace, there is a view through a window onto a courtyard where trees grow. Divided by a slim pillar, it resembles an open book. The room is detailed, refined and subtle; its elaborate decoration represents Islamic architecture at the height of its sophistication. We know the religion of Islam is itself indissolubly linked to a book, a scripture containing layers of esoteric or inner meaning. Since much of the architecture and art of Islam is symbolic, the room's interior might be said to represent this other dimension. Nature, then, which can be seen through the open "pages," is seen in just this way because of the presence of these other "books." In this book within a book within a book metaphor, to first open the book of religion, then the book of esoteric knowledge, reveals the book of Nature, the essence of which is Beauty.

POSTSCRIPT

Many of the great traditional cultures of the world refer to a cyclic movement of time, akin to the passage of the seasons yet vast in scope. In Hinduism there are four successive ages, or *yugas,* the last of them, the *Kali Yuga,* in which, it is said, we now live, is the darkest because in it a knowledge of our true nature has been all but eclipsed. In the Greco-Roman tradition, it was accepted that a remote "golden" age had long ago given way to one of "iron." Nor was the state of humanity perceived any differently in the Abrahamic religions, where a sense of imminent doom pervaded Western consciousness until the Renaissance. And if, as was anticipated, this darkest of ages inaugurates a new cycle, it is not before a degenerate humanity has brought destruction to the world. Thus, the American Indian tradition foresees a "purification day" when the damage wrought to the earth will be redressed.

The mechanism for a destruction of biblical proportions is now evident. Global warming, if it continues to escalate, may bring not only flood, but fire, famine, and pestilence. Assuredly, it is humanity that is to blame. And, if we take the traditionalist stance that a spiritual crisis lies at the root of the ecological crisis, then the reason we are implicated is because an ignorance of our nature has allowed us to acquiesce to a dangerous paradigm of thought, the outward manifestation of which must be implicated in the world's ruin.

Yet, as Philip Sherrard says, no one is making us pursue this suicidal path. Likewise, "no one can stop us from changing our own self-image and consequently our world-view except ourselves."[1] If our worldliness does not permit us to believe in a miraculous reinstatement of a golden age, still we may embrace the logic inherent in the view of cyclic time. A return to what *was,* implies a return to a past understanding, and so an understanding of the past. And while faith in a linear progress would once have made us shy from this return, the world we have brought into existence by our actions should allow us to recognize such faith as misplaced and delusionary.

---

[1] Sherrard, *Human Image: World Image,* p. 4.

An engagement with the programme that ecophilosophy has set itself was the initial impulse behind the imaginative travel into the past. An awareness of the exigencies we face, a mistrust of current thought, and a willingness to survey as wide a landscape of wisdom as possible, has provided ecophilosophy with the means to acquire, from the past, a vision for the future. Of all modern movements, it is capable of resetting the course that Western civilization has been compelled to follow for over four hundred years, abandoning the desolate seas of modernist thought, and making our way towards a re-encounter with a genuine metaphysical tradition. This is a lot to ask of a philosophy that is often captivated by the view around it, and by the siren song of science. However, the re-emergence of the *sophia* today may be seen as fortuitous for environmental thought. For, it is as if the past had come halfway to meet it, and brought, too, the same vital scepticism of the ultimate worth of rational empiricism that ecophilosophy often professes. It is in the esoteric dimension of traditional thought that we can discern the affirmation of precisely the qualities within humanity and within nature that have been denied through the overextension of reason. To find that tradition speaks of an intuitive perception, the supreme value of the natural world, and the mysterious "feminine" quality of beauty, is to be made aware of what the rational mind has silenced. It is to be made aware, too, of a clear point of convergence for both tradition and the environment movement.

The three elements, or strands, which seem to define this movement— a profound response to nature, disaffection with the modernist paradigm, and an intuitive aspiration towards an essential wisdom that might guide our lives and heal the earth—are echoes of those sentiments brought forth by Romanticism, wherein an initial revolt against scientism, together with the impact of esoteric thought, re-shaped the vision of nature. Too weak to resist the heroic impulse of science, however, this earlier movement fell apart.

An opportunity now exists to braid the three strands in a cord which will not break. This must be our aim. Beauty, that mysterious quality which explains the emergence of each strand, can also be what draws them together. The *perception* of beauty is like a secret revealed—it is both evidence for an essential reality and for the unfolding of consciousness. When the beauty that dwells at the heart of nature is seen to be the same beauty in our inmost heart, beauty is revealed as a winged messenger moving between two worlds, unveiling as it goes. It becomes both the best of guides and the very means by which we travel.

We can always point to the benefits of modern science, and even debate the relative influence of science on the shaping of the modernist worldview. But we should be aware that modern science paralleled the demise of the *sophia* in the West, and that today the very operation of science—its faith in reason, empiricism and measurement as the means to knowledge—obscures both an understanding of the Intellect, and the alternative vision of the world that it gives. To lose the vision of the Intellect is to lose a vision of nature as a supremely beautiful presence. It is to lose the vision of earth as paradise.

The tragedy of the world today is not just that there are ever fewer opportunities to experience the transforming quality of nature, but progressively less inclination. The beauty of this world is fast disappearing and we cannot expect ever to create an equivalent. Indeed, the consciousness that is heedless of its destruction has had beauty drained from it, and to be unable to register beauty is to be unable to produce it either. While the power of nature's inner beauty would once have been all that was necessary to instil a love for the world, it can no longer be relied upon. Now that the discursive, rational mode of consciousness has become pre-eminent, we are as sleepwalkers blundering towards our doom, mindlessly wielding the firebrand that must seal it. In the absence of real vision, we are in desperate need of an imaginative vision—an alternative view of ourselves and the world—to invigorate the nascent intuitive sense that lies at the heart of the environment movement. This could be achieved by providing a metaphysical foundation for this movement—by ecophilosophy abandoning an outdated and increasingly restrictive paradigm and drawing instead from the wisdom of tradition.

BIBLIOGRAPHY

Abrams, David. *The Spell of the Sensuous*. New York: Vintage, 1977.

Adorno, Theodor. *Aesthetic Theory*. London: Continuum, 1997 (1970).

Angus, Max. *The World of Olegas Truchanas*. Hobart, Tasmania: Olegas Truchanas Publishing Committee, 1975.

Bacon, Francis. *Advancement of Learning*, ed. W. A. Wright. Oxford: Oxford University Press, 1900.

Bakar, Osman (ed). *Critique of Evolutionary Theory: A Collection of Essays*. Kuala Lumpur: Islamic Academy of Science and Nurin Enterprise, 1987.

Behe, Michael. *Darwin's Black Box*. New York: The Free Press, 1996.

Berry, Wendell. *Life is a Miracle: An Essay against Modern Superstition*. Washington DC: Counterpoint, 2000.

———. "Christianity and the Survival of Creation". In Barry McDonald (ed), *Seeing God Everywhere*, 2003, pp. 53-70.

Bertell, Rosalie. *Planet Earth: The Latest Weapon of War*. London: Women's Press, 2000.

Birch, Charles & Cobb, Jr., John B. *The Liberation of Life: From the Cell to the Community*. Cambridge: Cambridge University Press, 1981.

Blake, William. *Jerusalem: The Emanation of the Giant Albion*. 1820.

———. *The Marriage of Heaven and Hell*. Oxford: Oxford: University Press, 1975.

Bohm, David. *The Special Theory of Relativity*. New York: W.A. Benjamin, 1965.

———. *Wholeness and the Implicate Order*. London: Routledge, 1983.

Bookchin, Murray. "Social Ecology versus 'Deep Ecology'". *Green Perspectives: Newsletter of the Green Program Project*, 4/5 Double Issue, Summer (1987): pp. 1-23.

———. *Re-Enchanting Humanity: A Defense of the Human Spirit against Antihumanism, Misanthropy, and Primitivism*. London: Cassell, 1995.

Briggs, John P. & Peat, F. David. *Looking Glass Universe: The Emerging Science of Wholeness*. London: Fontana, 1985.

Bronowski, Jacob. *The Ascent of Man*. London: BBC, 1976.

———. *The Origins of Knowledge and Imagination*. New Haven: Yale University Press, 1978.

Brown, Bob. *Lake Pedder.* Hobart, Tasmania: The Wilderness Society, 1985
———. *Tasmania's Recherché Bay.* Hobart, Tasmania: Green Institute, 2005.

Brown, Joseph Epes. *The Sacred Pipe: Black Elk's Account of the Seven Rites of the Oglala Sioux.* Norman: University of Oklahoma Press, 1989 (1953).

Bryson, Bill. *A Short History of Nearly Everything.* Doubleday: London, 2003.

Burckhardt, Titus. *Mirror of the Intellect.* Cambridge: Quinta Essentia, 1987.
———. *The Universality of Sacred Art.* Colombo: Sri Lanka Institute of Traditional Studies, 2001.
———. *Sacred Art in East and West.* Bloomington, Indiana: World Wisdom, 2001.

Burke, Edmund. *A Philosophical Enquiry into the Origins of our Ideas of the Sublime and Beautiful.* Oxford: Oxford Paperbacks, 1998 (1757).

Callicott, J. Baird. "Conceptual Resources for Environmental Ethics in Asian Traditions of Thought: A Propaedeutic". *Philosophy East and West* 37(2), April, (1987): pp. 115-121.
———. "The Land Aesthetic". In J. Baird Callicott (ed), *Companion to A Sand County Almanac.* Madison, Wisconsin: University of Wisconsin Press, 1987, pp. 157-171.
———. "What's Wrong with the Case for Moral Pluralism." Paper presented at the Sixty-Third Annual Meeting of the American Philosophical Association, Berkeley, California, March 23, 1989.

Capra, Fritjof. *The Tao of Physics.* London: Fontana, 1983 (1975).
———. *The Turning Point.* London: Fontana, 1990 (1983).

Carlson, Allen. "Nature and Positive Aesthetics". *Environmental Ethics* 6 (1984): pp. 3-34.
———. *Aesthetics and the Environment.* London: Routledge, 2000.

Carson, Rachel. *Silent Spring.* London: Hamish Hamilton, 1963.

Chadwick, Henry. *The Early Church.* Harmondsworth: Penguin, 1990 (1967).

Chryssavgis, John. "The World of the Icon and Creation". In Barry McDonald (ed), *Seeing God Everywhere.* Bloomington, Indiana: World Wisdom, 2003, pp. 253-266.

Clark, Emma. *Underneath Which Rivers Flow: The Symbolism of the Islamic Garden.* London: The Prince of Wales' Institute of Architecture, 1996.

Clark, Kenneth. *Civilisation.* London: BBC, 1969.

Clarke, J.J. *Oriental Enlightenment: The Encounter between Asian and West-*

ern Thought. London: Routledge, 1997.

Coleridge, Samuel Taylor. *The Complete Poems of Samuel Taylor Coleridge.* London: Penguin, 1997.

Coomaraswamy, Ananda. *The Bugbear of Literacy.* Bedfont UK: Perennial Books, 1979.

———. *What is Civilisation?* Ipswich: Golgonooza Press, 1989.

Coomaraswamy, Rama. *The Destruction of the Christian Tradition.* London: Perennial Books, 1981.

——— (ed). *The Essential Ananda K. Coomaraswamy.* Bloomington, Indiana: World Wisdom, 2004.

Cooper, J.C. "The Yin and Yang in Nature". In Barry McDonald (ed), *Seeing God Everywhere,* Bloomington, Indiana: World Wisdom, 2003, pp. 227-238.

Cornford, Frances MacDonald. *The Republic of Plato.* London: Oxford University Press, 1955 (1941).

Crick, Francis. *Of Molecules and Men.* Washington DC: University of Washington, 1966.

———. *The Astonishing Hypothesis.* New York: Simon & Schuster, 1995.

Cutsinger, James. *Advice to the Serious Seeker.* New York: SUNY, 1997.

Dante Alighieri. *The Divine Comedy,* trans. Mark Musa. Harmondsworth: Penguin, 1986.

Davies, David. *The Last of the Tasmanians.* Sydney: Shakespeare Head Press, 1973.

Davies, Paul. *The Mind of God.* London: Penguin, 1992.

Davies, Peter. "Mururoa: How Safe are the French Tests?" *Quantum* television documentary produced by Australian Broadcasting Corporation, August 23, 1995.

Dawkins, Richard. *River Out of Eden.* London: Phoenix, 1995.

———. *Unweaving the Rainbow.* London: Penguin, 1998.

———. *The God Delusion.* London: Bantam, 2006.

Denton, Michael. *Evolution: A Theory in Crisis.* London: Burnett, 1985.

Dewar, Douglas. *The Transformist Illusion.* New York: Sophia Perennis Et Universalis, 1995 (1957).

Dubos, René. *Reason Awake.* New York: Columbia University Press, 1970.

Dyer, Colin. *The French Explorers and Aboriginal Australians 1772-1839.* St. Lucia: University of Queensland Press, 2005.

Eaton, Charles Le Gai. *King of the Castle: Choice and Responsibility in the Modern World.* Cambridge: The Islamic Texts Society, 1990.

Eddington, Arthur. *The Nature of the Physical World.* New York: Macmillan, 1928.

Edwards, Philip (ed). *The Journals of Captain Cook*. London: Penguin Books, 1999.

Egler, F.E. *The Way of Science: A Philosophy of Ecology for the Layman*. New York: Hafner, 1970.

Ehrenfeld, David. *The Arrogance of Humanism*. New York: Oxford University Press, 1981 (1978).

Ehrlich, Paul. *The Machinery of Nature*. London: Collins, 1986.

Emoto, Masaru. *The Hidden Messages in Water*. New York: Atria, 2004 (2001).

Flood, Josephine. *Rock Art of the Dreamtime*. Sydney: Harper Collins, 1997.

Fox, Warwick. "Deep Ecology: A New Philosophy of our Time?" *The Ecologist* 14 (1984): pp. 194-200.

———. "The Meanings of Deep Ecology". *Island Magazine*, 35 (1988): pp. 4-6

———. *Toward a Transpersonal Ecology*. Boston: Shambhala, 1990.

Godfrey-Smith, William. "The Value of Wilderness". *Environmental Ethics*, 1 (1979): pp. 309-319.

Goldsmith, Edward. *The Way: An Ecological Worldview*. London: Random Century, 1992.

———. "Editorial". *The Ecologist*, 30(1) (2000): p. 3.

Goldsmith, Zac. "Discomfort and Joy". *The Ecologist*, 30(7) (2000): pp. 35-39.

Goodpaster, Kenneth. "On Being Morally Considerable". *Journal of Philosophy*, 75 (1978): pp. 308-25.

Griffin, Susan. *Woman and Nature: The Roaring Inside Her*. New York: Harper Collins, 1978.

Guénon, René. *Orient et Occident*. Paris: Trédaniel, 1924.

———. *Man and His Becoming According to the Vedanta*. New Delhi: Oriental Book Reprint Corporation, 1981.

———. *The Reign of Quantity and the Signs of the Times*. New York: Sophia et Perennis, 1995 (1945).

Hagger, Nicholas. *The Fire and the Stones*. Shaftesbury, Dorset: Element, 1991.

Harding, Stephan. "Exploring Gaia". *Resurgence*, No. 204 (2001): pp. 17-19.

Hawking, Stephen. *A Brief History of Time*. London: Bantam, 1988.

———. *On the Shoulders of Giants*. London: Penguin Books, 2003.

Hay, Peter. *Main Currents in Western Environmental Thought*. Sydney: University of New South Wales Press, 2002.

Hobson, John. *The Eastern Origins of Western Civilisation.* Cambridge: Cambridge University Press, 2004.

Hume, David. *Enquiries Concerning Human Understanding and Concerning The Principles of Morals.* Oxford: Oxford University Press, 1983 (1777).

———. "Of the Standard of Taste". In *Four Dissertations,* 1757.

Huxley, Aldous. *The Perennial Philosophy.* London: Chatto & Windus, 1969 (1946).

Johnson, Philip. *Darwin on Trial,* Downers Grove, Illinois: Intervarsity Press, 1993.

Jung, C.G. *Collected Works.* Vol. 10, London: Routledge, 1969.

Kant, Immanuel. *Critique of Judgment,* trans. Werner S. Pluhar. Indianapolis: Hackett Publishing, 1987 (1790).

Keeble, Brian. "Ananda K. Coomaraswamy: Scholar of the Spirit". *Sophia,* 2 (1), 1996, pp. 71-91.

Kiernan, Kevin. "I Saw My Temple Ransacked". In Bob Brown, *Lake Pedder,* Hobart, Tasmania: Wilderness Society, 1985, pp. 18-23.

King, Ynestra. "The Ecology of Feminism and the Feminism of Ecology". In J. Plant (ed), *Healing the Wounds: The Promise of Ecofeminism.* Philadelphia, Pa.: New Society, 1989, pp. 1-28

Kuhn, Thomas. *The Structure of Scientific Revolutions.* Chicago: University of Chicago Press, 1977 (1962).

Laing, R.D. *The Voice of Experience.* Harmondsworth: Penguin, 1983.

Lane, John. *Timeless Beauty.* Dartington, England: Green Books, 2003.

Lean, Geoffrey. "Global Warming to Speed Up as Carbon Levels Show Sharp Rise". *The Independent,* January 15, 2006, p. 1.

Leopold, Aldo. *A Sand County Almanac.* New York: Oxford University Press, 1989 (1949).

Lewis, C.S. *The Abolition of Man.* Glasgow: Fount Paperbacks, 1978.

Lings, Martin. *Ancient Beliefs and Modern Superstitions.* London: Unwin, 1980 (1965).

———. *Muhammad: His Life Based on the Earliest Sources.* Kuala Lumpur: Foundation for Traditional Studies, 1983.

———. *The Eleventh Hour: The Spiritual Crisis of the Modern World in the Light of Tradition and Prophecy.* Cambridge: Quinta Essentia, 1987.

———. *Symbol and Archetype.* Cambridge: Quinta Essentia, 1991.

———. *A Sufi Saint of the Twentieth Century.* Cambridge: The Islamic Texts Society, 1993.

————. *The Sacred Art of Shakespeare*. Rochester: Inner Traditions, 1998 (1984).

Lovelock, James. *Gaia: A New Look at Life on Earth*. Oxford: Oxford University Press, 1995 (1979).

————. *The Revenge of Gaia*. London: Penguin, 2006.

Majzub, Justin. "Martin Lings: Collected Poems". *Sophia*, 5 (2), 1999, pp. 73-104.

Malyon-Bein, Angela. *In Search of the Timeless Wisdom: An Inquiry into the Ecological Implications of the Loss of Tradition in Western Civilization*. Ph.D. thesis. Hobart, Tasmania: University of Tasmania, 2001.

Mascaró, Juan. *The Bhagavad Gita*. Harmondsworth: Penguin, 1975.

————. *The Upanishads*. Harmondsworth: Penguin, 1975.

Mathews, Freya. *The Ecological Self*. Maryland: Barnes & Noble, 1991.

————. *Reinhabiting Reality: Towards a Recovery of Culture*. Albany: SUNY, 2005.

Matthiessen, Peter. *Indian Country*. London: Fontana, 1986 (1979).

McDonald, Barry (ed). *Seeing God Everywhere: Essays on Nature and the Sacred*. Bloomington, Indiana: World Wisdom, 2003.

McKibben, Bill. *The End of Nature*. Harmondsworth: Penguin, 1990.

Merchant, Carolyn. *The Death of Nature: Women, Ecology and the Scientific Revolution*. San Francisco: Harper Collins, 1980.

Naess, Arne. "Identification as a Source of Deep Ecological Attitudes". In Michael Tobias (ed), *Deep Ecology*. San Diego: Avant Books, 1985, pp. 256-70.

————. "Self-Realization: An Ecological Approach to Being in the World". *The Trumpeter*, 4(3) (1987): pp. 35-42.

Nash, Roderick. "Aldo Leopold's Intellectual Heritage". In J. Baird Callicott (ed), *Companion to a Sand County Almanac*. Wisconsin: University of Wisconsin, 1987, pp. 63-88.

————. *The Rights of Nature: A History of Environmental Ethics*. Sydney: Primavera Press, 1990.

Nasr, Seyyed Hossein. *Knowledge and the Sacred*. Edinburgh: Edinburgh University Press, 1981.

————. *Science and Civilization*. Cambridge: The Islamic Texts Society, 1987.

————. *Man and Nature: The Spiritual Crisis in Modern Man*. London: Unwin Hyman, 1990 (1968).

————. *The Spiritual and Religious Dimensions of the Environmental Crisis*. Temenos Academy Paper 12, London, 1999.

————. "Man and Nature: Quest for Renewed Understanding". *Sophia* 10 (2) 2004, pp. 5-14.

Needham, Joseph. *Within the Four Seas*. London: George Allen & Unwin, 1979 (1969).

Nicks, Oran W. (ed). *This Island Earth*. Washington DC: NASA, 1970.

Northbourne, Lord. *Religion in the Modern World*. Ghent, New York: Sophia Perennis, 1994.

————. *Looking Back on Progress*. Ghent, New York: Sophia Perennis, 1995.

Oldmeadow, Kenneth (Harry). *Traditionalism: Religion in the Light of the Perennial Philosophy*. Colombo: Sri Lanka Institute of Traditional Studies, 2000.

Oldmeadow, Harry. "The Firmanent Sheweth His Handiwork: Reawakening a Religious Sense of the Natural Order". In Barry McDonald (ed), *Seeing God Everywhere: Essays on Nature and the Sacred*. Bloomington, Indiana: World Wisdom, 2003, pp. 29-50.

————. *Journeys East: 20th Century Western Encounters with Eastern Religious Traditions*. Bloomington, Indiana: World Wisdom, 2004.

————. *The Betrayal of Tradition*. Bloomington, Indiana: World Wisdom, 2005.

Pallis, Marco. *Peaks and Lamas*. London: Cassell, 1939.

Penrose, Roger. *Shadows of the Mind*. Oxford: Oxford University Press, 1994.

Perry, Whitall (ed). *A Treasury of Traditional Wisdom*. Cambridge: Quinta Essentia, 1991 (1971).

Plomley, N.J.B. (ed). *Friendly Mission: The Tasmanian Journals and Papers of George Augustus Robinson 1829-1834*. Hobart: Tasmanian Historical Research Association, 1966.

Popper, Karl R. *The Logic of Scientific Discovery*. New York: Harper & Row, 1968 (1934).

————. *Objective Knowledge: An Evolutionary Approach*. Oxford: Clarendon Press, 1974.

Raine, Kathleen. *Autobiographies*. London: Skoob Books, 1991.

————. "The Vertical Dimension". *Temenos* 13, 1992, pp. 195-213.

Randall, John Herman. *The Making of the Modern Mind*. New York: Columbia University Press, 1976.

Regan, Tom. *The Case for Animal Rights*. Berkeley: University of California Press, 1983.

Rosenhead, Jonathan. "Prison Control and Catastrophe Theory". *New Scientist* 72, 1976, p. 120.

Rousseau, Jean-Jacques. *Reveries of the Solitary Walker*, trans. Peter France. Harmondsworth: Penguin, 1979.

Russell, Bertrand. *Why I am Not a Christian*. New York: Simon & Schuster, 1957.

———. *A History of Western Philosophy*. London: Unwin, 1984 (1946).

Ryan, Lyndall. *The Aboriginal Tasmanians*. Sydney: Allen & Unwin, 1996 (1981).

Sagan, Carl. *The Dragons of Eden*. London: Hodder & Stoughton, 1977.

———. *The Demon-Haunted World*. London: Headline, 1996.

Salleh, Ariel Kay. "Deeper than Deep Ecology: The Eco-Feminist Connection". *Environmental Ethics* 6, 1984, pp. 339-45.

Scarry, Elaine. *On Beauty and Being Just*. Princeton, New Jersey: Princeton University Press, 1999.

Schaya, Leo. "Creation, the Image of God". In Barry McDonald (ed) *Seeing God Everywhere: Essays on Nature and the Sacred*. Bloomington, Indiana: World Wisdom, 2003, pp. 241-251.

Schimmel, Annemarie. *The Celestial Garden*. Washington DC: Dumbarton Oaks, Trustees of Harvard University, 1976.

Schneider, Pierre. "Optics at Chartres Reported Ruined". *New York Times*, January 1, 1977, p. 3.

Schumacher, E.F. *A Guide for the Perplexed*. London: Abacus, 1995 (1955).

Schuon, Frithjof. *Islam and the Perennial Philosophy*. World of Islam Festival Publishing Company, 1976.

———. *Sufism, Veil and Quintessence*. Bloomington, Indiana: World Wisdom, 1981.

———. *From the Divine to the Human*. Bloomington, Indiana: World Wisdom, 1982.

———. *Castes and Races*. London: Perennial, 1982.

———. *The Transcendent Unity of Religions*. Wheaton, Illinois: Quest Books, 1984.

———. *Logic and Transcendence*. London: Perennial Books, 1984.

———. *Light on the Ancient Worlds*. Bloomington, Indiana: World Wisdom, 1984.

———. *Spiritual Perspectives and Human Facts*. Middlesex: Perennial Books, 1987.

———. *The Feathered Sun*. Bloomington, Indiana: World Wisdom, 1990.

———. *Esoterism as Principle and Way*. Bloomington, Indiana: World Wisdom, 1990 (1981).

———. *To Have a Center*. Bloomington, Indiana: World Wisdom, 1990.

————. *Understanding Islam.* Bloomington, Indiana: World Wisdom, 1994 (1963).

————. *Language of the Self.* Bloomington, Indiana: World Wisdom, 1999.

————. "Seeing God Everywhere". In Barry McDonald (ed), *Seeing God Everywhere: Essays on Nature and the Sacred.* Bloomington, Indiana: World Wisdom, 2003, pp. 1-14.

Schweitzer, Albert. *My Life and Thought.* London: Unwin, 1966.

Shah-Kazemi, Reza. "Verily God Is Beautiful and He Loves Beauty: Aesthetics in Islamic Metaphysics" (unpublished and undated article).

Sherrard, Philip. *The Sacred in Life and Art.* Ipswich, England: Golgonooza Press, 1990.

————. *Human Image: World Image.* Ipswich, England: Golgonooza Press, 1992.

————. "The Science of Consciousness". *The Scientific and Medical Network Newsletter*, No. 48, April 1992, pp. 5-7

————. *Christianity: Lineaments of a Sacred Tradition.* Boston, Massachussets: Brookline, 1998.

————. "For Everything that Lives is Holy". In David Cadman and John Carey (eds), *A Sacred Trust: Ecology and Spiritual Vision.* London: Temenos Academy Papers 17, 2002, pp. 1-32.

————. "The Desanctification of Nature". In Barry McDonald (ed), *Seeing God Everywhere: Essays on Nature and the Sacred.* Bloomington, Indiana: World Wisdom, 2003, pp. 109-130.

Shute, Evan. *Flaws in the Theory of Evolution.* Nutley, New Jersey: Craig Press, 1961.

Singer, Peter. *Animal Liberation: A New Ethics for Our Treatment of Animals.* New York: Random House, 1975.

Smith, Huston. *Beyond the Post-Modern Mind.* Wheaton, Illinois: Quest, 1989.

Smith, Wolfgang. "Bell's Theorem and the Perennial Ontology". *Sophia*, 3 (1) 1997, pp. 19-38.

Stone, Christopher. "Should Trees Have Standing? Toward Legal Rights for Natural Objects". *Southern California Law Review* 45 (1972).

Tacey, David J. *Edge of the Sacred: Transformation in Australia.* North Blackburn, Victoria: Harper Collins, 1995.

Tarnas, Richard. *The Passion of the Western Mind: Understanding the Ideas That Have Shaped Our Worldview.* New York: Ballantine, 1991.

Thoreau, Henry David. *Walden.* New York: Harper & Row, 1965 (1854).

Teilhard De Chardin, Pierre. *The Future of Man.* London: Collins, 1973

(1959).

Uždavinys, Algis. *The Golden Chain: An Anthology of Pythagorean and Platonic Philosophy*. Bloomington, Indiana: World Wisdom, 2004.

White, Jr., Lynn. "The Historical Roots of our Ecological Crisis". In Ian G. Barbour (ed), *Western Man and Environmental Ethics: Attitudes Toward Nature and Technology*. Reading, Massachusetts: Addison Wesley, 1973, pp. 18-30.

Whitman, Walt. *Leaves of Grass*, Jerome Loving (ed). Oxford: Oxford University Press, 1998.

Wilson, Colin. *Starseekers*. London: Granada, 1982 (1980).

Wilson, E.O. *Consilience: The Unity of Knowledge*. New York: Vintage, 1999.

ACKNOWLEDGMENTS

From whence comes the inclination to dwell upon, let alone write about, the disappearing beauty of the world? In no small way it arises from the inspiration of those people for whom the Earth has become part of their being, and who write about it with passion. Of many, I single out those who especially guided the form this book takes.

Peter Hay, under whose thoughtful guidance writers may flourish. Mary Jenkins, an environmental traveler from the "beginning," whose friendship and assistance is ever ready. The traditionalist writers, Frithjof Schuon, Seyyed Hossein Nasr, Philip Sherrard, and Kathleen Raine, whose special insight into the ecological crisis helped illuminate the metaphysical landscape. Satish Kumar, whose whole life is a lesson in earth wisdom. And Angela Malyon-Bein, a companion in life, whose love, encouragement, and wise counsel never fails.

Grateful thanks go to all those at World Wisdom who have made this book possible, especially Mary-Kathryne Steele, Stephen Williams, and Clinton Minnaar.

Picture credits are as follows: "Lake Pedder, Tasmania" by Gordon Griffin; "Lake Pedder from Frankland Range, Tasmania" and "Showers, Frankland Range, Tasmania" by Olegas Truchanas, reproduced by kind permission of Melva Truchanas; "Weld River, Southern Tasmania" by Phil Griffin; "Morning light on Little Horn, Cradle Mountain, Tasmania" by Peter Dombrovskis, reproduced by kind permission of Liz Dombrovskis; "Christ Pantocrator, Sancta Sophia, Istanbul, Turkey" and "Two birds, copper rendition of 16th-17th century ceramic tilework, Hotel dû Grand Monarque, Chartres, France" by the author; "Patio de la Acequia, Generalife Gardens, Alhambra, Spain" by Emma Clark and Khaled Azzam; "Trisul, Himalaya, India," "The Blue Virgin Window, Chartres Cathedral, France," and "Mirador de Lindaraja, Alhambra, Spain" by Angela Malyon-Bein.

INDEX

For a glossary of all key foreign words used in books published by World Wisdom, including metaphysical terms in English, consult: www.DictionaryofSpiritualTerms.org.
This on-line Dictionary of Spiritual Terms provides extensive definitions, examples, and related terms in other languages.

BIOGRAPHICAL NOTES

JOHN GRIFFIN was born in Tasmania, Australia. Although still a youth when he witnessed the destruction of Lake Pedder in the heart of the Tasmanian wilderness, the experience left a deep impression upon him. Growing up, he explored many of Tasmania's wild areas. An abiding love of nature combined with a concern for the plight of the environment influenced his later academic career. An Honors' Degree in Environmental Studies was followed by a Ph.D. in Environmental Philosophy. His book, *On the Origin of Beauty*, is an adaptation of his dissertation (which won the Dean's Prize for 2007).

He has travelled widely, seeking out places where traditional ways of life are still to be found, in such countries as India, Morocco and Turkey. Traditional architecture and timeless ways of building have been inspirational, and on returning from these travels, he spent several years in Australia building homes from natural materials—earth, stone, and timber. And in England, together with a partner, he built a stone sunken garden in the grounds of Schumacher College, Devon.

He now lives on a small farm in the hills of northern Portugal, engaged in rehabilitating old stone-walled terraces, tending an organic vegetable garden and orchard, and devoting any spare time to writing.

SATISH KUMAR was born in Rajasthan, India, in 1936. He later settled in England in 1973, taking on the editorship of *Resurgence* magazine. He is the guiding spirit behind a number of ecological, spiritual, and educational ventures in Britain. In 1991, Schumacher College—a residential international center for the study of ecological and spiritual values—was founded, with Kumar acting as the Director of Programmes for many years. He is the author of *Path Without Destination, You Are Therefore I Am*, and *No Destination*.

Other Titles in the Perennial Philosophy Series by World Wisdom

The Betrayal of Tradition: Essays on the Spiritual Crisis of Modernity,
edited by Harry Oldmeadow, 2005

Borderlands of the Spirit: Reflections on a Sacred Science of Mind,
by John Herlihy, 2005

A Buddhist Spectrum: Contributions to Buddhist-Christian Dialogue,
by Marco Pallis, 2003

*A Christian Pilgrim in India: The Spiritual Journey of Swami
Abhishiktananda (Henri Le Saux)*, by Harry Oldmeadow, 2008

The Essential Ananda K. Coomaraswamy,
edited by Rama P. Coomaraswamy, 2004

The Essential René Guénon, edited by John Herlihy, 2009

The Essential Seyyed Hossein Nasr,
edited by William C. Chittick, 2007

The Essential Sophia,
edited by Seyyed Hossein Nasr and Katherine O'Brien, 2006

*The Essential Titus Burckhardt: Reflections on Sacred Art, Faiths, and
Civilizations*, edited by William Stoddart, 2003

Every Branch in Me: Essays on the Meaning of Man,
edited by Barry McDonald, 2002

Every Man An Artist: Readings in the Traditional Philosophy of Art,
edited by Brian Keeble, 2005

Figures of Speech or Figures of Thought? The Traditional View of Art,
by Ananda K. Coomaraswamy, 2007

A Guide to Hindu Spirituality, by Arvind Sharma, 2006

*Introduction to Traditional Islam, Illustrated:
Foundations, Art, and Spirituality*, by Jean-Louis Michon, 2008

Introduction to Sufism: The Inner Path of Islam,
by Éric Geoffroy, 2010

Islam, Fundamentalism, and the Betrayal of Tradition:
Essays by Western Muslim Scholars,
edited by Joseph E.B. Lumbard, 2004, 2009

Journeys East: 20th Century Western Encounters with Eastern Religious
Traditions, by Harry Oldmeadow, 2004

Light From the East: Eastern Wisdom for the Modern West,
edited by Harry Oldmeadow, 2007

Living in Amida's Universal Vow: Essays in Shin Buddhism,
edited by Alfred Bloom, 2004

Maintaining the Sacred Center: The Bosnian City of Stolac,
by Rusmir Mahmutćehajić, 2011

Of the Land and the Spirit:
The Essential Lord Northbourne on Ecology and Religion,
edited by Christopher James and Joseph A. Fitzgerald, 2008

Paths to the Heart: Sufism and the Christian East,
edited by James S. Cutsinger, 2002

Remembering in a World of Forgetting:
Thoughts on Tradition and Postmodernism, by William Stoddart, 2008

Returning to the Essential: Selected Writings of Jean Biès,
translated by Deborah Weiss-Dutilh, 2004

Science and the Myth of Progress, edited by Mehrdad M. Zarandi, 2003

Seeing God Everywhere: Essays on Nature and the Sacred,
edited by Barry McDonald, 2003

Singing the Way: Insights in Poetry and Spiritual Transformation,
by Patrick Laude, 2005

The Spiritual Legacy of the North American Indian: Commemorative Edition,
by Joseph E. Brown, 2007

Sufism: Love & Wisdom,
edited by Jean-Louis Michon and Roger Gaetani, 2006

The Timeless Relevance of Traditional Wisdom,
by M. Ali Lakhani, 2010

The Underlying Religion: An Introduction to the Perennial Philosophy,
edited by Martin Lings and Clinton Minnaar, 2007

Unveiling the Garden of Love:
Mystical Symbolism in Layla Majnun and Gita Govinda,
by Lalita Sinha, 2008

The Wisdom of Ananda Coomaraswamy:
Selected Reflections on Indian Art, Life, and Religion,
edited by S. Durai Raja Singam and Joseph A. Fitzgerald, 2011

Wisdom's Journey: Living the Spirit of Islam in the Modern World,
by John Herlihy, 2009

Ye Shall Know the Truth: Christianity and the Perennial Philosophy,
edited by Mateus Soares de Azevedo, 2005